The Little Wonder

Also by John Winton

We Joined the Navy
We Saw the Sea
Down the Hatch
Never Go to Sea
All the Nice Girls
H.M.S. Leviathan
The Forgotten Fleet
The Fighting Téméraire
The Little Wonder
Sir Walter Ralegh
One of Our Warships
Hurrah for the Life of a Sailor!
Good Enough for Nelson
The Victoria Cross at Sea
Aircraft Carrier
Jellicoe
Convoy
The Good Ship Venus
A Drowning War

The Little Wonder

150 Years of the Festiniog Railway

Revised Edition

John Winton

Michael Joseph
LONDON

First published in Great Britain by Michael Joseph Ltd
44 Bedford Square, London WC1
1986

Winton, John
　　The little wonder: 150 years of the Festiniog
　　railway.—Rev. ed.
　　1. Festiniog Railway—History
　　I. Title
　　385.'52'0942929　　HE3821.F4/

ISBN 0 7181 2712 9 (h/b)
　　　0 7181 2728 5 (p/b)

Typeset in 10/11½ Palatino by
Cambrian Typesetters, Frimley, Surrey
Printed and bound in Great Britain by
Billing and Sons Limited, Worcester

Illustrations

Map of the Festiniog Railway   *vi and vii*

PHOTOGRAPHS

Between pages 80 and 81
The Cob under construction in 1810.   The Festiniog Railway in about 1840.   William Alexander Madocks.   Samuel Holland MP.   Robert Francis Fairlie.   Livingston Thompson in about 1885.   A pair of first-class observation four-wheelers in 1887. *The Prince* in 1887.   Portmadoc Harbour in about 1878. *Little Wonder* at Harbour station. *The Princess* with a down passenger train. *Little Wonder* at the head of an up-train.   Charles Spooner's 'Boat'. *The Princess*.   On the Festiniog Railway. Festiniog Railway poster by Norman Keene.   Dduallt before the First World War. *Taliesin* in 1933.

Between pages 144 and 145
Boston Lodge workshops in the early 1950s.   Allan Garraway, Robert Evans and Morris Jones on the Simplex in 1954.   A party of volunteers in the mid-1960s on board *Mary Ann*.   Part of the 'Bog Railway' on the Deviation, with Tunnel Mess. Going home at the end of a day's work on the Festiniog Deviation.   Work on the Deviation. *Mountaineer* entering the tunnel in 1977.   The 'Spiral' on the Deviation, with *Blanche* and a down-train. *Earl of Merioneth* in 1982, on the resumption of services to Blaenau Ffestiniog. *Linda* at Portmadoc. *Merddin Emrys* in 1979, the twenth-fifth anniversary of the Festiniog Railway Society. *The Prince* in 1980.   The new double Fairlie engine, *Earl of Merioneth*.   Late afternoon sunshine at Minffordd. *Merddin Emrys* and *Earl of Merioneth*. *Linda* at Hafod-y-Llyn.

Festiniog Railway

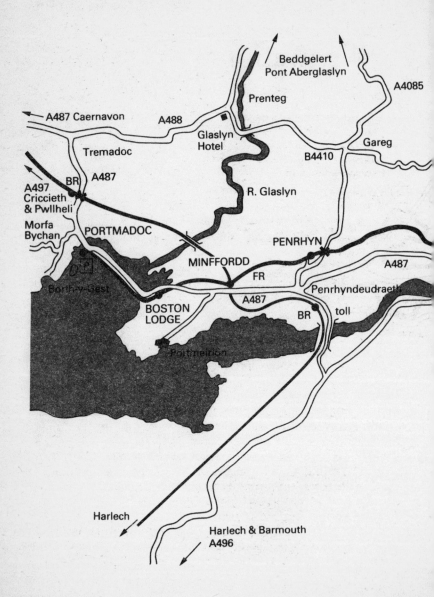

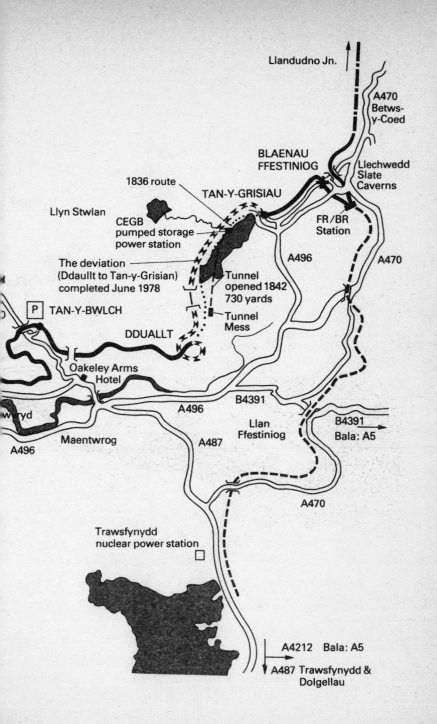

Prologue to the 1975 Edition

In the summer of 1973, I drove down again to Portmadoc, after an absence of many years. I came by Ysbyty Ifan, over the moors and mountains which I still think of as 'The Hump'; even now, going to Portmadoc is to overcome mental obstacles of altitude and distance. Whether by Ysbyty Ifan, or from Bala, or from the North Wales coast over the Crimea Pass, one descends into the Maentwrog Vale, into one of the most fertile and idiosyncratic landscapes in the British Isles. Oaks and chestnuts arch over the main road. Black cattle graze by the river's edge. Demented motorists with Birmingham number-plates overtake coal lorries on blind bends. The trees and the grass have a healthy, well-washed look, as so they should in a part of the country where it rains most afternoons, sharp at three. Again I saw the Cob, that astonishing man-made causeway across the Traeth Mawr, with an amazing little train puffing across it. There were people waving at it, and grinning, as they always do. That was the Festiniog Railway.

To me, the attraction of the Festiniog is not what I call the 'flange-wheels' – what size and shape the boilers were, or what colour ticket you bought to take a parrot with you in 1896 – but the story of the people who worked on it.

On 2 August 1946 the Festiniog Railway Company sent identical letters to their few remaining staff. One of those letters still survives, and it can still be seen in the museum at Portmadoc Harbour station. It was addressed to T.J. Roberts, at the time living in Tunnel Cottage, near Blaenau Ffestiniog, and was signed by the General Manager.

Dear Sir,
There will be no further traffic conveyed over this Railway and the service of the Staff is dispensed with. I therefore regret having to inform you that your services will not be required after tomorrow the 3rd instant.
Yours faithfully, Robert Evans.

And that was that. Nothing else: no newfangled nonsense about golden or copper handshakes, or redundancy pay, no sentiment, no thanks for a working lifetime spent in the Company's service. The railway stopped dead, literally in its tracks. The last slate train from Blaenau Ffestiniog stood in Harbour station. Passenger services had stopped years before, at the outbreak of the Second World War. The rolling-stock simply stayed where it was when the wheels stopped turning. The Festiniog Railway stood still, as though under an enchantment.

In the fairy story the Sleeping Princess's castle was soon overgrown. Much the same thing happened to the Festiniog Railway. The wagons and rails in the marshalling-yard at Minffordd were covered in a thick, thorny carpet of brambles, waving like prairie grass in the wind. It was impossible to see what was down there. Higher up the line, in the woods, rhododendrons filled the cuttings from wall to wall with a dense, shiny mass of vegetation that was very beautiful in the spring. Weeds ran riot on the permanent way. Trees grew from shoots to saplings as thick as a man's leg. Drains and ditches were blocked up. After heavy rain, rushing streams carried away stretches of the track. In a few years the railways reverted to nature and became a wilderness. Wooden fencing and boards rotted away. Walls crumbled. Cuttings became water-filled. Water poured constantly from the hillside into the Long Tunnel. Sleepers and keys were stolen for firewood. The line was taken over by the sheep. Here and there, near Blaenau, local residents trundled private wagons on private errands. In the engine works at Boston Lodge the floors fell in, the roof rafters sagged and rested where they lay on top of abandoned carriages. Doors rotted on their hinges. The works, a priceless example of Victorian industrial history, lay open to wind and rain and trespassers. Thieves, vandals and souvenir-hunters broke or walked in, and took away copper, lead and brass fittings, nameplates, tools, anything portable and reminiscent of the past. They smashed what they could not take. In Harbour station local children played amongst the marooned carriages. Inside the station building hundreds of workmen's timesheets dating back for nearly a century littered the floors ankle-deep, together with documents by the thousand, record and account books, photographs, posters, tickets, clothing, badges, lanterns, station furniture – all the sad and rather touching impediments for date-stamping tickets was still set for the last day passenger services had run: 15 September 1939.

So the railway rested. But it was not forgotten. It was one of the oldest narrow-gauge railways in the world, with a long and a romantic history. From time to time visitors from England ('knaves from over the border' the local Welsh press called them) used to come and discuss the possibility of restoring the railway. But they all retired, appalled by the financial and administrative difficulties, their spirits quite depressed by the sheer physical decrepitude of everything. Some pretended interest, as an excuse for being shown around and taking away with them anything they could get. After a time the general manager, the only surviving member of the staff, understandably began to discourage visitors.

The railway could not profitably be restarted, because it was worth far more as scrap than as a going concern. It could not be sold for scrap, because an Act of Parliament prevented the sale. Nor, for the same reason, could it be officially abandoned. The situation seemed hopelessly deadlocked. But in any case it did not seem to matter very much. In those days there was far less interest in restoring the past than there is today. Except for a few sentimental individuals, nobody bothered very much. Old railways, like old canals, old buildings and the old British Empire, could be allowed to fall into disrepair.

All that was in the early 1950s, when Portmadoc and the district around used to be a depressed area of North Wales. Portmadoc itself was a grim little town, of unkempt houses and hushed streets where grass grew between the paving-stones. If you had a hundred pounds in your pocket you could buy any house you fancied; if you had a thousand you could buy the whole street.

But when I returned I could see that things had changed in Portmadoc. Clearly, there were precious few property bargains still to be picked up. The whole place looked as though it had had several coats of expensive paint. There were gift shops, and coffee shops, and antique shops and boutiques. There was no doubt that prosperity had come to Portmadoc. A large part of it was due to the general rise in living standards and prosperity in the whole country, but just as much was due to the railway.

From a derelict relic of industrial archaeology, the Festiniog Railway has been transformed into the fifth most popular tourist attraction in Wales, with more than 400,000 passenger journeys a year, and a gross annual turnover of nearly £250,000. There are about ten miles of track in regular use, and another three under construction; six locomotives, and scores of items of rolling-stock, from first- and third-class bogie carriages to wooden slate wagons; and a permanent staff of over forty, boosted by volunteer effort to eighty in the high summer season. At peak periods there are thirteen passenger trains a day, up the mountain and back again. The Railway Society has more than six thousand members. There are plans for new rolling-stock; new buildings going up at Boston Lodge and at Harbour station, and schemes for new buildings at Blaenau Ffestiniog; a thriving mail-order business; a profitable trade for philatelists in first-day railway covers; a new automatic telephone system; new rails, new ballast, newly-repaired bridges, benches and walls, newly-painted railings and boards; and new links with coach companies, Butlins Holiday Camps, British Rail, countryside nature trails, and with conducted tours round the Llechwedd Quarry at Blaenau Ffestiniog.

The local press call all this the 'Festiniog Miracle'. It is not a bad description. Like all the best miracles it happened quite unexpectedly and against all the odds – and it was free. By far the greatest share of the time, labour, expertise and equipment that was needed to restore the railway was given for nothing by volunteers.

Obviously, something really extraordinary has been going on down at Portmadoc in the last twenty years.

Prologue to the 1986 Edition

When, in the summer of 1985, I next drove across 'The Hump', to see and write about the railway and its people again, it was clear that the extraordinary happenings had continued over the last decade or so. For a start, the railway has yielded to pressure from Welsh Nationalists and the Welsh Language Society to accept a dual name: Rheilffordd Ffestiniog Railway, except in circumstances where the Company itself is referred to, when it remains (by Act of Parliament) Festiniog Railway.

Similarly, Portmadoc has now been transmogrified into Porthmadog, a Welshification which has not the slightest historical basis. Portmadoc was always Portmadoc, from the beginning. However, when the GPO allocated postal code numbers and changed the postal name of the town, the railway agreed, for the sake of local harmony, to use the new name, and Portmadoc does now wear a faintly archaic air.

It still rains in the vale of Maentwrog many afternoons at about three, and the countryside still has that healthy well-washed look, although most of the black cattle seem to have been sold off to market and replaced by sheep. Demented motorists still career along the roads, which have been much widened; many fine trees have been lost, with at least one act of sheer vandalism: the wanton destruction, to save a few seconds' travelling time, of one half of a splendid avenue of mature chestnut trees which used to line the short straight across the Vale, from the bridge to the Oakeley Arms Hotel.

Harbour station is much enlarged and includes 'The Little Wonder', a name seldom used except in an historical context until recently, but now bestowed upon a cafeteria. The museum has moved to larger, though darker, premises along the platform. To seaward of the station, where the old slate wharves used to be, there is now an estate of modern holiday homes. Across the harbour is a new Civic Centre, and Gwynedd Maritime Museum. At the other end of the town, the Welsh Highland Railway is stirring into a new life.

Old faces have gone. New faces have arrived. The Festiniog now has a new General Manager, David Pollock, from Westinghouse Brake. Allan Garraway, who both ruled and served the railway as Manager and Engineer for some thirty years, has retired to Scotland with his memories, his MBE, and his Moyra, taking with him the thanks and respect of two generations of staff and volunteers. Dick Wollan, seconded from ICI, was Chief Executive from April 1979 until September 1983, when he brought management systems and techniques of the 1980s into an industrial structure dating from the 1930s (or even, some might say, the 1830s). The National Union of Railwaymen has come to the Festiniog in force and, with Warren Shephard as the FR Staff Representative Committee Secretary, ran its first gauntlet of redundancies in the long hot summer of 1983.

In recent years there have been new people on the line – not permanent staff, not volunteers, but professional tunnelling engineers for the new tunnel, contractors' staff to build the formation behind the power station, and Manpower Service Commission employees, working on the top end of the line towards Blaenau Ffestiniog.

Over at Boston Lodge, the numerals on the works clock still spell J-O-L-L-Y-G-O-O-D-F-U-N, but there have been many changes. *Prince* is once more back in steam, embodying a colossal technological leap across the years – here is an 122-year-old locomotive with a radar speedometer. There is now a new double Fairlie engine, *Earl of Merioneth/Iarll Meirionnydd*, built at Boston Lodge and completed in 1979 as the first Fairlie built since 1911. *Merddin Emrys* is being rebuilt to traditional double Fairlie Festiniog lines, and a new diesel is being built, or rather rebuilt – *Trematon Castle*. *Linda* is coal-fired again. The new engine erecting shed is complete and in service, and there is a new carriage-building shed, Fort Boughey.

For the railway and its Society, there have been landmarks. In 1975 there was a royal visit. In June 1978 the Deviation up to Tan-y-Grisiau was finished. In 1979 the Society celebrated its Silver Jubilee. In April 1983 the seven millionth passenger journey was recorded. Alan Pegler (whom God preserve) is President but Bill Broadbent, after thirty years' taking part in

Society and Company affairs, stepped aside to become a Vice President. A Society member, Paul Allott, played cricket for England. A sponsor has appeared, with enough money to influence events.

Just as the Israelites after the Diaspora annually prayed 'Next year in Jerusalem', so for over a quarter of a century the Festiniog Railway has looked forward to a return to Blaenau Ffestiniog. Services were triumphantly resumed to Blaenau in May 1982 and the line and station officially opened a year later. Many supporters of the railway stood on the bridges of Blaenau in a bitter wind, hardly daring to believe what they saw as *Earl of Merioneth* swung across the Glan-y-Pwll road and surged up the final rise to the new terminus.

But the return to Blaenau has left the railway, the Company and the Society on a plateau of achievement, seemingly unsure which way to go next. There are fresh financial difficulties. Traffic figures have retreated since the palmy days of the early 1970s, and the grant money has dried up, now that the projects have been completed. With the Deviation complete, all those who worked on it, not for any liking for railways but simply because they enjoyed shovelling, have tended to lose interest. Even those who are interested in railways find these days that they can work on a railway without travelling as far as North Wales. The volunteers themselves (who are by no means all members of the Society) are in general an ageing workforce. Society membership is virtually static. So, in this 150th year after its opening, the Festiniog Railway is trying to find the answer to the question 'What makes the Festiniog special?' – and, having found it, to market it.

There was some criticism of the 1975 edition, notably from members of the Company Board, that 'it had too much history in it'. However, this opinion was not generally shared, indeed many readers said or wrote that they liked to have the railway set in its historical context. In this edition, the historical content has been reduced, but it has also been amended according to the latest research by the Festiniog Railway Archivist Michael Seymour, and others.

Chapter 1

That sad little letter of August 1946 was the Festiniog Railway's epitaph, published after a long process of decay. The railway had in fact been quietly dying on its feet for years. The end could have been foreseen at any time after a brief resurgence in the slate trade had subsided – this time for good – at about the turn of the century.

In the high and palmy days of the 1880s and the 1890s the Festiniog carried well over 100,000 tons of slate and about the same number of passengers almost every year. Regularly paying a dividend of eight per cent or more, the railway appeared in Victorian eyes as a solid, copper-bottomed investment, as sound as the Bank of England. But even then, the forces leading to dissolution were already at work. Fashions in roofing materials were changing. The manufacturers of roof tiles, and later the importers of foreign slates, were preparing to take advantage of continuing labour troubles in the Welsh slate industry. Other railways pushed through to Blaenau Ffestiniog and took away Festiniog traffic. In the First World War the railway benefited from a system of state control of finance which amounted virtually to a form of subsidy, but after the war the railway declined ever more rapidly. The five and a half per cent Preference shareholders were paid no dividends after 1921 (and they were much luckier than the holders of the four and a half per cent shares, who received nothing after 1913).

In the 1920s and the 1930s the patterns of rural life in Wales were changing. Roads were improved. The railway steadily lost passengers to the rural bus companies. Tourists still travelled on the Festiniog in increasing numbers, but they came only in the summertime and there were never quite enough of them. The railway's management, though always

1

supremely self-confident and autocratic, were also curiously inept and allowed the railway to fall into a vicious circle of falling income, falling investment and falling traffic. As revenue dropped, less was spent on maintenance, leading inevitably to a drop in reliability, loss of goodwill, fewer passengers, and hence another drop in revenue. Between the wars the Festiniog's record was mostly a wretched tale of poorly-kept track, spreading woods and undergrowth barely kept at bay, neglected fences and stoneworks, badly-maintained locomotives burning rotten coal, trains regularly running two or three hours late or not at all, and often with only one long-suffering passenger still on board. The railway still preserved a certain flourish. The Festiniog undoubtedly had style. Local people who travelled on it remember the shining brasswork of the engines and the bright livery of the carriages. But this was just the smart paint on the skull.

At about this time the Festiniog became associated with the neighbouring Welsh Highland Railway, an organization with an even more precarious financial future. The liaison was quite disastrous. Alone, the Festiniog might conceivably have survived; with the Welsh Highland wrapped like an albatross round its neck, it was doomed. The Welsh Highland's last passenger services were withdrawn in 1936 and the lines were taken up in 1941. The money invested was lost, leaving only a lasting local bitterness against narrow-gauge railways.

Meanwhile, by 1939, the Festiniog's annual total of slates carried had sagged to 30,000 tons. Passenger services were suspended shortly after war broke out in September. In the event, they were never resumed. The railway somehow struggled on through wartime difficulties and restrictions (the financial help of the first war was not repeated in the second). In the seven months of 1946 before closure, the Festiniog carried a mere 9,000 tons of slate. The end was not far off, and when it came the railway subsided with hardly a whimper.

The hard truth was that by the 1940s the Festiniog Railway had long since lost its meaning and its purpose. To start again, the little railway would need fresh faces, fresh money, fresh ideas.

Astoundingly, it found them, and just in time. The Festiniog has always had an extraordinary talent for survival. Whatever happens, it somehow goes on. There is some mysterious quality in that little railway which constantly leads men to lavish their time, money and efforts upon it. Somehow, the right men, with the right ideas and the right skills, have always appeared at the right time.

The first, and vital, idea was the brainchild of William Alexander Madocks. Although he is almost unknown in the United Kingdom at large, he is something of a historical celebrity in his own part of North Wales. He was actually born in London, in 1773, into a wealthy Denbighshire landowning family. He went to Oxford, and he became a Fellow of All Souls. For eighteen years he was Member of Parliament for Boston, in Lincolnshire. He knew Shelley, and Tom Sheridan the playwright's son, and Samuel Rogers, the diarist. He had many friends and acquaintances in London society. By all accounts he was a most genial and sociable character, very good company, a great party-goer and giver. He loved watching, and acting in plays. He composed some moderately witty doggerel verse and some atrocious puns.

Madocks was one of those rare men who have one foot in town and one in the country. He loved North Wales, which in his day was as remote as Kamchatka. Roads were few and bad. Most travellers went on foot, just as George Borrow still did fifty years later. The countryside was rugged, poor and mountainous, and inhabited by a secret people, the Welsh. They spoke their own incomprehensible language and thought their own inscrutable thoughts. They tolerated the English, while still indulging in, and hugging to themselves, their ancient and impenetrable sense of humour – just as they do today.

Madocks loved it all, people, countryside, climate. He bought a house and some land at Dolmelynllyn in the valley of the Eden River. Here he entertained his friends from the South, known as the 'Chaotics', wrote verse, rehearsed plays, rode and swam and looked at the scenery. In 1798 he bought another small estate on the Traeth Mawr (the Great Sands) of the estuary of the River Glaslyn, at Tan-yr-Allt.

The house Madocks built at Tan-yr-Allt was occupied later by Shelley and, later still, by members of the Greaves family. The house is still there, long and low and white, on the hillside above Tremadoc, with a view across the whole Traeth Mawr.

Madocks's portrait shows a dark, thoughtful, sensitive face, with a somewhat rounded and pugnacious chin, jutting at a firm angle. There is perhaps a touch of the dandy in the tying of the cravat, the locks of curly hair and the bushy sideboards. His features suggest a man of ideas with enough practical drive to be able to have his notions translated into action. He was a visionary with a grip on reality.

Certainly, he had ideas. He was a pioneer among town-planners. He had projects for improving farming and the use of the soil. He had ambitious schemes to improve his own property and the locality as a whole. The Traeth Mawr was then a wide stretch of sand, sea-grass and sea birds, almost a wasteland. There was a bridle path across it, but it was difficult to find and to follow. Riders and footmen needed local knowledge; they were subject to delays and, at certain stages of the tide, to real danger on their way across. In 1800 Madocks had built a small embankment which ran from Clog-y-Berth to Portreuddyn, reclaiming about a thousand acres of the north-western part of the estuary. Here, Madocks designed and laid out the little township of Tremadoc. The town, too, is still there as Madocks willed it. With its wide main street, its gracefully designed and placed buildings, it is a model township, a little gem.

From this minor success Madocks went on to the concept of a much bigger embankment, one that would stretch right across the Traeth Mawr, reclaim thousands more acres and greatly improve communications. It might even become a part of a new and faster route through from England to the boats for Ireland.

In 1807 Madocks obtained an Act of Parliament which empowered him to begin the work and which vested the rights of any land reclaimed in himself. Work began the following January.

The embankment was, as Madocks's friend the diarist Richard Fenton said, 'a gigantic undertaking'. It employed between three and four hundred men and over a hundred horses. Madocks himself thought the work would take about eighteen months and would cost about £23,000. When, at first, work went very well it seemed he might be right. But, like those who were to revive the Festiniog Railway over a hundred years later, he really had no idea of the difficulties he faced. Perhaps that was as well, for if he had known the time, money and work that would be required he might never have begun.

The embankment was made of stone, which was quarried at both ends, from the eastern, Merioneth side at Penrhyn Isa, and from the western Caernarvon side at Ynys Towyn (where the town of Portmadoc begins today). The stones were carried out by boat, or along the top of the completed part of the embankment, and dumped into the bed of the estuary. A coloured aquatint of 1810 by H.W. Billington shows work in progress and apparently at a fairly advanced stage. Horses are plodding along the embankment drawing wagons on a tram-

4

way. There is a somewhat improbable arrangement of points in the foreground. The tramway had iron 'round' rails, as they were known, made in Wrexham and probably of about three-foot gauge. There was also a mysterious device called a 'Towyn machine', which is not described in the records but was very probably a kind of incline with rails for handling the stone on the Ynystowyn (Portmadoc) end of the Cob.

At the eastern end of the embankment a place called Penrhyn Cottage was built, with workshops, offices and stabling for the horses. It was occupied in January 1809. In May 1811 it was renamed Boston Lodge in honour of Madocks and his constituency in Lincolnshire. The name, and the building, still survive in the Festiniog Railway Works.

Urged on by Madocks crying, 'More wagons, more wagons,' the wagons would dump about 600 loads of stone in a good day. Madocks had good reason for urging them on. It was his money they were using and it was steadily being swallowed up in the sands of the Traeth Mawr. The stones either vanished into the soft silt or they were swept away by the tides and currents in the River Glaslyn. The project tended to be self-defeating. The more of the embankment that was completed, and the nearer the two ends came together, so the more fiercely and destructively the water rushed through the narrowing gap that remained.

At last, in July 1811, after three and a half years of hard work and frustrations, after the worst that the Welsh weather, the tides and the currents could do, after being badgered and encompassed about by a great cloud of creditors and doubting Thomases, Madocks finished his great embankment – the Cob, as it is nearly always called. It was 1,600 yards long and some ninety feet wide at its base, narrowing to about eighteen feet at the top, which stood about twenty-one feet clear of the water. Sluices, to control the rush of the tidal waters, were built at the Ynys Towyn end. For its time and place, it was a marvellous feat of civil engineering, and was rightly called one of the 'Wonders of Wales'. It cost £60,000 and left William Madocks very nearly penniless.

But however parlous the state of Madocks's finances (and the Sheriff in Caernarvon was being bombarded at that very time with orders to distrain his goods) Madocks still determined to entertain his friends on a scale worthy of a Roman emperor. He opened his Cob with a Jubilee celebration in September 1811. Guests hastened to Tremadoc from all over England and Wales to join what the *North Wales Gazette* called 'our Cambrian

Nobility, Clergy and Gentry' in a programme of jollifications which began on Monday 16 September and lasted most of that week. There was something for everybody; races on the Race Ground, plays at the Tremadoc Theatre, free meals at the Madock Arms Tavern, bardic recitals, community singing in Tremadoc Square, a service of dedication in the new Church, a great Ball (by invitation) in Tremadoc Town Hall, and an Eisteddfod. A fine fat ox was slaughtered, roasted whole in the square, and then taken to the Cob where carved slices were presented to the workmen and anybody else who passed.

All the tinkers, pedlars and gypsies in Wales joined members of the racing fraternity for the races. At the Eisteddfod, a Mr David Owen from Llanystumdwy won a prize for a poem about Welsh agriculture. A harpist called Hercules won a silver cup. The local press was in ecstasies. The man from the *Gazette* had to search for words approving enough to describe the meal provided by Madocks at a booth on the Cob. It was 'a most sumptuous collation' of wines, meats and other dishes, of 'the choicest description'. As for the races, 'never was there seen better running'. The 'Ordinary' (the meal served to all comers in the Madock Arms) was 'crowded beyond all description; and the unremitting attention of Mr Madocks, who would not be seated until he saw all the company comfortably employed, exceeds all panegyric'. 'The solemnity of church service,' the reporter considered, 'was rendered particularly impressive by the addition of Choral Service, performed under the direction of Mr Pring, of Bangor.' A procession of fifty carriages formed up, headed by a band of music, and the rear was 'brought up by about 300 of the workmen employed in the embankment, uniformly clothed by the munificence of W.A. Madocks Esq.' The evening concluded with the Ball, 'where "the light fantastic toe" moved on until Chanticleer gave notice to retire'. The reporter, who evidently had a splendid time himself, ended by spraying compliments in all directions, but especially at Madocks. 'We congratulate the public at large,' he wrote,

> on the completion of a work which stands unrivalled in the history of the world. That a single individual should attempt, persevere in, and at last (after four years exertion) accomplish, so stupendous an undertaking appears truly astonishing! and it only requires ocular demonstration to convince the incredulous of its superiority over every other work of the kind now extant.

6

It certainly was William Madocks's great day. He must have felt that all the work and anxiety had at last been worthwhile. The diarist Samuel Rogers, who was in Tremadoc for the Jubilee, wrote that Madocks was 'a great Lord in his little city of Tre Madoc'. A comet was seen in the sky that week. The omens seemed good for the Cob and for Madocks.

The only sour note was struck by the novelist Thomas Love Peacock, who was then living at Maentwrog. He did not conceal his opinion that the embankment was a visual disaster. There is more than a casual resemblance to William Madocks in Squire Henry Headlong of *Headlong Hall*, published in 1816, and one famous passage in the novel gives an eyewitness account of the Traeth Mawr while the Cob was being built. The Cob, Peacock thought, might or might not turn out to be useful but meanwhile it was definitely spoiling the view. The Traeth Mawr, he wrote, was

> a scene which no other in this country can parallel, and which the admirers of the magnificence of nature will ever remember with regret, whatever consolation may be derived from the probable utility of the works which have excluded the waters from their ancient receptacle . . . The mountain-frame remains unchanged, unchangeable: but the liquid mirror it enclosed is gone.

Holding these views, Peacock probably felt a gloomy satisfaction in February 1812 when a storm washed part of the Cob away. The horse-drawn tramway which had been dismantled, prematurely as it turned out, had to be relaid again. That comet had evidently meant disaster, not triumph. Though encouraged and approved of by Shelley, then living at Tan-yr-Allt, Madocks's shortage of money meant that repairs went very slowly. The Cob was not in fact rebuilt and opened again until 1814.

In the same passage of his novel Peacock had written that 'the waters within, retained by the embankment, poured through its two points in an impetuous cataract, curling and boiling in innumerable eddies, and making a tumultuous melody admirably in unison with the surrounding scene'. In time, and quite unforeseen by anyone, these melodic cataracts in their curling and boiling progress had a far-reaching effect upon the Traeth Mawr and, eventually, upon the surrounding countryside. Madocks's motives in building the Cob had been the reclamation of land and the improvement of communications. But after a few years it was found that the River Glaslyn, racing through its sluices at Ynys Towyn, was scouring out a deep passage – deep enough, with a little more work, to make a harbour. Madocks asked himself, why not make a harbour, big enough to take ships, big enough to export some of the local slate? This was the second, vital idea, which led to the Festiniog Railway.

Chapter 2

To the average Englishman slate is the stuff that comes off roofs in a gale of wind. It is hard for us to see slate as the Welsh see it, as not so much a commodity, more a way of life. But to approach any understanding of the early history of the Festiniog Railway one must grasp the importance of the slate industry to North Wales. Slate working has a history of greed and exploitation, of hardship and disease, and of appalling living and working conditions for the quarrymen and their families, relieved only by the natural humour and dignity of the Welsh.

Slate has been used in Wales since the earliest times. The Romans knew it and used it at Segontium (their Caernarvon). The oldest worked quarry in North Wales was probably Cilgwyn, near Nantlle in Caernarvonshire. There were quarries at Glynceiriog in the seventeenth and at Llansannan in the eighteenth centuries. The industry was primitive, but by 1748 some four million slates a year were being exported to Ireland.

The first 'slate baron' was Richard Pennant, later Lord Penrhyn, who built Penrhyn Castle, near Bangor. In 1765 he married Anne Susannah Warburton, who was heiress to half the Penrhyn estate in Caernarvonshire. By 1785 Richard had bought the other half, including thousands of desolate acres of Snowdonia, where some Welsh quarrymen were hacking slate out of the hillsides, selling the slates locally, and exporting some to Ireland. These early quarrymen had little capital, and worked by themselves or in teams of two, three or four men. The slates were packed in panniers, sixty-four to a load, and taken down the mountains by ponies to small creeks or to Pennant's own wharf on the Menai Straits. The quarrymen paid a royalty of one-eighth the value of the slates, and later, a rent of £1 a year

9

for a twenty-one-year lease. This system brought Pennant in about £80 a year.

Pennant bought the quarrymen out for a total of £160 but kept them all on as hired labourers. He leased more sites, improved the roads, built Port Penrhyn and a railway to it, and joined quarries together into one vast quarrying complex – eventually the world's biggest – at Bethesda.

Pennant's neighbour, Assheton Smith, followed his example. He built his own port at Dinorwic and a railway. In 1806 he got an act through Parliament which gave him four-fifths of the common land adjacent to his own estate of Dinorwic, and rights over the slate. The quarrymen tried to resist but they had no money and no influence. They were finally forced out by the Enclosure Acts of the nineteenth century.

In Merioneth the slate industry began rather later and was much more influenced by businessmen and capital from outside Wales. In 1755, so the story goes, a certain Methusalem Jones had a dream telling him to walk across the mountains from Nantlle and start quarrying near Ffestiniog. He obeyed, and with a small consortium (if that is not too grand a word) of five fellow Welshmen, including William Morris, the first of many men to die in a Blaenau quarry accident, he began to dig at a slate outcrop on a hillside which later became the Diphwys quarry. In those days there was no town of Blaenau Ffestiniog (which means 'the cliffs above Ffestiniog'). There was nothing there at all except very poor farming land, and bleak moors supporting a few hardy grouse.

In 1800 that hillside worked by Methusalem was put up for auction by the owner, an absentee landlord who lived further south in Merionethshire. It so happened that an Englishman called William Turner was in the district, possibly on a walking tour of Wales.

The history of the Festiniog Railway has been much influenced by people who just happened to be walking by at the right time. The appreciation of scenery and mountains for their own sake was a major change in sensibility in the eighteenth century. Until then the medieval view had prevailed, that mountains were monstrous excrescences placed there by God to make more difficult the lot of sinful man. It was Thomas Pennant (a relative of Richard Pennant) with his famous *Tours in Wales*, published in 1773, who led the way. He was followed by dozens of other tourists who afterwards set down their impressions (for example Cradock in 1777, the Reverend

10

Bingley in 1798, Richard Fenton in 1804 and of course George Borrow much later in 1862).

Diphwys was knocked down to William Turner for £1,000. Methusalem Jones's bid was too low and too late. Turner and his partners, the brothers Casson, worked the quarry for a number of years before selling it to the Diphwys Casson Company for £120,000.

Turner was the first of many. The Ffestiniog slate was there and it was of the highest quality. It only needed to be exploited. Quarries began to open one after the other. Near the Diphwys was the farm of Rhiwbryfdir (meaning 'the hill infested with fruit flies' – many quarry names reflect Blaenau's pastoral history) which William Oakeley, a local landowner, leased in 1819 to a Liverpool slate dealer called Samuel Holland – another name to conjure with in the history of the Festiniog Railway. Holland put in a man from Liverpool, Peter Whitehead, as clerk of works. But Whitehead evidently did not like Wales. Like Gershom, he was a stranger in a strange land. Eventually he took to the bottle, and on one of his visits Holland heard that Whitehead was getting drunk at the hotel every night and discharged him. He sent for his son Samuel Jr to run the quarry instead. Young Samuel arrived in March 1821, having walked most of the way from Liverpool. The nineteen-year-old Samuel took over the quarry and developed it from what he himself called 'a small hole in the ground with only a few men' into a prosperous concern which he was able to sell, with the help of an uncle in Baring's Bank, to the Welsh Slate Company which had Lord Palmerston and Nathan Rothschild on its Board. (Such names as Baring, Rothschild and Palmerston showed the degree of fashionable metropolitan interest in Ffestiniog slate soon after its development.) Holland kept, and named after himself, another quarry higher up the same mountain and continued to work it. By 1831 its output was 650 tons a year. Holland slates were the first to be carried by the Festiniog Railway.

In 1830, three years before the construction of the Festiniog Railway started, another young man arrived in the vale to seek his fortune: John Whitehead Greaves, yet another man who was to become famous in the Festiniog saga. He was the fourth son of a Warwickshire banker and was on his way to emigrate to Canada (the third son had already emigrated to New Zealand). He had walked from Liverpool (yet another of those astonishing pedestrians passing through who were so crucial in the Festiniog's history) and happened to be in

Portmadoc when he heard about the prospects for slate mining. He decided to stay and try his luck. In partnership with Edwin Shelton he leased the Glynrhonwy quarry near Llanberis from Lord Newborough and another quarry called the Chwarel Lord, at Blaenau Ffestiniog, after the previous tenant had gone bankrupt.

The way John Greaves made his fortune is a romantic story, and is probably true. He, too, is supposed to have had a dream – that the really rich vein of Ffestiniog slate lay, still untouched, between himself and the Rhiwbryfdir on a hillside known as Llechwedd (which means 'hillside'). Greaves backed his hunch. He had to wait fifteen years before he could buy out all the leaseholders who held the grazing rights on the hillside, and it was 1846 before he could start prospecting properly. By that time he had married and had a young family and was almost penniless. Edwin Shelton had taken out his £25,000 loan and gone. Greaves had tried in several places on the hillside, with no luck, when his foreman, one of two workmen who agreed to work for nothing and whom John Greaves afterwards supported for life, suggested another place. The story has become a legend in the Greaves family, of how, one evening in 1846, the children heard the sound of a horse galloping up the drive of Tan-yr-Allt. Their father told them that this messenger would bring them either ruin or a fortune.

It was fortune. When the door opened, there was the foreman, on his knees. 'Now is the time to praise God,' he said. They had struck the famous 'Old Vein' from which Llechwedd slates went to roof houses and public buildings all over the world. At an exhibition in 1862 John Greaves won a medal with a piece of Old Vein slate from Llechwedd ten feet long and one foot wide, one sixteenth of an inch thick, which could be bent and twisted like veneer.

The profits, and the expenses, of slate mining were both enormous. In the 1830s Assheton Smith told a friend that Dinorwic cleared him £30,000 a year profit, and this trebled by 1860. On the other hand, the Mr Roberts who leased Hafoty Cwmbowydd and Chwarel Lord from Lord Newborough and failed, thus giving Greaves his chance, had spent £30,000 before going bankrupt. It was either boom or bust.

One problem shared by all the Ffestiniog quarry-owners was transport. For years the slates were carried in panniers, in batches of sixty to eighty, on the backs of mules or ponies down the rough hillside tracks and slopes to Congl-y-Wal, where they were transferred to carts hired from local farmers (at huge profit

12

to them) and taken to jetties along the banks of the river Dwyryd. Some of the jetties can still be seen today. The slates were once more transhipped into barges, each carrying a load of about six tons.

The barges were manned by men called Philistines. No picture of them seems to have survived but their appearance was obviously remarkable enough to be remembered. They were picturesque-looking gentlemen in gamekeepers' clothes and tall felt top-hats which gave them a generally outlandish appearance. The Philistines were independent-minded people, known and feared for their physical strength and 'degree of difference'. They formed a mysterious, isolated community, notable even in mysteriously isolated nineteenth-century Wales.

The derivation of the name 'Philistine' is one of those romantic stories of early Festiniog history. In the latter part of the eighteenth century a Jewish chandler who had married a Welsh girl and set up business in Ludlow used to send his eldest son Dafydd to market his wares in Welshpool. There, Dafydd met, fell in love with, and eventually married Ffilys Iorwerth, the strapping, black-eyed, beautiful daughter of a Maentwrog farmer. When the farmer died Dafydd and Ffilys took over the farm. They had six children; Ebenezer the eldest son who helped to work the farm; three more sons, two of whom became fishermen and the third a boat-builder; and two daughters who both inherited their mother's looks and were married in their teens to local farmers.

Ebenezer had his mother's strong will but not her business sense. Ffilys was something of a despotic matriarch, and when Ebenezer announced he was going to marry a girl she disapproved of Ffilys banished him from the family hearth. Ebenezer renounced his interest in the farm and the rest of his family, who had all sided with Ffilys. He married the daughter of another local farmer, an enemy of Ffilys's.

When the slate quarries opened at Blaenau Ffestiniog it was Ffilys who thought of a scheme for transporting the slates by barge to the coast. Under her direction, the family built a flat-bottomed sailing barge and a stone pier on their land where it touched the Traeth Bach.

Ebenezer, meanwhile, whose father-in-law had died, now also owned part of the Traeth Bach shore lower down the estuary. He went into opposition, with a barge of his own.

The barges, and the family feud, were well known in the district. The local people, who almost all supported Ffilys, used to turn out in numbers to see which of the barges was going to be first. Everybody could tell if it was Ffilys's barge because she used to make her crew wear tall felt hats to avoid head injuries when loading and unloading. So, the tall-hatted crew would be cheered and welcomed with shouts of 'here come the Ffilys Steins' (as opposed to the Ebenezer Steins). Hence 'Philstine'. Like many Festiniog Railway stories, if it is not true, it ought to be.

Every fortnight at spring tides the Philistines worked their barges down the river, over the sandbanks and through tidal currents, and normally dead in the eye of the prevailing south-westerly winds, to the exposed anchorage of Ynys Cyngar which had room for only two or three barges at a time. Here the slate was transferred for the third time into the holds of coastal sailing ships bound for Liverpool. The slates' journey from quarry to customer was therefore inconvenient, complicated and expensive. It might have satisfied Methusalem Jones, but it would not do for long for Holland and the other English quarry-masters. Samuel Holland Sr, in fact, soon made his own arrangements. To the fury of the Philistines he had two boats of his own made in Liverpool. The first was sailed round to Portmadoc by an old sailor, W. Jones, who then walked back to Liverpool for the second. Samuel Sr also had a sloop built to carry about twenty tons, provocatively called the *Experiment*, which used to carry wheat-flour up the river to his warehouses at Trwyn-y-Garnedd.

Something clearly had to be done about transporting the slates. It was here that Madocks's idea of a harbour began to look so attractive. He already had powers under his original Act of 1807 to construct a harbour at Ynys Cyngar, but this was obviously not the solution the slate trade was looking for. Far better to take advantage of the dredging which was already being fortuitously done by the River Glaslyn. In June 1821 Madocks obtained another act enabling him to build a harbour at what is now Portmadoc, which is called after him (contrary to the romantic theory that it was named after Prince Madoc, who sailed from those parts to discover America before Columbus).

The first quays were ready in 1824, and the first one was rented by Samuel Holland on 21 October.

Once the harbour was built the next obvious step was to connect it by railway to the slate quarries. At least, it seems obvious, but somebody had to have the idea first and it seems as likely as not to have been William Madocks again. He appears to have been mulling over the idea of a railway for some time before. As early as May 1820 he had written to John Williams, his agent, asking his opinion on the best line for a railroad from the quarries down through Dol-y-Moch to Tan-y-Bwlch. This would cut out the pony- and mule-trekking portion of the journey, though still leaving the Philistines in business. Madocks had married in 1818 a young widow, a woman of property, a Mrs Roderick Gwynne (née Eliza Anne Hughes). Her home was at Tregunter, near Talgarth in Breconshire where there was a railway, the Hay Railway, completed in 1818.

Madocks may have had the idea there, but in any case railways were very much in the air at that time. As Lord Newborough's solicitor said, 'the rage for railways is gaining a footing in the Principality'. The plan that eventually emerged for the Festiniog Railway was for a very much longer scheme than Madocks's suggestion – to run from the quarries directly to the slate wharves at Portmadoc harbour. Several schemes for a Festiniog Railway appeared at much the same time.

The struggle between the various factions to decide which railway scheme would be built, and who would have control over it, is a fascinating revelation of local feelings and local personalities of the time. It was an early nineteenth-century power-game, involving men of high imagination and low scoundrels, peers and pigmen, good ideas and bad debts, excellent engineering and preposterous proposals. Each scheme had its devoted supporters and its bitter opponents. As the sides manoeuvred to find an advantage, there were meetings and betrayals, accusations and counter-accusations, petitions and cross-petitions. There were rumours of take-overs, and regroupings, and reconciliations. Charges of trespass were brought. There was even a threat of horse-whipping. The managing director of one company defected to its chief rivals in an atmosphere of general recrimination. In a litigious age, the parties were all ready to go to law at the drop of a slate. People published accusing pamphlets, and wrote furious letters to the local press who, meanwhile, danced excitedly up and down on the sidelines, cheering on first one side and then the other. The rival teams were so evenly matched for so long that it was a wonder the Ffestiniog quarries ever got their railway at all. As it was, internal strife delayed it for nearly a decade.

By 1824 two main schemes had emerged. The first was actually called the Festiniog Railway. It was promoted by what the draft of the act calls 'Several Owners and Occupiers of Slate Quarries and also Owners and Occupiers of land'. These almost certainly included Lord Newborough and, most likely, Madocks himself. Their scheme served the Blaenau quarries by means of inclines which joined where Blaenau Ffestiniog now is, and then dropped very steeply (falling some 700 feet in three miles) by means of three inclines to Dol-y-Moch on the valley floor. The railway then ran almost level along the north bank of the river, crossed the headland at Minffordd and then followed the present route to the Cob.

The rival line was called the Festiniog and Port Madoc Railway. This one was promoted almost certainly by W.G. Oakeley and very likely at this stage by Holland who was, after all, renting his quarry from Oakeley. Their railway ran from a farm called Maenyferram, just below the Diphwys, and went round the Moelwyn to the farm of Creuau, down the hill at Rhyd to the present level of the Festiniog Railway and then at a steady gradient down to the Cob.

Both routes were perfectly feasible, but both bills were rejected by Parliament, together with a third bill sponsored by Madocks, to consolidate his grip on his harbour and to raise money by mortgaging the rates. In spite of his marriage Madocks was still chronically short of money.

However, the need for transport was still there; in fact it became yearly more pressing. Welsh slate boomed in 1825. 'Bubble' companies were formed, speculators flocked to float them. One new company was the Welsh Slate Company, which bought Holland's lease of Rhiwbryfdir. The chairman was Lord Palmerston, and other directors included Lord Sidmouth (who as Henry Addington had been Prime Minister), John 'Bubble' Wilks, a well-known promoter of dubious companies, and William Lloyd Caldecot, who had at one time looked after Madocks's pigs. George Homfray was managing director.

Madocks and Lord Newborough transferred their support to Oakeley's Festiniog and Port Madoc Railway. Homfray, on behalf of the Welsh Slate Company, was also involved. They intended to present another bill when, suddenly, there was a threat from powerful newcomers. To the dismay of the local partisans it was found that Baron Nathan Meyer Rothschild, no less, had formed the Royal Cambrian Company to work mines and quarries on Crown lands throughout Wales. The company's surveyor, Benjamin Smith, began to go prospecting over the hills above Rhiwbryfdir. Oakeley promptly slapped a notice for trespass on the Royal Cambrian. The company proposed a railway which would cross the north and west faces of the Moelwyn before descending to Portmadoc. This one was to be called the Moelwyn and Portmadoc Railway. Madocks was by now in a state of considerable alarm, being convinced that Rothschild had designs on his harbour.

16

The line was surveyed by James Spooner – another name of power in Festiniog history (but not for this line). His survey was a bold series of straight lines, apparently disregarding topography or contours. The line ran north-east along the Traeth Mawr and then shot up the face of Moelwyn Mawr in a series of inclines.

Now, events quickened and insults flew thick and fast. Homfray defected to the Rothschilds. Caldecot published a blistering attack on the Moelwyn Railway Company, and had a violent argument in public with Homfray, threatening to horsewhip him. Rothschild did not appear in court to answer the charge of trespass. Oakeley and other landowners petitioned against the Moelwyn Railway, and the bill for that, too, failed.

When all the dust had settled the Ffestiniog quarries still had no railway. The slate boom collapsed. Quarrymen in Ffestiniog were forced to find work metalling the roads. Madocks died in 1828 in Paris. Samuel Holland Jr started to work another quarry, and quarrelled with Homfray.

In the lull that now followed there appeared the unlikely figure of Henry Archer, the man who, with Samuel Holland as a kind of *éminence grise* in the background, really built the Festiniog Railway. Born in 1799, Archer was a member of a prominent Irish family. They were lawyers in Dublin and had produced three lord mayors of the city. His stepbrother George was town clerk of Dublin.

It is difficult now to estimate the importance of the part Samuel Holland Jr played in the building of the Festiniog. His own memoirs show that he played a major role, but his surviving letters to Archer suggest that theirs was a formal business relationship only. His memory is demonstrably at fault at times. However, he certainly can claim the credit for introducing Archer to the idea of a railway. Nobody knows what Archer was doing or why he had come to North Wales. He seems to have had no regular business or profession. In the best Festiniog tradition, he just happened to be passing through when in December 1829 Holland met him in the parlour of a pub in Pen-y-Groes. They began to talk and Archer said he was looking for something to do and was thinking of renting 'the little Horse railway', the Nantlle, which ran from the quarries at Talysarn to Caernarvon. 'I advised him,' Holland wrote in his memoirs,

> to have nothing to do with it; but that if he really wished to undertake a railway, he had better come over to my neighbourhood and plan a railway from the Ffestiniog

17

Quarries to Port Madoc. He asked many particulars about it. I advised him to come over and see and stay with me, when I would point out the proposed line to him. He did not know where I lived and knew nothing about our neighbourhood, quarries etc., etc., so, he agreed to come, but without fixing a day. I told him how and which way to come.

Archer arrived at Holland's house unexpectedly at dusk on New Year's Eve. He stayed for several days, while Holland showed him round.

He and I walked over what I thought would be a good line to make the rail, and when I was much engaged about my own affairs, he went over the proposed line himself and thought it feasible. He said it must be a *single* line about two feet wide that would cost much less, and less to pay for land taken.

One evening Archer mentioned that he had been looking around the quarries and had met someone who 'was conversant with engineering and laying out lines and had partly engaged to meet him to walk over and lay out the Line with him'. Holland asked who it was, and to his consternation Archer said, 'Mr Benjamin Smith'. This was the Smith who had been surveyor for the Royal Cambrian, and Holland's foe. Holland wasted no time in steering Archer away from such a man. 'I told him that would never do. He asked *why* – I gave him my reasons, and said if any one in the neighbourhood was to be employed it must be Mr Jas. Spooner.'

They went to see Spooner, who was living at Tan-yr-Allt Isa. At first Spooner declined the offer. He said 'he was not a sufficient engineer to do it', which, on the evidence of his grotesque survey for the Moelwyn line, was only too true. Holland told him he must accept and he would have the help of a good man, Thomas Prichard, who had worked under Robert Stephenson. So Spooner reluctantly agreed.

Spooner and Prichard surveyed and laid out the line together, with the help of two of Spooner's sons, probably James Swinton the second son and Charles Easton (to be one of the great Festiniog Railway personalities) the third. The line they surveyed was much as it is today, except for the stretch where the Long Tunnel replaced double inclines over the saddle of the Moelwyn. The line was in the greatest contrast to Spooner's former monstrosity in the Moelwyns, but this may well have been due to the steadying hand of the experienced Thomas Prichard, who was to work on the Festiniog for the next thirty years.

Meanwhile, Archer set about raising the necessary finance. All the capital was subscribed in Dublin. Archer himself put up £11,905, a cloth merchant called James Smith £5,400, and £100 each came from Henry's stepbrother the town clerk George, another ex-lord mayor, an alderman, a magistrate, and three barristers. Thus, ironically, the original money for the Festiniog Railway was not English or even Welsh, but Irish.

Archer went to London to see about promoting a bill in Parliament. Holland went with him to help. But they failed. Although a railway would ultimately be to the good of the whole area, local opinion was almost unanimously against it. The farmers, carters and Philistines opposed it because it would deprive them of business. Turner and the Cassons would have nothing to do with it. Lord Palmerston and the Welsh Slate Company objected to it. John Madocks objected, on behalf of his uncle's estate. All those who had wanted a railway to Portmadoc down the other side of the Moelwyns opposed it.

Archer had to make three attempts to get the bill through Parliament. On the third occasion he was forced to incorporate safeguards for the Madocks estate and for the Bankes estate. But the tide of affairs was running on Archer's side. The railway could no longer be held up. Archer's bill had an unopposed passage in January 1832, and received the Royal Assent on 23 May. Curiously, now that the railway was a possibility, local opinion changed. Mrs Madocks had always campaigned for the railway. 'The Welshmen,' she wrote to Spooner after Archer's bill passed through the Commons, 'have already made Moelwyn blaze, to celebrate the fortunate progress Mr Archer's Bill has made.' Perhaps the local people realised that the railway had to come. Perhaps some of them also now realised, belatedly, that there was money in it for them. Perhaps they were bought off, or scared off. The local press was once again in ecstasies and in no doubt that this was good news. 'We congratulate our readers,' said the *Caernarvon Herald* on 26 May (as in Madocks's day, the press sprayed compliments in all directions), 'on the fair prospect of this important undertaking being speedily carried into effect. Mr Archer has entitled himself to the gratitude and respect of the neighbourhood, and indeed of the country, and especially of the industrious poor.'

That was well said. It now only remained to build the railway.

Chapter 3

One of the features of the Festiniog Railway which so much impressed those first volunteer workers of the early 1950s, and one of the factors which probably inspired and sustained the effort needed to retore it, was the sheer excellence of its civil engineering. It was a wonderfully well thought out and well laid out little railway, with a scope and a style of its own. The skill and care expended on the undertaking showed in the way the line neatly followed the contours of the hills to give a reasonable downward gradient. Bridges were built, earth and stoneworks erected, curves eased, to preserve that steady gradient all the way from Blaenau Ffestiniog down to the sea.

Allan Garraway first visited the Festiniog on a July afternoon in 1951. He and a friend, Bill Harvey, who was then British Railways shedmaster at Norwich, climbed up through the woods above the Oakeley Arms and reached the line above Tan-y-Bwlch. There, above the tree-line, the track was fairly clear. They could get some idea of the state of the line and its design. At that time they were both much involved with the restoration of the Talyllyn Railway, forty miles to the south, at Towyn. Garraway was immediately struck by the difference between the two lines. 'The Talyllyn was in such a decrepit state it was a wonder it still worked. The permanent way was just two bars of metal embedded in the turf, no more. But this was different. I said to Bill, *this* is the railway we ought to be restoring. This is a *proper* railway.'

A proper railway needs a proper beginning and ending, and now, at last, the Festiniog Railway has a station terminus again at both ends, at Porthmadog by the sea, and at Blaenau Ffestiniog up in the hills. At Blaenau, the return of the little trains to the centre of the town in May 1982, bringing the first passengers from Porthmadog in more than forty years, has helped to promote the first stirrings from what has been a very long economic trance. Some Blaenau business and trades people claim, obviously for tax purposes, that the Festiniog has brought nothing to the town. But any casual bystander on any day between May and September can see crowds of people, who are clearly not Welsh natives, walking up and down the main street of a town which (especially on Sundays and Bank Holidays) is still not exactly sure how to welcome visitors.

In Blaenau, there are some modern shops, next door to some whose frontages, decor and, it seems, articles for sale, have not changed since the 1930s. There are chapels, in an amazing range of architectural styles, from grim little buildings, unmistakably dedicated to an unforgiving God, to luxuriantly Italianate or baroque temples, transported piecemeal from Rimini or eighteenth-century Verona. In the background, there is Blaenau's almost lunar landscape of towering rock faces and vast slopes of shattered slate and rubble. On gloomy days, in summer and in winter, rain descends upon everything, trains, visitors, shops and chapels, with monsoon ferocity.

Blaenau Ffestiniog, the joint British Rail/Festiniog station, is something of a disappointment. There were pipe-dreams of a Welsh Grand Central, with a shopping and amusement arcade serviced by rail and road. In fact, years of hopes, hours of discussions and reams of paper have produced two bleak platforms; one, on the town side, for British Rail, and the second, on a central island approached by a great, gaunt footbridge, for the Festiniog.

Nearby, in the town, to make more room and a better access for a car park, the old Queens bridge has been demolished. New bridges have been built over the railway for the Benar Road and the A496 road to Maentwrog, and the roads themselves diverted for short distances.

The Festiniog's share of Blaenau Central is nothing but functional. Booking-office, café, and shop are on the ground floor of Isallt, a Victorian merchant's villa facing the main road; from a window there, a television camera scans the platform for the arrival of trains and/or vandals. On the platform itself: toilets, a small shop, and a station shelter brought from Acton in west London.

On the left, as the line moves out from Blaenau Central, under the two bridges towards Glan-y-Pwll, there is the seven acre site of what might have been. It looks, as Sam Snead once said of the Old Course at St Andrews after he had won the

Open there, 'the sort of real estate you couldn't give away'. In fact, this is the site of Stesion Fain, where it was at first intended that the Festiniog's terminus in Blaenau could (and some still maintain *should*) have been built.

From a carriage window, much of Blaenau still looks as it must have looked a hundred years ago. The peripatetic Blaenau sheep still wander everywhere, in and out of alleyways, back yards and gardens, eating everything green except the 'Blaenau rhododendrons', stunted bushes which grow on slate but seem never to flourish and never to die. Glan-y-Pwll level crossing is still there, where for very many years the original track was left embedded in the road tarmac (to safeguard the railway's right of way against the day of return). But the crossing is now automatically controlled, with flashing lights and audible warning signals. The crossing keeper's house has been renovated and now incorporates a volunteers' hostel. Behind it is a kind of fortified storage space: tools, stores, equipment, various assorted items of rolling stock and a huge pile of scrap iron are kept behind a high zareba of wire.

Every proper railway must pass, somewhere along its route, beside rows of small terraced houses, with tatty back yards, sooty washing lines, decaying sheds, and rusting, abandoned vehicles. From Glan-y-Pwll to Tan-y-Grisiau the Festiniog passes among some of the tattiest back yards, sootiest washing lines, most decadent sheds and most comprehensively rusting and terminally abandoned motor cars in the railway world. But this dereliction is more apparent than actual, more a matter of expectation and image than reality. In fact, a closer look shows many of the front doors and window-sills to be freshly painted and roofs newly repaired. Houses in one terrace at Barlwyd have been individually redecorated, to compose an ensemble of different colours and shapes and textures which would have pleased Lowry. Even as the train passes, one of the most hopelessly abandoned cars suddenly starts up and drives away.

Opposite, on the other side of the Afon Barlwyd, the great background slope of slate and rubble remains, but the ground in front, once desolate acres of marsh and reeds, has been reclaimed by spoil tipped from Glan-y-Don in 1976; a row of small trees, in a neat plantation, stands beside the river. Barlwyd bridge has been completely rebuilt, in what Brian Hollingsworth, civil engineering consultant to the FR Company, calls 'a fine piece of *cottage* engineering'; massive timber beams, supporting old rails laid transversely close together, a layer of tarmac, and finally, fresh ballast, sleepers and track. This bridge-work raised the track slightly. But very close by is a footbridge, at Groesffordd, under which the track has to pass with sufficient clearance for coaches. These two requirements mean that this very short length of track (two chains, or forty-four yards) has the steepest gradient of any part of the railway.

Now noticeably going downhill, the formation winds across the face of the hillside, following the contours towards Tan-y-Grisiau. On either side there are small cottages, many once derelict or vandalised, but now sold and restored. One or two were then *re*vandalised by arson, in the name of Wales, because they are or were thought to be 'second homes'. One sad little house in particular had for a long time blackened window sashes and heavy boards over the window spaces. Its Welsh owner, physically handicapped, had hoped to retire there. Anti-English graffiti scrawled on the walls held out similar threats for the future.

At Pen Craig there was one of those minor Festiniog miracles of recovery. In November 1975, there was a heavy fall of rock from under the line which damaged a cottage called Penlan below. Here, the railway ran along a narrow shelf under an overhanging outcrop of unstable rock. The fall was a serious threat to the railway's progress back to Blaenau. But international consultants Ove Arup designed what amounted to a new piece of hillside, and contractors McAlpine (known in Festiniog hagiography as the Blessed Robert) secured it in place with gigantic steel bolts, and underpinned it with cement. The only signs of the repair now are a short section of concrete cradles, laid side by side, and cupping the track as though pulling it safely into the hillside.

A few chains further, there was yet another threat to the railway's continuity, at Dolrhedyn bridge. The original structure was removed in 1957, with undertakings that it would be replaced. So it was, in 1980, but only after a great deal of bureaucratic activity. Honour on all sides was eventually satisfied, but the Dolrhedyn bridge episode was a typical example of how threats to the railway could arise seemingly out of nothing, and how complicated and time-consuming a process it was to resolve them.

The last mile or so of formation, the upper reach from Tan-y-Grisiau to Blaenau, was perhaps the Festiniog volunteers' finest achievement in all the three decades of the restoration. A supreme effort of organisation and labour was needed to prepare the track, and to restore what is known as the

23

'geometry' of its curves and slopes and gradients. A great deal of the work was funded by the Development Board for Rural Wales, and carried out under Manpower Service Commission schemes – a new source of manpower for the Festiniog.

Above Tan-y-Grisiau there were four footbridges to be rebuilt, heightened and strengthened, hundreds of yards of crumbling retaining walls to be rebuilt, scores of culverts, drainage channels and manholes to be designed, positioned, or repositioned, and built. Here and there, the works have unobtrusive decorations – a frill of slates along the top of a wall, or a pleasing little arch over the water-channel – as the 'signature' of men, such as Howard Bowcott, who built them.

Tan-y-Grisiau was the railway's terminus (the fourteenth terminus, somebody has calculated, since the restoration began) from 1978 until 1982. But those days of bustle and excitement are now over. Its buildings, never more than temporary, have now gone and Tan-y-Grisiau, like Dduallt, like Penrhyn and even Tan-y-Bwlch and Minffordd, is not much more than a halt, where some passengers get on or off some of the time.

At Tan-y-Grisiau the line of the old railway meets the new Deviation. When the top portion of the Festiniog was amputated by the electricity pumped storage scheme and its reservoir, the railway painfully set about growing another, which became known as the Deviation. As the line sets out upon the Deviation, towards the power station, on the right is one of the wonders of the Festiniog, the Cwmorthin Falls, and below the train is one of the wonders of the Deviation, the Cwmorthin bridge. Made of three giant fifty-five-feet long concrete beams, the bridge was finished in 1978 and cost only £6,000. It was put in the wrong place, leading to what Brian Hollingsworth, also the Deviation's historian, calls 'a little extra voluptuousness in the curves on each side as well as some pleasurable intellectual exercise for the man who set them out'.

From Cwmorthin the gradient is actually uphill, to a point just before the power station, where the new formation was raised to give adequate clearance above the pumped storage scheme 'penstock' pipes laid underground. This section of the line, including 'Summit Cutting' was built by contractors, at the insistence of the Central Electricity Generating Board, and not by volunteers.

The CEGB went to some trouble to make their power station as unobtrusive as possible, taking care over the disposal of spoil, landscaping and planting of trees. The main pumping and generating building is made of local Vale of Ffestiniog stone, and is very probably the largest building to be built with that stone since Harlech Castle.

The Ffestiniog scheme was the first hydro-electric pumped storage power station to be built for the CEGB. It is still their only daily pumped storage scheme and is one of the largest in the world. National demand for electricity varies from summer to winter, and from day into night. The problem is that electricity cannot be stored on a large scale. But pumped storage provides an ingenious indirect solution. The nation's power generating plant is steam-driven and is most efficient if operated at constant output. During the night, when demand for electricity is lower, excess power is used to pump water from the lower reservoir at Tan-y-Grisiau up to another reservoir at Stwlan some 1,000 feet above. Next day, when demand is greater, the water flow is reversed and the hydraulic head of water is used to generate power in a water turbine. Normally, the scheme pumps for six or seven hours every night, and generates power for four hours every day. Such a scheme can provide extra power to the national grid at very short notice (as when, for instance, a popular TV programme ends and half the population suddenly gets up to put an electric kettle on to make tea). The lower Tan-y-Grisiau reservoir and the main building, created in the 1960s, cut off the Festiniog Railway from its proper terminus at Blaenau Ffestiniog – and thereby hangs the tale of one of the longest law cases in British legal history.

Emerging from behind the power station, the line runs along the west bank of the reservoir. From above, the waters are still, peaty, almost Marmite-coloured and, in some curious way, vaguely hostile, as though they concealed some monster as menacing as Grendel's mother and the fishermen on the banks are there at their own risk. In fact, the CEGB stock it with thousands of rainbow trout every year reared at the Board's fish farm at Trawsfynydd nuclear power station. The reservoir is one of the best fisheries in Britain and holds Welsh records for rod-caught trout of over ten pounds.

From the power station onwards, for the next two miles, is the heart of the Deviation. The labours of the Deviationists (only twenty per cent of them members of the Festiniog Railway Society and most of them not interested in railways but in shovelling) over more than thirteen years can be seen (although they are not all by any means obvious) in the new cuttings, new embankments, new culverts, new walls and ditches. To appreciate the skill and labour involved one often has to get down off the line and look at it from below.

Above the western shore, a now almost imperceptible widening of the formation shows the site of Llyn Ystradau Halt, perhaps the shortest-lived of all the Festiniog termini: the single platform came into service, was used, and removed, all within a year. The site was then levelled, to conform to landscaping requirements, and now only a siding remains. But standing there, one becomes aware of an odd-looking group of trees down to the left by the water's edge. It is an experimental plantation, to find which trees can best put up with the constant rise and fall of the reservoir level, as the pumped storage effect takes place. Other trees have been planted to see how tolerant they are when flooded for long periods. Some even have specially induced 'roots' grafted on to their stems, to help them get the oxygen they cannot get from the soil!

In the very early mornings, when the reservoir water level is at its lowest, one can still cross the valley floor by the old line of the railway, which will be flooded again later in the day, to the entrance of that legendary 'Long Tunnel' through the Moelwyns. The tunnel is blocked now, sealed for ever by tons of cement, but its very close clearances, grimy walls, constant dripping water, and stifling smoke clouds (supposed by the locals to be a sure cure for whooping cough) have passed into Festiniog mythology. Before the tunnel, a water-wheel hauled the slate wagons up an incline. Water for the wheel was provided by a dam, known as Archer Dam, built in 1836. The railway passes between two remaining portions of the dam as it heads for the northern entrance of a new tunnel. Opened in June 1978, after over a year of hard and sometimes anxious work, the 'New Tunnel' is shorter than the old; but, with its shot-creted interior, cemented portals and walkway beside the track, it is higher, wider and altogether more handsome.

From Tunnel South the line goes still downhill, around the curves of the various Deviation working sites, each with its well-remembered, distinctive name, through woods of Coed Dduallt, sweeping in a great spiral down and into Dduallt, which was the Festiniog terminus for some ten years. Trains used to stop there for ten minutes, while the engine ran round and took up its position in the front of the train again for the journey down. Ten minutes at Dduallt was enough for most people, especially when it rained. There is a station platform, a view point, with a slate viewing table set up in 1970, a small house, a signal box, and a patch of marsh, with bog cotton and reeds. It is a lonely and a somewhat depressing place; before a Light Railway Order reduced it to 'halt status' in 1923, Dduallt actually had a station-master. There was little for him to do or see and it was no wonder that occasionally incumbents became quietly unstable and had to be taken away.

From Dduallt the gradient seems more noticeable to the untutored eye, down through Tro Peudy (meaning 'cowshed bend' – the actual cowshed is on the right), down again to a glimpse of grey roofs and some magnificent upstanding fir trees, below on the left. This is Dduallt Manor House, dating from the fourteenth century. This was Colonel Andrew Campbell's house, with a barn which was once a Deviation Mess – the subject of many a song and saga. The Colonel's name is still remembered on the railway. Three memorial stones on Dduallt platform commemorate his long friendship with the Festiniog, and there still, above his house, is Campbell's Platform with the siding where the Colonel kept his diesel engine, used regularly in the days when the Manor House was only accessible by rail.

The line continues downwards, past Coed-y-Bleddiau, where the line superintendent Hovenden once lived. So, once, did other celebrities: the composer Sir Granville Bantock, and St John Philby, explorer, author, father of Kim Philby. Then, a sound rather like 'Wha-a-a-arp': this is Garnedd Tunnel, the 'Short Tunnel', the 'Tunnel Fach' which was once strengthened with steel hoops taken from the hulls of surrendered German U-boats after the Great War. Far below on the left (downhill is always on the left all the way down as far as Minffordd) is the steep slope of Tafarn trip, with a sight of swans on Llyn Mair, a small lake, beautiful but bogus, dating only from the nineteenth century.

And so into Tan-y-Bwlch station, looking just like something out of one of those inimitable railway stories by the Reverend Wilbert Vere Awdry. It is all there: the large station clock, the train destination indicator, the bright red geraniums in tubs, by courtesy of the Festiniog's horticultural consultant, who for many years was A.B. Vaughan of Dolgellau; green platform benches, made and presented by the Sheffield Group of volunteers; white railings, made and presented by the North Staffordshire Group; notice-board by the Bristol Group; the cross-over bridge for pedestrians, made and erected by several groups; the Olde Tea Shoppe, sticky buns, postcards, tea and tickets; the water tank; and the station-master's cottage, which in the distant past used to be the booking office and waiting-room. There, for many years, John Harrison, or 'Lord North' as he was known on the railway, was the station-master, with his gilt-peaked cap such as all proper station-masters used to, and ought to wear, and his small dog Sally, star of so many TV pictures of the railway. John Harrison has left the Festiniog, but his presence still seems to brood over the landscape at Tan-y-Bwlch.

The station-master gives the 'Right away' and the train moves off across the road bridge, iron cast at Boston Lodge in 1854, so it says on the side, and so into another world on the Festiniog, known to all as 'The Woods'. Aficionados of the Festiniog often say this is the part they love best. In wintertime, the woods and hillsides on the Festiniog have a peculiarly chilling bleakness all their own, but in spring and summer they are transformed by bluebells, primroses and rhododendrons. This is the world of the sessile oak, the pine and the larch, the home of the squirrel and the badger. Meanwhile, the train is still descending, through the typical cuttings of the Festiniog which are very narrow, with only just room enough for the train to pass. The guard locks carriage doors to prevent the unwary passenger opening one and impaling himself on passing rocks, or worse still, doing some damage to the carriage. Festiniog cuttings are dim and cool and mysterious. There are shining rock faces, wet with damp, trailing ferns, foxglove spikes, vivid tufts of green grass and, in one place, the scrawled graffiti and initials of men who worked on the railway over a hundred years ago. One always thought of slate as grey; the cutting slate is blue and black and brown and dark green and yellow. By now the alert passenger, equipped with all the Company's guide-books, can pick out some well-known landmarks, as the Vale of Maentwrog spreads out below. There is Llan Ffestiniog at the head, the roofs of Plas Tan-y-Bwlch through the trees, once the home of the Oakeleys, now the Snowdonia National Park Centre. There is Harlech Castle, the jetties on the river Dywryd where the slates used to be loaded into barges, and high across the valley, almost at eye-level, the great edifice of the nuclear power station at Trawsfynydd. It is supposed to have been built in the most unobtrusive site, and in a way to attract the least attention; if that is true, then the good Lord help North Wales if the Atomic Energy Authority ever want to get themselves noticed. As it is, Trawsfynydd looks as though it was built by Edward I to keep the Welsh in order.

The Festiniog must be one of the most closely studied railways in the world. People are always racking their brains over the history and the significance of what they can see from the carriage window – all those tracks in the woods leading to abandoned workings of old lead and copper mines, with

28

occasionally a ruined cottage, a fenced mineshaft, and an odd triangular-shaped clearing which once was the site of an old Festiniog station, Hafod-y-Llyn.

At Cei Mawr, literally the 'Great Quay', the train crosses a small valley on the largest civil-engineering feat of the line, a sixty-foot-high stone embankment. Every landmark, every curve and cutting and straight, sometimes one feels every knob and stone on the line, has its own name. Some are obviously derived from a physical feature. Others commemorate accidents and incidents. Thus there is Linda's Leap, scene of a notable derailment, and Blanche's Bump. There is Whistling Curve, and Tyler's Curve and Milestone Curve and Gysgfa Curve ('sleeping place curve', it used to be a favourite spot for Sunday afternoon siestas) and Tro Bagl ('shepherd's crook curve') and Tro Ffatri ('factory curve'). Some are plate-layers' names reflecting climatic and working conditions on the railway: Cutting Budr ('dirty'), Cutting Gwlyb ('wet') and Cutting Naddu ('hewn', that is, not blasted).

On the bare and windswept hillside of Rhiw Goch ('red bank') where there is a passing loop, completed in 1973, the line finally leaves the woods and approaches houses, cars, roads – all the signs and trappings of life outside the railway. At Penrhyn, where the old station building has been imaginatively converted into hostel accommodation for volunteer railway workers, the train passes beside neat back gardens – anemones, aubretia, Star of Bethlehem and later fuchsias and dahlias, a world away from Glan-y-Pwll. There are faces grinning and hands waving at Penrhyn level-crossing. Here the Festiniog touches the other world. The impact is sometimes painful and unexpected. One evening in the very early days after the restoration a motorist from Beddgelert, driving a blue Reliant three-wheeler, saw a train, heard its warning toot, but still drove onto the station occupation crossing, where the engine hit him square amid-ships. Eye-witnesses said the three-wheeler was converted into a U-shape, with a foot trimmed off each end. When asked, did he not hear and see the train, the motorist said, 'Oh yes, but I thought to myself, the Lein Bach doesn't run any more, this must be a ghost train.'

To those who live and work on the railway the familiar places come thick and fast upon each other now: Minffordd station, a prime example still of Victorian narrow-gauge railway architecture; Minffordd crossing, with Lottie Edwards the crossing-keeper standing at the gate. Over the years hundreds of volunteers have spent their evenings in Lottie's cottage

29

parlour, drinking her tea and talking interminably about railways. Next is Minffordd Cemetery, the last resting place of many Festiniog railwaymen, including Bill Hoole, one of the most famous of Festiniog drivers.

Passing Boston Lodge Works there is a long glance, intoxicating for all railway enthusiasts, of assorted rolling-stock, heaps of scrap metal, and ramshackle but obviously quite vital buildings, with perhaps a double-engine locomotive blowing off clouds of steam and self-importance, and groups of men standing in statuesque poses wearing shiny grease-caps, filthy overalls and intensely sombre expressions.

The last lap is out across the Cob, with a view inland which has not changed much since William Madocks's day. It is a sight which has often inspired travel-brochure writers to eloquence. But the travel writers are a part of the Festiniog tradition, too, and a good example of the *genre* is by somebody called Twells Brex, writing between the wars. He was, he said, in the studio of a landscape painter when the conversation turned on the question, which was the finest view in the world? Somebody said Mont Blanc, somebody else the Golden Horn, others said Rio, Niagara, Richmond Hill, Derwentwater. But there was one view that Twells Brex thought surpassed them all. 'I had barely started to speak of it,' he wrote, 'when the landscape painter intervened. "I know," he cried, "what you are speaking of; it is the view of Snowdonia from the bridge over Portmadoc estuary; I have travelled the world and I know nothing to equal it." ' So, wrote Twells Brex,

> whenever I think of North Wales, that picture comes back to me – the cattle standing in pools set like turquoises in yellow sands; the folding in of the hills to the gorge of Aberglaslyn; and then ridge upon ridge, shoulder above shoulder, the stairway of the mountains to the spire of Snowdon.

Journey's end and journey's beginning, is the Harbour station at Portmadoc, the railway's administrative centre and the Company's registered address. It once was a grim little granite building, with its own characteristic smell. One lady once said, 'My *dear*, it smells *just* like a *French* station'.

In recent years the station building has been almost doubled in size, with an enlarged booking office and lobby, a much bigger bookstall and shop, the Little Wonder buffet, and a suite of offices on the floor above. But in high summer as one's train draws in, Harbour station platform is still an amazing and even faintly alarming sight. There is what seems like an unbroken rank of faces, three deep, all longing to get on board so much they barely allow one space to get off. The platform is milling with people of all sorts: sunburned men in blue anoraks, surrounded by children, and shouting 'Caroline, for God's sake where's Caroline got to now?'; very large women with very loud voices asking where the 'Ladies' is; anxious Germans fretting about their cameras; men and women with Midlands accents wearing (unwisely) loudly-patterned shorts and 'Engine-Driver' caps. All this excitement and activity began with an Act of Parliament of 1832.

Once Samuel Holland and Henry Archer (who became managing director under the Act) had their Parliamentary approval, tenders were put out for the construction of the railway. The contract was won by James Smith of Caernarvon. For the sum of £6,972, to be paid in instalments as each eighth of the work was completed, Smith was to build the formation, supply the stone sleepers and lay the track. The Festiniog Railway Company (given one 'f' in the Act and ever since) would provide the rails, chairs and rolling-stock. They would also pay the foreman and the engineer. The specification of the line was attached to an Agreement of 22 December 1832. A technical description of one of the oldest narrow-gauge railways in the world makes interesting reading:

1. The Railway to be formed for the reception of Iron Rails, according to the plan or Specification furnished by Mr Spooner to Mr James Smith the Contractor for forming the Railway and by which the same James Smith formed his estimate and will be required to enter into a Contract for completing same.

2. An inclined plane to be formed over that part of the line where a tunnel had been proposed to be formed with a Water Wheel of twenty-four feet Diameter, and three feet wide with all the necessary Machinery dams and other works for the purpose of conveying the Trucks over the said inclined plane.

3. Wrought Iron rails and chairs to be procured for and laid on the entire line of said Railway being nearly fourteen miles which rails and chairs are to be of the same weight as those used on the Caernarvon and Nantlle railroad, that is forty pounds to the yard.

4. The rails and chairs to be laid on proper Stone Blocks or Sleepers.

5. All land required for the said Railway or Tramroad to be purchased and paid for.

6. The present surface of the Embankment on Traethmawr to be widened by three feet at the least in case Mrs Elizabeth Madocks does not consent to form a new Carriage way, and give up the present Carriage way over the said Embankment to the said Company.

7. One hundred wagons each to contain Twenty-three hundred-weights of slates to be made for the use and benefit of the said Company.

8. And finally the Railway is to be completed in a workmanlike manner for the Conveyance and carriage of slates and other goods by means of Trucks or Railway Waggons.

Mr W.G. Oakeley laid the first stone on 26 February 1833 near the farm of Creuau, above Tan-y-Bwlch, and work began at each end of the line. But the conditions of Clause 8 were not fulfilled, or at least not at first, and soon there was trouble. By April 1834 Smith had abandoned his contract and left the line unfinished. Archer dismissed him for allegedly failing to keep to his contract. There was a dispute over Smith's payment; he insisted he had completed seven-eighths, but the Company said he had only done three-quarters. There was another lawsuit, which went to arbitrators who awarded nominal damages of 14s. 4d. against the Company, and this award was upheld by the Court of Common Pleas.

The Company decided to finish the line themselves, with James Spooner in charge. Some figures for the financing of the railway still survive. The Company were authorized to raise capital of £24,185. 10s., which was the amount Spooner had originally estimated the railway would cost. As they were virtually penniless when the line was finished, this is probably very near the sum actually spent. The work left undone by Smith and repairs caused by his shoddy workmanship cost £4,314, and another £5,209 was spent on alterations and on work which Smith was not responsible for. The authorized capital can be broken down in more detail from surviving records. Excavating, embanking, forming and fencing cost £14,275. 9s. 9d.; culverts and bridges £337. 3s.; rails, blocks, chairs, and laying and bedding them £8,400. The purchase of the necessary land cost £1,172. 18s. 3d.

The earliest Company pay-sheets date back to April 1834 (when the Company took over from Smith) and they show that James Spooner as engineer and Thomas Prichard as foreman were paid £100 and £65 a year respectively. At its peak the building of the railway employed about 150 men of several different trades. Because so many of the men had the same surnames and Christian names, the pay-sheets often distinguished individuals by their home towns. Some came from Ffestiniog and the Vale of Maentwrog, others from Caernarvon and as far away as Holyhead, Pwllheli and Bala. There were up to nine gangs of track-layers and labourers, each gang with ten or more men. Some men worked in partnership with each other. They were known as 'bargain-men' and were paid a form of piece-work for digging cuttings and drains, building walls and embankments. There were men called 'block-getters' who supplied the sleepers; boatmen, to ferry the stones up the river; and carters, to carry building materials to the higher stretches up the line. The work was done entirely by man- and horse-power. It was a case of picks, shovels, wheelbarrows, horses and carts. The men found lodgings locally, the bachelors often living near the line in the week and walking home at weekends. Some local smallholders also worked on the railway, perhaps two or three days a week, and were paid by the day.

Railway enthusiasts and historians have had many hours of innocent amusement over the years arguing about the origins and exact dimensions of the Festiniog Railway gauge. Archer had decided that the Festiniog should be 'about two feet wide'. Even today it is still colloquially called 'a two-foot gauge'. But it is not, in fact, two feet; it is the odd measurement of one foot eleven and a half inches. This is so near sixty centimetres that it has been suggested that the Festiniog Railway gauge was an early example of metrication. In 1856 Charles Spooner (James's son, and successor on the railway) said that the line was 'twenty-five inches from centre to centre'. With rail one and three-quarter inches wide, that made twenty-three and three-quarter inches inside measurement, rail to rail. But in 1869 Spooner was saying on oath before the House of Lords Select Committee that 'the line was absolutely one foot eleven and three-quarter inches . . . called the two-foot gauge'. The ensuing Act certainly gave the measurement as twenty-three and three-quarter inches. In a paper of 1870 Spooner said that 'it is termed two foot gauge but in reality it is somewhat less'. Anyway, one foot eleven and a half inches it was and has remained. The measurement may have been taken originally from the Penrhyn quarry line, or from some other line – or Spooner may have just thought it up. Railway enthusiasts can debate. It looks, and is, just about right.

The kind of track, that is to say the size and shape of rails, chairs and sleepers, has also exercised railway experts for years. The best and shortest description is in Dr M.J.T. Lewis's excellent little book *How Ffestiniog Got Its Railway*, which is indispensable reading for the history of the railway at this time.

> The specification laid down that the 'rails and chairs are to be of the same weight as those used on the Caernarvon and Nantlle railroad, that is forty pounds to the yard'. The forty pounds refers to two yards of 15½lb. rail and two 4½lb. chairs, although in the event the track was made slightly heavier. The fish-bellied rails, weighing 16lb. per yard, came from Dowlais and from Jevons Sons and Co. of Liverpool, at about £9 per ton. The chairs were cast by Thomas Jones of Caernarvon, who, to deal with this large order of about 50,000, apparently set up a branch foundry at Portmadoc, which was continued by his son John to become Glaslyn Foundry. The chairs, which varied in weight, were mostly either 5lb. or 6lb., and cost 15s. a hundredweight. The only known track which is certainly original (recently excavated in Boston Lodge) has 5lb. chairs. Slate and granite sleeper blocks, one per chair, were collected from nearby hillsides and bored at 3s. 6d. a dozen. The process of fitting oaken pegs (17s. 6d. per thousand) into the holes and spiking the chairs down cost 6d. a dozen blocks. Spikes and iron keys were supplied by the resident nailer. Wooden sleepers were used only on the Cob. Points (called passbyes or turnouts indiscriminately) consisted of solid castings weighing a hundredweight with wrought-iron movable tongues.

By December 1834 money was very short and a reduced work-force was concentrated on the track. By July 1835 the line was just about finished, except for the fencing, building a lower road across the Cob, and the quarry inclines at Blaenau Ffestiniog. The inclines taking the line across the flank of the Moelwyn (later replaced by the 'Long Tunnel') also needed to be rebuilt.

In January 1836 there was another row, one of many that were to rock the railway and enliven life for those who worked on it right up to modern times. Many of those connected with the Festiniog Railway over the years have had high tempers and low flashpoints. It may be that there is some abrasive element in the very business of running a railway which so often causes men to blow off steam as vigorously and as freely as their engines.

This row, between Henry Archer and the rest of the Board, was a serious one. The cause of it is not clear from the records and correspondence which still survive, but it was enough for the Board to press Archer to resign. He refused. However, he did agree that Edward Carreg of Tremadoc, the Treasurer, Captain James Gandon and Livingston Thompson (a young lawyer from Dublin who was to be a notable personality in the Festiniog) should have what was termed 'the entire control of every matter'. But obviously the trouble rumbled on, for in July Spooner was sending in his resignation because of the way Archer had behaved towards him. It was suggested that Archer had tried to provoke Spooner to resign so that he, Archer, could run the line more economically without him. Spooner was evidently persuaded to withdraw his resignation (he was by then a vital figure on the railway, carrying out the duties of general manager) but later in the year Archer was again at loggerheads with the Board. He claimed they owed him back salary and money for the purchase of some of his shares. The Board offered £500 as a peace gesture. Archer refused it. The matter went, once again, to arbitration. The arbitrators could not agree but at last, in a most unfortunate atmosphere of general hostility, the Company were ordered to pay Archer a large sum. From this time, Archer began to drift away from the control of the railway. He seems to have remained a director, intermittently, until as late as 1860 when the Company granted him an annuity of £100 a year. He had sold all but ten pounds' worth of his shares by 1844. He became involved in schemes for building a harbour at Porthdinlleyn, on the Caernarvonshire coast, to improve communications with Ireland. Henry Archer is also remembered by philatelists for having invented a machine for perforating postage stamps. He died, in Pau in south-western France, on 2 March 1863. He left the Festiniog in a manner which was to be repeated so often in the railway's history; personal disagreements, followed by the disappearance of one party in the dispute. So often those who began an enterprise were not there to see it completed.

A cause of Archer's dispute with the Board may have been the design of the inclines taking the railway over the Moelwyns; there has always been an element of mystery about them. Local magistrates signed completion certificates for the Caernarvonshire section of the railway on 30 June 1836, and for the Merionethshire section on 1 July. These, if they meant anything at all, meant that the railway was complete and open for traffic from top to bottom. The first recorded tonnage is for the period to 30 June, when 1,195 tons were noted for the payment to Mrs Madocks of her halfpenny per ton due on slate carried across the Cob; this, presumably, was the total tonnage brought down the line between the opening date and 30 June 1836. Yet the cable drums for the inclines were only installed in May of that year and the water-wheel (mentioned in the specification of December 1832 and essential to provide power to work the inclines) was not in place until September. Some other temporary arrangement must have been in use, probably animal haulage. In July and August Richard Lloyd was paid 11s. 7d. for 'Traces for Donkey' and 'Jno' Lewis, sadler, 10s. for 'harness for Donkey'. The original inclines had been built by James Smith and were actually finished in August 1834. Of the two inclines, the north one required load-hauling against the grade; the south side was balance-worked, the downhill loaded wagons pulling up the empty wagons. These inclines must have been unsatisfactory, because by June 1835 another quite different plan was being approved – possibly designed by Robert Stephenson; the Company paid him a bill of £21 the following year for a plan of an incline. Archer was certainly involved in the incline designs. In January 1836 the other directors were urging him to resign his responsibilities for them. All the inclines were made redundant in late May 1842 when a tunnel 730 yards long – it had been started in December 1839 – was opened for traffic. The bill for the celebration drinks, dated 24 May 1842, still exists.

The Company did not wait for the inclines to be finished before opening the railway. Some haste may have been forced on them because the four years' completion limit laid down in the Act expired in June 1836. By that spring the fencing was largely complete. The lower road across the Cob had also been finished. On 20 April the Company threw a party. Samuel Holland was there, and described the 'grand opening day' in his Memoirs:

> I had a short Train of Waggons loaded with slates and a great number of carriages laden with people, workmen and others (not only those engaged on the line, but many of the Quarrymen) of course, my own Family (sisters) and some guests who were staying with us, Archer, Spooners, Mathews, Greaves, and sister, Baines, West and others, all went up to the Inclines in the Carriages, drawn by Horses, but we all came down without Horses, the inclination being sufficient to enable us to do so.
>
> There was great cheering and Rock Cannon firing, all along the line and on our arrival at Port Madoc over the Embankment we were drawn by Horses until reaching the Embankment – the Horses rode at the tail of the Train, in

Boxes made purposely, feeding all the way. At Port Madoc we were met by Crowds of People, Bands playing and the workmen had a good dinner given them; all the better Company were entertained at Morfa Lodge by Mr Spooner and ended the day with a Dance.

Chapter 4

Business on the railway was very slow indeed at first. Once a railway had been built connecting the quarries with the sea, one would have thought that the owners would have fallen over themselves to make use of it. Not so at all. Samuel Holland agreed in August 1834 to use the railway but he was the first and, for some time, the only quarrymaster to do so. The rest held aloof. Negotiations were carried on in an atmosphere of petty squabbling, backbiting and absurd displays of temperament. Local landowners like W.G. Oakeley behaved like petty tribal chieftains exacting tribute from the caravans passing through their domains. Oakeley had insisted that provision should be made in the railway's Act for walls to be built four feet six inches high along the line where it passed through his land. For some 500 yards, nearest Plas itself, the walls were to be built ten feet high! Archer had a far-sighted appreciation of the railway's possibilities for those who loved to look at scenery. He seems to have had very early ideas about carrying passengers. 'If the stone walls were built throughout,' he wrote to Oakeley in 1834, 'the public would be deprived of one of the finest Panoramic views in North Wales.' He pointed out that Oakeley, as landlord to Holland and to the Welsh Slate Company, stood to gain a great deal from the railway business. He offered Oakeley a penalty of £500 for not building the walls.

It was all in vain. Oakeley insisted. Not only that, but he revoked his earlier promise to allow an incline to be built over his land to serve Holland's quarry. Because of that promise, the Company had not made provision for the incline in the Act. Those wretched walls might even have been built had not Oakeley died in October 1835. His widow agreed to waive her rights in return for the £500. She did not allow the incline to be built until 1839, when the Company paid £250 out of the total cost of £796.

Slowly, business began to pick up. Agreement was reached with the Welsh Slate Company in December 1837. Inclines were built, extra rails laid, another wharf at Portmadoc commissioned and Welsh Slate Company slates travelled on the Festiniog Railway in October 1838. Lord Newborough's quarries soon followed suit. Incredibly, Turner and Cassons did not use the railway until 1860. Although much slate was still carried by the Philistines for some years, the tonnage of slate annually quarried leaped up eightfold, largely due to the railway, in forty years, from 11,396 in 1825 to 89,294 in 1865. The railway paid its first dividend in 1843 – seven per cent.

The Festiniog dropped some 700 feet in its length of some thirteen miles. The gradient was steepest at Duffws station, in Blaenau Ffestiniog, and slightest across the Cob. The average for the line was about one in a hundred. A wagon released at Blaenau would have rolled all the way down to Boston Lodge (if its speed had not derailed it by then). Given a following wind it might also have made a fair way across the Cob. The early trains did literally that – they rolled down to Boston Lodge, where horses then drew them across the Cob. Each train had brakesmen who ran up and down its length along the tops of the slate wagons, applying brakes as needed to regulate the train speed.

John Greaves's granddaughter Dorothy Drage, writing after the Second World War, has left a charming description of the whole process. 'The wagons,' she says,

> were started by a push and then the rest of the journey was achieved by force of gravity. When the trucks were very heavily loaded they needed a good deal of pushing and then once going, the pushers had to jump quickly on to the trucks and take the journey with them. The return journey in those days had to be done with the aid of an elderly horse who did not mind the tunnels.

At Blaenau the elderly horses who did not mind the tunnels would of their own accord walk across from the front of the 'up' train to the back of the 'down' and re-embark in specially made wagons with high flaring metal sides, called 'horse-dandies', for the trip back down to Portmadoc again. At the intermediate stage stations, the 'up' empty train would most likely stand alongside the 'down' loaded train, so that the horse-dandies would be side-by-side at the top end of each train. The horses would back down out of the 'down' horse-dandy and then turn round to be harnessed to the 'up' train alongside. One horse-dandy still exists and can be seen in the Museum at Porthmadog.

The Company employed specialist personnel, such as the brakesmen and the splendidly titled 'Weighmaster and Constable' who had a cottage at Boston Lodge, but after a short experiment of nine months or so of working the railway with direct labour the Company gave a contract to a local farmer to provide horses and wagons. The earliest contract to survive (possibly it is the earliest drawn up) is dated 6 November 1838. It gives Morgan Jones of Rhiw Goch Farm the right to work traffic over the railway. Whoever drew up the contract (very probably Spooner) reveals even at this very early stage in the Festiniog's history the true railwayman's almost obsessive urge to write everything down in dozens of rules and regulations. The contract fairly bristles with all the things Morgan Jones could not do, on pain of a fine of five shillings. He was not to stop any train by any means other than the brake, not to apply the brake by any other means than by hand, and not to lock the wheels; he was to oil the wagons (which the Company undertook to supply and repair) at his own expense. He would be fined for blocking the tracks near points, for taking wagons off the rails to unload them, and several other railway crimes. All this Spooner signed for the Company with Prichard as witness. Morgan Jones made his mark.

On his part Morgan Jones contracted to convey all the slates raised from Rhiwbryfdir to Portmadoc for 7d. a ton. The time allowed for the carriage of slate down was eighteen daylight hours from the time of loading.

Morgan Jones had the contract for some time, but whether he died, or retired, or was eventually oppressed by the restrictions, by 31 March 1849 the Company had a different contract, with Robert Roberts of Pensyflog. Roberts's rate was at first 5d. then rising to 6d. per ton of slate carried. He, too, was hedged in with cautions. He could not carry hay or straw in the trains. He was fined if any of the weigh-bills were lost. He had to be responsible for maintaining the axle-bearing 'bushes'. The train journey time was two hours down to Portmadoc and eight hours back up to Blaenau. One horse was reckoned to be able to pull eight wagons up at three mph. Trains went down at a restricted ten mph. Roberts ran a timetable (which still survives) of six and sometimes seven trains a day, up and down. There were four crossing-points on the line, where there were stables, at Caednyfydd, Rhiw Goch, Hafod-y-Llyn and the top tunnel. Trains could pass each other and the horses that did not mind the tunnel were changed. There were also stables and watering at Boston Lodge and at the Quarry Terminus in Blaenau. The Company continued to employ contractors (probably Robert Roberts) until the introduction of locomotives.

In time, techniques were perfected for working wagons on the inclines, known as 'crewling', and for marshalling the slate trains for the run down to Minffordd or Boston Lodge. The Festiniog served four main quarry inclines. They were the Oakeley and the Welsh Slate Company/Llechwedd at Dinas, and the Maenofferen and Votty and Bowydd at Duffws. Making up the trains was done at Dinas Junction (later at Glan-y-Pwll) and was the responsibility of the quarry employees working on the inclines. They were obliged by the rules to put two braked wagons at the head of the train and any wagons for the other branch at the rear, but otherwise the formation of the train was left to chance: normally there was about one braked wagon in every five. A Festiniog Railway employee, a brakesman, then took the train as far as Glan-y-Pwll. Later in the nineteenth century, when the LNWR and the GWR had reached Blaenau, wagons for these two lines were detached here. The Dinas section was then dropped through on to the main Festiniog Railway line and the Duffws section – including additions from Cwmorthin, Wrysgan and Craig-Ddu – would be coupled up for the run down to Boston Lodge or Minffordd. A Festiniog head brakesman or foreman would examine the train, some-times rearranging the braked wagons. The wagons started easily enough at Glan-y-Pwll, but the train would have to be given its head through the tight cuttings and blind curves behind Tan-y-Grisiau if it was not to stall before the false summit opposite the Moelwyn Mine, a little above the Long Tunnel. After that, it was a matter of keeping the train 'just not quite out of control'. Working a gravity train needed skill and nerve.

As the railway began to prosper the trains grew longer, and soon there were formations of over a hundred wagons, making a train over 300 yards long – clanking and thundering downhill, with two or sometimes (if there were more than eighty wagons) even three brakesmen on board, shinning over the tops of the slates to reach their brakes and regulate the speed. The leading brakesman would now and then wind a blast on his horn – a special kind of sawn-off hunting-horn. A fully loaded train was a fine sight, especially at night when its sound could be heard down the mountain long before its wagons came into view, bucking and snaking and throwing showers of sparks to each side. After some early accidents, ropes hanging from small gantries were placed to brush the heads and shoulders of the brakesmen, to warn them of oncoming bridges and other overhead obstructions. As traffic grew, there were many mishaps. Wagons were derailed because they were allowed to go too fast, or because of loose wheel-tyres, or broken axles. Trees fell across the line. Sheep were trapped in tunnels and cuttings. As the track wore down, so flanges jammed in points and coupling chains broke while wagons were being drawn up inclines. The track was improved, and relaid with heavier metals. Bends were smoothed, especially at Tan-y-Grisiau where a new embankment and an easier curve were built, and at Garnedd, where an awkwardly sharp bend across the face of the hillside was replaced by an easier curve running through a short tunnel.

To make sure that their regulations were carried out, the Company employed a policeman (probably that same weigh-master and constable of Boston Lodge). His name was George Doyle, and he was quick to leap upon, for example, the Caednyfydd driver for leaving sixteen minutes late with the train that should have left at 6.46 a.m. from Rhiw Goch (fined five shillings). On another occasion 'Will the Caednyfydd driver' brought a loaded train from Rhiw Goch station to opposite the workhouse (now the Bron-y-Garth Hospital at Minffordd) in eight minutes; consequently, he must have brought it to the weighing machine in fourteen or fifteen minutes. This was apparently bad, and he was fined five shillings for it. Again, 'Jack the Tavern Trip driver' brought the loaded train from the Little Tunnel to Hafod-y-Llyn station without 'the boy', who was, it seems, a kind of second or secondary brakesman. Anyway, his absence cost Jack another five shillings. Constable Doyle worked on a rising scale of fines. Two months later Will the Caednyfydd brought a loaded train to the weighing machine without 'the boy', who had got off to go to the smithy. This cost Will ten shillings. Late starting, travelling too fast or without the proper complement of crew, or without the proper weigh-bill, always brought retribution in a five shillings fine – a hefty sum in those days.

One of the earliest printed mentions of the Festiniog, and an indication that passengers were in some way carried at an early stage, is in a little book (the second edition was published in 1835), now fairly rare, called *Panorama of the Beauties, Curiosities and Antiquities of North Wales* by J. Hemingway, 'late

42

editor of the Chester Chronicle'. Although there were officially no passengers then, Hemingway describes the descent of the Festiniog from top to bottom as 'a most delightful ride, winding round mountains through deep cuttings in the rocks, and thickly planted woods, and over precipitous vallies [sic], fearful to contemplate in the transit'. Tourists and visitors, Hemingway goes on,

> have the opportunity of enjoying this high treat in perfection, and without personal fatigue, as a carriage has been placed on the line connected with the Oakeley Arms Hotel. The quarries, with which the railway is in connection, produce the best and most valuable kind of slate, which, in consequence of its freeness from spots, may be termed *virgin slate*.

It is quite probable that quarrymen and their families travelled free on the railway from its first days, although unofficial riding was discouraged and punished if discovered, but Hemingway's reference suggests a carriage for people to inspect the line while it was being built, which was later used for tourists. It is supported by another little guidebook of the time, *The Book of North Wales* by Charles Frederick Cliffe, published in London in 1850. 'A tramway,' he says '. . . runs along the mountains on the north-east behind Tan-y-Bwlch. We believe that a tram fitted for visitors belonging to the hotel has been placed on the line.'

That *virgin slate* had a galvanising effect upon the whole neighbourhood. It created the town of Blaenau Ffestiniog, converting a bare hillside into a town of more than 12,000 people (the largest in Merionethshire) by the end of the century. Slate and the railway also made Portmadoc. In 1800 there was a handful of cottages, a small hamlet, no more, at Ynys Towyn. As the century went on the population of Ynyscynhaiarn parish, which became Portmadoc, almost doubled every twenty years, to more than 3,000 by 1861. The slate trade made Portmadoc into a thriving port and shipbuilding town. The first ship of any size to be built there was the 120–ton brig *Lady Vaughan*, launched in 1826. In the next ninety years, until the last Portmadoc ship the schooner *Gestiana* was launched in 1913, some 260 ships of various kinds and rigs were built at Portmadoc to trade in slates, phosphates, copper and all manner of cargoes all over the world. The ballast from ships trading to and from European ports was often used on the Festiniog permanent way, where it was actually called for many years 'Hamburg ballast'.

All this prosperity was borne on the backs of the humblest. The working life of an early nineteenth-century slate quarryman was almost unbelievably hard. Quarrymen had families of eight or ten children to support on wages of twelve to sixteen shillings a week. It rains more in Blaenau Ffestiniog than in most parts of the British Isles. Weather conditions there were ideal for encouraging tuberculosis, rheumatism, arthritis and bronchitis. In winter work was often stopped by snow and frost. Underground at the slate face the air was constantly thick with fumes, smoke and dust. The men who trimmed and dressed the slates worked all day in what Richards calls 'narrow, low, dark, damp, draughty sheds'. Industrial accidents were frequent. Quarrymen were crippled for life by rockfalls. Lung diseases such as silicosis were endemic. There were frequent outbreaks of typhoid in Ffestiniog from 1835 to 1841; at one time the disease was actually known locally as *clofyd-'Sdiniog* (Ffestiniog fever). If a quarryman was incapable of work, his family faced starvation. There was no unemployment benefit.

The living and working conditions were bad enough. Worse still was the attitude of the management. Morgan Richards, one of the founders of the North Wales Quarrymen's Union, wrote in 1876: 'When I think of those hard times, and the volleys of insult that some managers used to pour on us, without reason or provocation, I feel, even now, my blood curdling, and my hair standing on end, in just indignation at such treatment.' But even Richards had something good to say about the managers. He was well aware that they drove because they themselves were driven, and were as frightened for their jobs as the quarrymen. Often a manager lived in fear of the owner and went on working with a quarrying system which he knew to be ultimately inefficient. Well into this century there were quarrymen in Blaenau who talked of ancestors who had ideas for some invention or improvement 'which might have saved the quarries' but which they had been too timid or unwilling to put forward. The only class of people for whom Richards had not one charitable word to say were the owners. They drew their royalties and contributed nothing, in his opinion; they gave nothing and took everything.

There was, of course, a brighter side. The spirit, intelligence and self-respect of the quarrymen rose above their surroundings. They were proud of being quarrymen, proud of being Welsh. They never for one moment thought of themselves as downtrodden or degraded. The quarries produced a native culture, and a way of life emerged as distinctly flavoured and as idiosyncratic as in the Welsh coalmining valleys. The most individual part of their natures, almost the essence of their Welshness, appeared in their 'Cabanau', named after the small slate hut, or 'caban', in which the quarrymen ate their dinners during their half-hour morning breaks. Over the years the men in a particular quarry's caban would form themselves into a regular society, with a chairman, a secretary and a treasurer. Minutes were taken and read. Debates were held, with all the formal ritual of the debating chamber, on a variety of political, religious and social matters.

In fact, the Cabanau touched some of the deepest chords in the Welshman's nature: his respect for learning, his tribal loyalty, his sociability, his love of an argument and his yearning for escape from the grim reality of quarrying life.

There seems to be no record of any railway equivalent of the Cabanau, probably because the Festiniog's employees were a more fragmented society. Their work spread them out along the length of the railway. But it is very likely they were at least honorary members of the Cabanau in the quarries they served, and they certainly shared the quarrymen's fierce family and community loyalties. There were 'railway families' on the Festiniog from the beginning, son following father, and eventually grandfather, into the Company's employ. (Some of these railway families survived into the post-war restoration. David Davies of Boston Lodge, for instance, was a Festiniog driver and his three sons, Tom, Will Dafydd and Evan, were also Festiniog drivers.) Like the quarrymen, the railwaymen were separated from their employers by a great divide – of them and us. The owners, the landlords, the employers, the Board directors – them – were all English, or at best anglicized Welsh. (Perhaps, more properly, 'they' were Irish; Irish board and share representation on the Festiniog was strong for over fifty years.) They spoke English as their first language, not Welsh; in fact, very few of them spoke any Welsh at all. They were Anglicans, not Nonconformists. The difference between them and us was a great social, ethnic and religious gulf constantly demonstrated in the difference between church and chapel, shoes and clogs, beef and bread and butter, whisky and stewed tea. This gulf has not entirely closed. A Welsh-speaking director is fairly unusual on any Board. A Welsh volunteer worker on the Festiniog is a rare bird, so that it is hard to disagree with Gerry Fiennes, the author of *I Tried to Run a Railway*, formerly of British Rail Eastern Region and once a Director of the Festiniog

Railway Company, when he says that 'the professional funny men are the Welsh, and the Festiniog is manned by deadly serious English'.

Morgan Richards overstated his case against the quarry-owners. Things were not quite so black-and-white. As a quarry-owner himself he believed in enlightened capitalism, and as the nineteenth century progressed there were some notable examples of enlightened philanthropy which greatly improved the quarrymen's lot. After they had built their own grandiose mansions in imitation of the great slate barons of Caernarvonshire, the Blaenau quarrymasters had money to spare to invest in the welfare of their employees' minds as well as their bodies. The two greatest figures in those enterprises were Samuel Holland Jr and John Whitehead Greaves. They were both Liberals, in a predominantly Tory countryside (Holland was Merioneth's second Liberal MP). Together they founded the Portmadoc Mutual Ship Insurance Company, and were involved in the foundation of Dr Williams's famous school for Young Ladies at Dolgellau. On a more plebeian level, William Turner started elementary education for quarrymen's children in Ffestiniog. Holland also started a savings bank, and Greaves the Blaenau Eisteddfod in 1854. With other quarry-owners he established the Gweunydd Band in 1864 (which still plays today as the Royal Oakeley Silver Band). A committee of quarry-owners, with Greaves as chairman, appointed Dr William Homfray as Blaenau's first medical officer of health in 1848. Over the years the quarry-owners financed or encouraged the building of schools, chapels, a reading-room, and a hospital at Rhiwbryfdir. The owners' wives interested themselves in the quarrymen's families, and particularly in their diet. John Whitehead's daughter-in-law Marianne, John Ernest Greave's wife, fought a twenty-year campaign with lectures, evening classes and posters to teach the womenfolk of Blaenau the benefits of a balanced diet. Until then the quarrymen existed chiefly on a diet of bread and butter and stewed tea.

Ironically, the quarrymasters' successful philanthropy encouraged the seeds of the very kind of social upheaval which their economic practices sought to stifle. In the nineteenth century, Welsh slate-mining communities presented an almost classical Victorian pattern – of apparent surface stability and rigidity being steadily undermined by powerful forces of change. Some of the most potent elements of that change were the mixed despotism and paternalism of the quarrymasters, the growing awareness of the potential power of trades unions and, not least, the escape route to wider horizons which was given to that closed community by the Festiniog Railway.

The railway was undoubtedly becoming a success. In his memoirs Samuel Holland said that eventually ten quarries (all except Turner's and Casson's at Diphwys) sent all their slates by the railway. The line, he wrote, had stations

> four in number where the Trains met, and exchanged Horses etc, the Horses drawing the empty waggons up, exchanged at the appointed station, and the line, being on a declivity all the way the Horses rode down in Boxes made for the purpose, at the tail end of the Train, all the way till about one third of the way over the great Embankment, they then had to be taken out of their Boxes and hooked on to the Waggons to draw them to the Port. The Horses were feeding all the way while coming down in their Boxes. At last the work increased so much that it was found Horse power could not do the work, that it would be necessary to have locomotive power.

Chapter 5

The last line quoted from Holland's memoirs was not strictly correct. As far as slate-carrying capacity was concerned, the Festiniog had no need to go over to steam when it did. Calculating from the capacity of the wagons and the timetables being used, the railway was still some way from making maximum use of its horse-drawn traffic when steam was introduced.

The real reason for the introduction of steam was that it was actually cheaper. In any case, horse-drawn tramways belonged to the eighteenth century; the nineteenth century demanded steam. For a railway that intended to expand its slate-carrying capacity in the future, and, above all, was considering carrying passengers, steam was essential. All that was required was a man on the railway sufficiently energetic and enthusiastic to bring the change about.

There was just such a man, in Charles Easton Spooner, James's son. James Spooner was secretary and engineer of the Railway Company. As early as 1850 he was reporting to the Board that six miles of track had been relaid with heavier metal, to prepare it for running locomotives. However, nothing much more had happened by James Spooner's death on 18 August 1856, when Charles Easton Spooner assumed his father's job and his mantle. Charles Easton Spooner was present at Board meetings in the early 1850s. He was elected Treasurer on security of £5,000 in 1847. When his father died he resigned as Treasurer and was appointed 'future Manager and Clerk'.

The question of introducing steam locomotives to the Festiniog had been considered before. Samuel Holland's diary, the main source of information, is ambiguous, implying that opinions of the late 1830s may have been expressed twenty years later (thus giving the impression, very creditable to

48

Holland and to Charles Spooner, that they had successfully introduced steam in the face of the best expert opinion). In fact, it seems virtually certain that it was in 1836–37, shortly after the line was opened, that Archer, James Spooner, Holland and Thomas Prichard walked the line with Robert Stephenson, then building the Chester and Holyhead Railway, and with John Urpeth Rastrick, joint engineer with Stephenson. As Holland's diary records, 'they took particular notice of the *Curves* as well as the gradient and they each declared that no Locomotive engine could be planned to work on such a line'.

However, railway technology had moved on in twenty years, and at Board meetings in August 1860 Charles Spooner was instructed to enquire about the practicability of using locomotives. He was recommended to visit the Neath Abbey Ironworks, to see their engines at work, and to get in touch with Charles Menzies Holland, Samuel's nephew. As his uncle said in his memoirs, Charles 'was brought up as a Mechanical Engineer . . . used often to go up and down the Line of the little Railway with me, and frequently expressed an opinion that Engines could be made to work up and down the Festiniog Quarry Line'. (Clearly it was a wise political move to have as engineer a relative of the railway's oldest and best customer.) Charles was then staying with his uncle, 'engaged in making a Line between the Terminus of the Festiniog Line at Blaenau, to Festiniog Village'. (This was the one-foot-eleven-and-a-half-inch Festiniog and Blaenau Railway, of which Samuel Holland was a director; it was opened in 1868, converted to standard gauge in 1883 and worked by the Great Western.) Holland's memory is sometimes faulty. At this time his nephew Charles was actually working in south London, on the Metropolitan Extension of the London Chatham and Dover.

Spooner and Holland corresponded for some two years, exchanging comments about possible designs of locomotives, improvements and alterations to the track, water and coal consumption, and other technical details. Spooner went to see the Neath Abbey engines in November 1861 and reported his visit to the Board the following February, when he submitted Charles Holland's specifications for a locomotive as 'more suitable' than others already supplied. The cost, it was thought, would now be nearer £1,000 per engine than the £750 Holland had first estimated. In August Holland advised Spooner that they ought to get one engine, just to start with, so that they could 'rectify defects etc.'. He said they ought to advertise for a builder in *The Engineer*, and if possible they should find a builder near London so that he, Holland, could supervise the work. He himself suggested George England and Company, of Hatcham Ironworks.

Holland went to see England who had apparently not been answering letters. It seems the reason was that England was understandably not interested in making only one engine. He would however be interested in making three, for £1,000 each. He and Holland would design it together but he, England, reserved the right to alter the design to suit his own methods. In any case, he objected to being tied down to time and price. The first engine was to be ready in four months.

On 10 October 1862 the Company advertised in *The Engineer* and in a month they had had twenty-nine replies from engine-makers from Leith to Bury St Edmunds, and from Carlisle to Devizes. England was not among them, but by March 1863 the Company had accepted Holland as engineer and had agreed to buy three engines from England, the first two to cost £1,000 each, the third £800. George England built the engines to a joint design of his own and Holland's. (Spooner had a number of freakish ideas, including one for an oval boiler, which England quietly suppressed or altered.)

There is a gap in the Company's correspondence for the summer of 1863, but two engines had certainly been delivered by 28 July. The Festiniog tradition, very probably true, says that two brothers, Harry and Job Williams, built a large cart at Beud-y-Gwyn, near Minffordd. Hitching up four horses they set off to Caernarvon which was then the nearest that the standard-gauge rail came to Portmadoc. They brought the first engine back on the cart. (Job was later crossing-keeper at Minffordd.)

Once again, the local press was there, and the *North Wales Chronicle* for 25 July 1863 had the story:

> The long-talked of and long-expected steam engine for the Festiniog Railway, and which is calculated to be of such immense advantage to this neighbourhood, arrived in the Port on Saturday last (18th July 1863). It was bedizened with evergreens and flowers as befitted the occasion, and as a matter of course created quite a sensation in the place. In about two hours after its arrival in the town it was placed on the line of the railway, and pushed across the embankment to the foundry, on the other side of the Traeth. I am informed that another engine is on its way to the Port as a sister engine.

In the railway accounts the cart built to carry the engines is described as 'locomotive truck £65. 0. 0.'. Payments for carriage

50

of locomotives from Caernarvon are listed: 'July 20, 1863, carriage of locomotives from Caernarvon, £24. 1. 0d.; Jan 6 1864, T.P. [Thomas Prichard] to pay Expenses of Carriage of Locomotive £17. 10. 0.; March 24, Prichard to pay for Carriage of Locomotive, £18. 0. 0.'. These accounts therefore suggest that the first two engines arrived in July 1863, the third early in 1864 and the fourth in March.

The name of the first Festiniog locomotive is another topic which is endlessly debated. Holland, writing long afterwards, says in his memoirs that one was *Lord Palmerston*, and the second was *Mountaineer*. A pencil note in the margin of Spooner's *Narrow Gauge Railways* leaves no doubt that it was *Mountaineer*. *Mountaineer* and *The Princess* were originally numbered 1 and 2.

The first trial was on *The Princess* on 4 August 1863. It did not go well. Spooner wrote to England that 'your man tried one of the Locomotives today for a couple of miles up the line on an Inclination of 1 in 82 with a couple of trucks behind it'. *The Princess* performed very unsatisfactorily. The injector would not work at all. Water flowed into the cylinders at such a rate that it was thrown out of the funnel 'in volumes'. The engine ran at about four mph with a steam pressure of sixty pounds. Eventually she came to a complete standstill, by which time there was about twelve inches of water in the tanks and the fire had to be put out. 'I fear,' said Spooner, 'there must be something wrong with the bearings for we had to go back over the before-named Inclination of 1 in 82 without steam and it was as much as the men could do to get the Engine back again.' The engine kept on priming. England said that the steam pipe was lying too close to the water-level. Holland admitted, 'I own it is a rather ticklish thing to manage.'

Meanwhile the whole vale was agog to see the first steam engine on the railway. There were several false alarms. The blacksmith in Minffordd was summoned to shoe some horses at Rhiw Goch, and on the way up lit the fire in his forge (he had a sort of mobile workshop on a wagon, just as the FR's Signals & Telegraph Department have today). Spying the clouds of smoke, local people flocked to the railway in the hope of seeing the new engine.

Between them, George England and Charles Holland produced a good working locomotive, although there were design faults. For those with a technical turn of mind, the design is perhaps best described by J.I.C. Burns, one of the pioneer historians of railway archaeology, in his history of *The Festiniog*

51

Railway. The two volumes are known to Festiniog buffs as 'Boyd's Bible'. Here is Boyd on *The Prince* and *The Princess*:

> These were four-coupled tank engines with auxiliary tenders for carrying coal; they had inside frames and outside cylinders whilst water was carried in side tanks whose tops were level with the top of the boiler lagging. The chimney was bell-mouthed, there was a front weather-board curved towards the top, brass dome with whistle thereon, safety valve in a brass cover on the firebox whilst the foot-plating was curved at front and rear presumably to give adequate clearance between vehicles on curves.

According to Charles Spooner, the engine ends were curved so that the engines could open gates on the line, but he does not say what gates were on the line or where they were, or how the engines could open them without damaging them.

A fourth engine was ordered and the numbering is generally taken to be No. 1 *The Princess*, No. 2 *The Prince*, No. 3 *Mountaineer*, and No. 4 *Palmerston*.

Most of the teething-troubles on the engines had been cured by September 1863. Extra steaming space was provided by giving both engines a large dome. The Company now felt bold enough to have one of their traditional outings. On 16 October Charles Spooner sent out the invitations:

> Bron-y-Garth, Portmadoc,
> October 16th 1863
>
> The Festiniog Railway Company propose opening their Line for traffic by Steam, on Friday 23rd instant, and intend starting a Train from Port Madoc, at 10, on the morning of that day to the Quarries.
> They hope to have the pleasure of your company up the Line, and return to Dinner at 3 o'clock, at the Town Hall, Port Madoc.

There is an eyewitness account of that first steam trip, written by Richard Richards of Bangor, in a chapter called 'Portmadoc and Festiniog Railway' in his *Miscellaneous Poems and Pen and Ink Sketches*, published in 1868:

> Two trains started from the Portmadoc station, with an engine attached to each, the number of persons altogether being about two hundred.
> The reader need not be possessed with any lively fancy to imagine to himself the laughable incidents which would be likely to occur on a line of railway when twenty carriages or so, for the first time since the creation, bounded along faster than any stage coach and with no visible propelling

power; for there were hundreds of people in the neighbourhood who had never before seen a steam engine, although, of course, they had heard of one. Horses galloped about the fields like distraught animals, when the puffing engines passed along, so confused and amazed were they at the noise, and the phenomenon altogether and the more timid cows and sheep seemed equally as astonished. All along the line of rails, at every available spot, crowds of wondering people were collected in groups, from the aged crone of ninety years, to the demure little damsel of three. When the trains arrived at the terminus at Blaenau Ffestiniog, we were greeted by hundreds of quarrymen, who were perched on the rocks many yards above us, who cheered lustily and uproariously, and as only Britons can. The engines were piloted by Mr Holland and Mr England, and they must have been deeply gratified with the successful results of their skill and labour.

Also deeply gratified, the Company wrote off to the Board of Trade in June 1864 to give notice that they intended to operate a passenger service. Meanwhile, passengers could travel free, but at their own risk.

The Board of Trade inspection was carried out on 27 October by their Inspector, Captain H.W. Tyler, Royal Engineers (the same Tyler of the Curve). Tyler was a typically energetic and resourceful Victorian. He inspected and reported on railways all over Europe and in North America. He was involved with early schemes for a Channel tunnel. He was MP for Harwich and later for Great Yarmouth. His advice saved the Town Hall in Great Yarmouth from collapsing because of waterlogged soil. He went to Peru when he was nearly seventy; eight days before his death at the age of eighty he was in his office as usual, and signed 1,600 cheques in one morning.

His inspection was exhausting and exhaustive. He walked every inch of the line, banging at the rails with the hammer specially fitted on the end of his walking-stick. His report, a typically thorough and perceptive summary of the Festiniog as it then was, recommended better layout and accommodation for passengers at stations; installation of telegraphs at the Long Tunnel and at Cwmorthin Incline near Tan-y-Grisiau, where there was a danger of runaway wagons; safety guards to be fitted to rolling-stock, because there was so little clearance at bridges and cuttings; stop-blocks on sidings; level-crossing gates across roads; semaphore signals which were invisible to signalmen to have repeaters; missing track pins on chairs to be replaced, and drains cleared.

53

One would have thought that most of these recommendations were obvious and hardly needed a Board of Trade Inspector to point them out. However, the report does show the great gap that lay between the primitive Festiniog Railway standards and those required for 'mainline' passenger working. Cut off in remote Wales, some way from any standard-gauge railway, the Festiniog Railway needed an expert view from outside. The Company put the recommendations in hand and were informed by the Board of Trade on 28 December that they could go ahead. The official opening took place on Thursday 5 January 1865 when a train carrying directors, officials and guests made the first passenger trip from Portmadoc. Unfortunately there was a tragedy when John Roberts, an engine cleaner, rashly jumped off an engine at Boston Lodge, tripped and was struck by the first carriage. He died later of his injuries. Free travel was granted on the rest of that day and passenger services began on the next.

There were to be three classes of passenger, with the quarrymen's traffic, which began about the end of 1866, making a cheap class of its own. The carriages were probably painted royal purple for first class, and red with white roofs for second and third, although nobody can now be sure. At first the quarrymen travelled in what were really open wagons, which later had temporary roofs fitted, with two openings each side for the men to get in and out. Parliamentary third class traffic started in the half-year ending 31 December 1882. One of the two-doored quarrymen's carriages still survives on the line – as a plate-layers' hut at Llechwedd-Coed, near Plas Halt.

The original coaches of 1863–4 were four-wheeled 'boxes', very wide and appearing hardly to clear the ground, to keep the centre of gravity low. They had one large compartment, with a single seat running down its length. These were soon supplemented by four-wheelers with two compartments and lateral seating. Two open observation cars were introduced with the passenger service (the roofs were added later). Five of the four-wheelers still exist; one of them, the restored open No. 7, is now in the Festiniog Railway Museum.

To match its new status as a passenger-carrying line, the Festiniog gave the staff suitably magnificent uniforms. The Reverend Tim Phillips, whose father worked at Boston Lodge, writing in the *South Caernarvon Leader* in 1946, said that the most gorgeous uniforms of all were given to the station-masters.

This important official was arrayed in a vesture which consisted of a frock coat, waistcoat and trousers, of dark navy-blue cloth, excellent in quality, and a cap of the 'cheese-cutter' pattern – all adorned with thick gold braid. He walked up and down the platform with grave dignity, carrying a baton [the staff] in one hand, and flourishing a carriage-key in the other. Not less spectacular was the uniform of the Passenger-Guard. Early photographs depict him as wearing a well-tailored frock-coat. The cap was of a different pattern – one similar to the one worn by the Czar of Russia. His uniform was adorned with silver braid, and he carried a broad, highly-polished black morocco strip across his right shoulder, which formed the receptacle of a big silver chronometer.

At first there were four stations – Portmadoc, Penrhyn, Hafod-y-Llyn (about 600 yards, or in railway terminology thirty chains, downline from Tan-y-Bwlch) and Dinas, which was opposite the Oakeley Quarry and highly inconvenient for everyone except those who worked at the quarry. Another Blaenau station at Duffws was soon opened and Dinas eventually closed down in the autumn of 1870. Stations were opened at Tan-y-Grisiau in 1866, at Minffordd in 1872 and at Tan-y-Bwlch in 1873 (Hafod then being abandoned). The Oakeleys at Plas Tan-y-Bwlch had a private station of their own. No definite dates are known for Dduallt station. An agreement of 1864 required trains to stop there daily, and station repairs for Dduallt are listed for the mid-1870s.

As annual figures of slate tonnage and passenger traffic rose, there was no doubt that the Festiniog was a commercial and technical success. Here was a steam-hauled, narrow-gauge railway operating successfully, in defiance of all the experts. But now that the Festiniog had proved them wrong, the experts hastened to show that it had proved them right. They proclaimed that they had known all along that it would work and there was some heated correspondence to and fro in the technical press of the time.

The technical press were fascinated by narrow-gauge railways. In the 1860s to 1880s journals such as *Engineering* carried article after article about the Festiniog. They wrote about it in editorials, published pictures of Festiniog engines and rolling-stock (some of them detailed manufacturers' drawings), and reprinted addresses on the Festiniog by Spooner and Tyler. In a paper read on 11 April 1865 to the Institution of Civil Engineers just after he had inspected the railway for a second time to examine the results of his first visit, Henry Tyler gives a good general description of the railway. By that time the Company's four engines had run 57,000 miles, 'without leaving the rails'. This must have given him great satisfaction for, as he says, the practicability of running locomotives on the line had often been discussed 'but more than once abandoned, in consequence of the apparent difficulties and of the adverse opinions expressed by the engineers who were consulted'. Tyler himself had no doubts. In his report of October 1864 he had stressed the cheapness, economy and safety of the line. He forecast (quite rightly) that such narrow-gauge lines had a great future in India and the Colonies.

On 24 September 1869 *Engineering* reprinted Tyler's paper in which he gave a good crisp account of how passenger and slate traffic were combined.

> In ascending from Portmadoc the passenger carriages are drawn by the engines with other vehicles, the passenger carriages being placed between the empty slate trucks, which are always last in the trains, and the goods wagons, which are next behind the tender. In descending, the loaded slate trucks, with empty goods trucks attached behind them, run first in a train by themselves; the engine follows, tender first; and the passenger vehicles, detached from the engine and the tender, and at some little distance behind them, bring up the rear, with a brake van in front, and a guard on a platform outside it. The speed is limited to about 6 miles per hour, in passing round the sharpest curves, and 10 miles per hour on other parts of the line.

In the same issue of *Engineering* the editorial described the Festiniog: 'If we were asked to draw a plan of the line from memory, we should simply repeat the letter S many times. A moderately long train may be on three curves at once'.

In 1867 George England built two more engines for the Festiniog, *Welsh Pony* and *Little Giant*, Nos 5 and 6. A year later six passenger trains a day were running. In that year there were 126,745 passengers carried over a distance of 46,732 train-miles, both figures being an increase on the year before. Running expenses were about fifty per cent of revenue. The figures show that in an era of low wages a railway could be very profitable indeed. The Festiniog was carrying more passengers and more slates, opening up new inclines, building new engines, new coaches and new slate wagons – and still making money. Understandably, the technical press were intrigued. In 1868 the Festiniog declared a half-year dividend of six per cent. 'Hear that!' exclaimed *The Engineer*,

> hear that, ye holders of ordinary railway stock! 12 per cent
> per annum from railway property. Why is this result
> obtained? Simply because the line which gave it was
> cheaply made and is cheaply worked. It is adapted to the
> purpose; it is not too big for its purpose.

By a further Act of Parliament of July 1869 the Company were
given fresh powers: to widen the line to double track (which
was never done); to run a branch from Minffordd down to the
Cambrian Railways (which was); to connect the two termini of
Duffws and Dinas by a short link, which was, eventually, done
in 1880; and to build a low wall along the Cob, to stop the steam
engines frightening the horses.

But success brought its problems. Even the new engines
were not up to their task. In a Board of Trade trial in September
1869 *Little Giant* was set to draw a train of fifty-one tons; forty-
one slate wagons, five passenger coaches and a brake van, a
rail-bending machine and Charles Spooner's own private boat-
shaped 'inspection saloon'. There were thirty passengers on
board, who could not have been reassured. According to the
report, *Little Giant* crept 'caterpillar-like', up the steep road. She
shouldered her work 'in a very curious fashion. She gets over
the road not steadily as she should do, but in a series of efforts
rapidly repeated.' As each cylinder drove the engine so that
side advanced before the other. The head of the engine sidled
across the rails with a most curious crab-like motion. At
anything like a high speed there was such a severe vibration
that all engines of this type were nicknamed 'Boxers'. When
working hard the engine blasted its fire to bits, giving a heavy
coal consumption. Wherever the track was old or rough it was
not possible to go more than about nine miles an hour at the
most 'without incurring the risk of breaking springs or
loosening the driver's teeth'.

In fairness to *Little Giant* it must be said that she had, after
all, been designed to haul only thirty-five tons at ten mph. For
the railway to progress, something new in the way of engines
was clearly needed. Once again in the Festiniog's history, the
hour produced the man.

Robert Francis Fairlie was born in Scotland in 1831. He
had a most fertile and inventive technical mind and was
something of a railway prodigy: he was superintendent of the
Londonderry and Coleraine Railway at the age of twenty-two.
For a time he went to India; when he returned to London he set
up as a consulting engineer. For him railways were in the
family. He married George England's daughter in 1862 and later

took over his father-in-law's works from him. Spooner and Holland both studied the technical press avidly and they must have seen Fairlie's paper 'Railway Management', read to the Royal Society of Arts and afterwards printed in *Engineering* in 1868. Fairlie was not one to hide his own light under a bushel. He was a vigorous propagandist, with radically advanced theories. When he hit on a good idea he pushed it as hard as it would go.

Fairlie had the answer to the Festiniog's problem, which was how to get more power onto the same set of narrow rails. His solution was a brilliant technical breakthrough. His patent locomotive was really two engines, placed back to back. There was one long boiler, but it had two fireboxes, two chimneys and two sets of controls, served by a common cab in the middle. There were also two sets of driving-wheels and cylinders, each set mounted on its separate bogie so that it could turn right or left, as demanded by the narrow track, independently of the main engine frame.

The first narrow-gauge Fairlie patent 'double engine' was delivered to the Festiniog by George England's successor, the Fairlie Engine and Steam Carriage Company, in July 1869. It had the perfect name – *Little Wonder* – No. 7 in the Festiniog numerology. It was indeed a little wonder. On trials it exceeded the wildest expectations. Here was no huffing and puffing and shouldering sideways. On a trial for the Board of Trade Inspector on 18 September (two days before *Little Giant*'s trial mentioned already) *Little Wonder* was set to pull a train of 111 slate wagons, six coaches, twelve goods wagons and sixty passengers, a total train weight of nearly 114 tons. The train set out from Portmadoc in a storm of wind and rain but *Little Wonder* simply 'walked away with it', as they say. The train 'rushed' Moelwyn tunnel in one minute five seconds, an average of twenty-three mph. Coming down the mountain again, twenty-five mph was easily achieved, and at one point they touched thirty-five mph. Everybody was amazed by the smoothness of the ride and the effortless way in which the engine rode the curves and hauled the load.

Little Wonder was a sensation in the technical press. So enthusiastic was the railway world that if anything the pendulum swung too far in the direction of narrow-gauge. Some actually suggested that standard gauge should be scrapped everywhere in favour of narrow-gauge.

Chapter 6

Charles Spooner was an adept at public relations, with a happy knack of keeping 'his' railway (as he thought of it) always in the news. In one notable publicity coup of February 1870 he arranged a series of trials to establish once and for all, and before an international audience, that the double Fairlies were better than all the others. It was a very important event for Fairlie and for the future of narrow-gauge. It is not too much to say that *Little Wonder*'s trials opened the golden age for narrow-gauge railways. There were about forty guests, all of them prominent figures in the railway world – including the third Duke of Sutherland, a great sponsor of railways in the British Isles; the Imperial Russian Commission headed by a descendant of Catherine the Great, Count Alexei Bobrinskoy; French officials from the La Vendée Railway and Russian officials from the Poti-Tiflis Railway; Carl Pihl, a narrow-gauge railway engineer from Norway; Herr Mulvany from Germany; C.P. Sandberg from Sweden; Henry Tyler, Lieutenant-General Sir William Baker and others from the India Office (who later adopted narrow-gauge); Count Szechenyi from Hungary; directors and representatives of the Cambrian, London and North Western, the Mid-Wales, Talyllyn, Brecon and Methyr, Neath and Brecon Railways; the Spooners; Livingston Thompson; Robert Fairlie; directors and employees of the Festiniog. The guests watched trials, went on trips up to Blaenau, heard addresses from Spooner at the Oakeley Arms, and were generally wined and dined. They also were treated to a demonstration of *Topsy*, Spooner's own miniature engine which ran on a three-and-one-eighth-inch-gauge track round his garden at Bron-y-Garth in Portmadoc.

Inevitably the technical and local press were present in force. *The Engineer* published a full report of the proceedings.

Nearer home, the *Oswestry Advertiser* reported that 'the absence of foliage on the trees so enabled passengers to look down in the yawning gulfs over which they passed, that a *soupçon* of danger helped to tickle the imagination'. *Little Wonder*'s feats eventually filtered through local folklore into the guidebooks of the time. *The Gossiping Guide to Wales*, 1874 edition, recorded that the visiting party 'did not hang about at Blaenau Ffestiniog. Nobody wished to stay long in so sharp an atmosphere'. The party returned to Hafod-y-Llyn and so down to the Oakeley, where there was dinner and 'afterwards Mr Charles Spooner read a paper on narrow gauge railways'. As late as 1890 the guidebooks were still exclaiming about the *Little Wonder*. The *Thorough Guide Series*, in their volume on North Wales published in 1892, had a section on the 'Toy Railway'. Of the Fairlie double engine it said:

> Its first appearance produced a sensation which put all the other 'Wonders of Wales' as deeply into the shade as an electric light puts an ordinary street lamp, and though the wonder has somewhat worn off, still no orthodox tourist visits Wales without taking a turn one way or the other, on the 'Toy' railway.

Like most of us, the writer could not resist making ponderous jokes.

> About here [Tan-y-Bwlch] the line is so tortuous as almost to render excusable the hyperbole that the engine driver of a long train can shake hands with the guard (at least the train need only be a mile and a half and the driver's and guard's arms an eighth of a mile long).

In return for having so boldly pioneered his invention (and no doubt also for the excellent exposure the Festiniog had given him in the media) Fairlie allowed the Company to build double engines free of patent licence fees. Over three hundred Fairlies were built, both standard and narrow-gauge, for service on railways all over the world. But the only examples which still survive in regular use are now on the Festiniog. It seems that *Little Wonder* was the peak of Fairlie's reputation. He went to Venezuela in 1873, fell sick there of malaria and sunstroke and came home more or less an invalid. However, various firms built Fairlie engines for railways all over the world until his death in 1885. The last was built in 1911, for a railway in Mexico – until *Earl of Merioneth* from Boston Lodge in 1979.

It was Charles Spooner who became the great apostle of narrow-gauge. He wrote a famous book, *Narrow Gauge Railways*, published in 1871, as well as dozens of pamphlets, letters to private individuals and contributions to the technical press. He delivered lectures and read papers by the score, tirelessly promoting narrow-gauge and forecasting a great worldwide future for it, wherever standard gauge was physically or economically impossible.

Henry Tyler's report of March 1870 freed the Festiniog from speed restrictions. It was a symbolic as well as a physical release, because the railway went on under Charles Spooner to flourish as never before and (rarely) since. The line was re-sleepered and relaid with new rails, heavier metal and fresh ballast. In December 1871 the editor of *Engineering* wrote, 'We never saw a piece of line of any length with the ballast in an equally perfect condition.' In 1869, with George Augustus Huddart, Spooner developed his own type of fish-plate, with the formidably tongue-twisting name of 'Double Socket-Joint Girder Plate'. He and his son George Percy Spooner designed a new bogie carriage for passengers, the first iron-framed bogie carriage in Great Britain to run in everyday service. He also laid out the branch sidings and interchange with the Cambrian Railway at Minffordd and produced an excellently designed yard for trans-shipping slates from one line (and one gauge) to another. Under Spooner, the new passenger stations were opened and more locomotives were built, all Fairlie-principled, but designed by Spooner's son George Percy; they were *James Spooner*, No. 8, in 1872; *Taliesin*, No. 9, in 1876; *Merddin Emrys*, No. 10, built at Boston Lodge in 1879; and *Livingston Thompson*, No. 11, also built at Boston Lodge, in 1886 (although the works plate reads 1885).

One of the most detailed accounts of the railway at the height of the Spooner era was written by an American, William H. Bishop, who visited Portmadoc and the railway in December 1878. His article, 'Over the Narrowest Narrow Gauge', appeared in *Scribner's Monthly* in August 1879. Mr Bishop met the Spooners, *père et fils*. He describes Charles as 'a hale, dignified gentleman of sixty. His son, a young man of energetic and companionable traits, my guide in the subsequent explorations, assures me that he is not beyond the ability to turn "cart-wheels" yet with the agility of youth.' The reporter picked up some interesting local gossip. James Spooner (Charles' father), he says, first came to Portmadoc from Yorkshire 'on a pleasure excursion. He hunted rabbits over most of the site where the town and the docks now are. There he fell in with ordnance surveyors, was pleased with the business, became an engineer,

61

and returned to assist Mr Madocks in his projects.' The latest research, by Michael Lewis, shows that the Spooner family came from Worcestershire. James was born at Powick, south of Worcester.

Bishop took the early Monday morning quarrymen's train leaving Portmadoc at six a.m.

> It was naturally much before daylight, at this hour of a mid-winter morning. Snow-flakes fell thickly at intervals. The quarrymen came trudging out of the silent streets with their ration of supplies in canvas bags knotted across their shoulders. They stamped the snow off their heavy boots in the station, and talked softly together in their strange tongue. Among them – the one touch of brighter sentiment in the scene – a rugged man, stiff in the joints from toil, had beside him a pretty child, a girl of ten, who carried in a satchel a part of his provisions. She was shabbily dressed, as became a quarryman's daughter; the small face was rosy with the storm, and the unkempt blonde hair had a genuine interest even apart from her circumstances. His only reply to compliments was the common *dim Saesnach* (no English) impassively spoken.

The snow that morning stopped traffic. 'The engine at the head of the long train of red-painted boxes slipped on the icy tracks and did not easily get under way. While it fumed and shrieked in the rage of ineffectual efforts, telegrams came down the line countermanding the train.'

However, Bishop did get a trip up the line on the footplate of *Little Wonder*, which he described as having 'an odd, aggressive-looking build', driven by one Williams, 'head of the machine-shops and the most trusted mechanic on the line'. Even Bishop gave way to the fatal tendency to make heavy jokes about the railway.

> The small wooden station at the end of Madocks' embankment has hardly more than the look of a sentry-box. One rather expects to find the tickets diminished in proportion, and the company's servants stunted in their growth. But the former are of the usual size, and porters, guards, and brakesmen bustle about with as important an air as if they had never been out of the service of Isambard Kingdom Brunell [sic].

The snow was not deep, but up at Tan-y-Grisiau they found *The Princess* derailed. '*The Princess*'s head was being lifted with small jack-screws, while a number of men mounted on the side, with their backs braced against the boiler, pushed against the wall, just as one might try to help a road wagon out of a rut.' Part of the trouble, Bishop thought, was 'the deficiency of the line in other snow-ploughs than old broom heads tied to the engine's head'.

Bishop had a sharp eye for the countryside.

> The quarries are vast abysses, gloomy as the pictures in Dante's Inferno. Slate is everywhere. It strews the slopes with debris, turning the light with slight bluish reflections; is set into the tops of walls instead of broken glass; and stands in irregular slabs like tomb-stones, for fences round outlying houses. The homes of quarrymen are for the most part in barrack-like structures on the heights. They are little given to revelry, and there is little in the villages to attract them down if they were. We passed the yellow van of a travelling show at one point, lying deserted in a field, melancholy as a grass-hopper in winter. Both horses and proprietor had turned out to work in the quarries.

Down in Portmadoc Bishop noted the Christmas preparations, the decorated parish church, the festivity known as 'tea-eating', the inn parlour 'festooned with holly and starred with oranges'. The band of the local volunteer rifle company played 'waits' in the evening in the principal quarters of the town. He was impressed by Portmadoc's sobriety. 'No sounds of revelry come out of the Quarrymen's Arms!' '"Temperance" signs prevail and chapels are so numerous as to be a special feature. A jack tar is never seen by any chance staggering under other than his legitimate burdens.' Bishop met a sail-maker, one William Roberts, styled Gwyllym Eryri, or William of Snowdon, who was the resident bard. He had three times won a prize at the national Eisteddfod and he composed for Bishop a special *awdl* (ode) on the Festiniog Railway. 'Thou art,' said William of Snowdon addressing the 'Narrowest Narrow Gauge',

> a monument to man's ingenuity. But more wonderful than man's masterpieces are seen around us, the towering mountains, the river and the valley. To the courteous director, Spooner, also, deserved praise is hereby offered. Without doubt he has been the occasion of great benefit to this our native town.

No doubt something has been lost in the translation.

Bishop seems to have had as shrewd an eye for business as for scenery. He saw that the Festiniog had a monopoly which was vulnerable. 'Both the North-Western and the Great Western are coming in with branches to its upper terminus. It looks as though the slates must turn and go the other way in good part, leaving the neat platforms and tipping tables, at Minffordd at least, with little to do.' The Festiniog was indeed just a little too successful for its own good in the end. The Board alienated Samuel Holland, their oldest customer, over rates to be paid for the carriage of slates. After the railway had lost a law case brought against them by the Diphwys Casson Co., Samuel also took legal action against them. Samuel had been the chief agency behind the Festiniog and Blaenau Railway and was its chairman. This line was worked at first by the Festiniog, until Samuel cooled towards them. He was also director of the Bala and Festiniog Railway which had been formed in conjunction with the Great Western. The Company do not seem to have behaved with the greatest consideration towards Holland, and perhaps he felt that he was not getting enough service from the Festiniog. Or perhaps he mistrusted, as a matter of principle, any monopoly, even though it belonged to friends. Holland now became a rival. After the narrow-gauge Festiniog and Blaenau had been converted to standard gauge, the Great Western eventually ran through to Blaenau without change of gauge in 1883. Actually, the Great Western never made money from the route, but the London and North-Western which reached Blaenau by the two-mile tunnel under the Crimea Pass, in 1879, certainly did. Both lines to Blaenau served to keep the Festiniog on their toes and remind them, as no doubt Samuel Holland wanted, that there were other railway lines in existence. Attempts were made in the 1880s to sell the Festiniog Railway as a going concern to either the LNWR or the GWR. But the mainline companies were apparently quite content to take the traffic, without the bother of buying.

It may be that Charles Spooner had too much power and influence over the Festiniog. It is not a good thing for one man to stay too long at the head of any concern. The fates were preparing a deliciously Victorian nemesis for Spooner. First, in 1879, his son George Percy got one of the housemaids 'into trouble'. Charles may have had the ability to turn cartwheels in lighter moments but on this occasion he played the heavy Victorian father. Evidently he told his son never to darken his doorstep again. As in all the best Victorian novels, Percy bit on the bullet and went off to India, if not to shoot tiger then certainly to run railways (his younger brother Charles Edwin also did, in Malaya). Percy returned to England years later and became a special constable at King's Cross. He died in 1917.

After the scandal of Percy, Charles Spooner's own reputation and infallibility were punctured by a mishap worthy of Mr Pickwick. Spooner had his own private inspection car. It was an amazing vehicle, probably built to his own design, with a 'prow' for opening gates. It looked like a boat on wheels (it was inscribed on its side *'Ni l'un, ni l'autre'*). On 12 February 1886 Spooner embarked in his car at Blaenau, together with a Mr and Miss Robinson and a Miss Tiddeman, a Spooner relative. Familiarity with the line had bred contempt, for he neglected to take up the single-line staff (installed by Spooner himself after Henry Tyler's inspection) which gave him the right to enter the section of line. Near the Moelwyn Tunnel. Spooner's 'boat' collided with an up passenger train. The 'boat' was smashed to pieces. Miss Robinson and Spooner himself were badly hurt. But the main injury might well have been to Spooner's reputation. Such a forceful outspoken character had enemies. It might have suddenly struck everybody that, after all, Spooner had very few shares and was only the Company Secretary. His position in the Company had no financial base. The year after the accident Spooner resigned as Secretary, being replaced by J.S. Hughes, with whom he had been 'double-banking' the duties of Secretary for some time. He died, at his home Bron-y-Garth, in 1889, aged seventy-one.

Charles Spooner came from a true Festiniog Railway family. He was born at Maentwrog, within sight and sound of the railway. His father worked for the Company. His son also worked for them and would have followed him had he not blotted his copybook. He ran the railway with a firm paternalistic hand. He was a strict disciplinarian, a hard man but a just one, who believed in summary punishments; Festiniog Railway legend has it that he thought nothing of hauling an erring signalman from his box and giving him a sound cuffing for his misdemeanours. He must have fallen out quite seriously with the rest of the Board, for his death was recorded in one terse paragraph in the minutes, in great contrast to the fulsome tributes often expressed when other directors died or retired. Nevertheless, the local press paid him generous tribute in his obituary, and men from the Festiniog Railway marched in his funeral procession all the way from Portmadoc to Beddgelert. For the Festiniog, his passing was the end of an epoch.

Chapter 7

In the late nineteenth century the Festiniog Railway enjoyed a period of high and splendid prosperity. It was to be an Indian summer, as it turned out, before the frosts came, but while it lasted it was good. The Railway paid a regular dividend, Victoria was firmly on her throne, the pound sterling was worth a pound backed by gold, and on the British Empire the sun never set. God was in his heaven and all was right with the Festiniog Railway.

In a sense, the physical appearance of the railway reflected its confidence in itself. It could be seen in the solid, prosperous railway architecture, in the design of the station buildings, the Gothic sloping cut of their slates, their fretted wooden roof fringes, their pillared portals, the Prince of Wales's feathers carved on stone plaques on the gables at Duffws, the colonial verandahs and covered awnings. The railway sign-boards were carefully lettered in an ornate black-shaded sans serif script. The granite gateposts had tops of quartz, and the railings, all of the best wrought iron, were capped with pyramids, or Trojan spears, or spades. There were three stations within half a mile of each other at Blaenau, two in the town and another at Glan-y-Pwll. There were eight passenger trains, up and down, every day. The quarrymen still had to endure fairly spartan conditions, but the first-class passengers were lapped in almost Byzantine luxury, with mirrors in their compartments, morocco leather seats, carpets, antimacassars changed daily, and copper foot-warmers in the winter.

A few accounts of travelling conditions on the quarrymen's trains still survive. James Parry, writing in *Caban*, the house magazine of the Llechwedd Quarry in 1960, described how as a boy of sixteen he used to get up at three o'clock on pitch-black winter mornings to walk the six miles to Portmadoc to catch the 'Tren Bach' up to Blaenau.

> The first picture that comes into my mind about that journey is one of a dozen or so men walking to the station, each one with his 'walat' over his shoulder. This 'walat' was a kind of white bag, similar to a pillow case, in which the men would carry their food etc., which would be necessary during their week's stay at the barracks. The middle of this 'walat' was placed on the shoulder with the food each side, one pack on the front, one on the back. The two ends of the bag were then tied underneath the opposite arm. The 'walats' usually contained a pound of butter, a dozen eggs, home bread, a cake and a pound of bacon.
>
> I remember reaching the station where the train stood like a row of chicken coops in the dark grey of the morning, then after getting a ticket, which was called the 'white ticket', into the darkness. There was room for about six to sit each end of the vehicle, and between the two doors there was something similar to an inverted washing tub which was called a 'mul' (mule). Everyone had their own place to sit in the train and I had to sit on the mule, seeing that I was the junior.
>
> Whilst looking around me on the train, I noticed a few crosses above certain persons' seats. I thought they were used as a way of identifying which seat was which. I hadn't been travelling for long before I found out the real reason for the crosses. When someone told rather a tall story one cross was placed above his seat. Lying would get two crosses and a white lie the worst punishment, three crosses.
>
> Although the train left in the early hours of the morning, winter and summer, there were no attempts whatsoever to heat the train or to light it. Rather than suffer the cold and darkness, the travellers had their own ways of making the train more homely. The carriage was lit by placing a small piece of candle on the wall by means of clay and a little warmth was to be had by tempting fate and burning a paper fire on the carriage floor.

The Reverend Tim Phillips also described the workmen's carriages which, he said,

> were box-like arrangements, each having a door, and a couple of windows on either side, with very little provision for comfort. They were designed to hold 16 passengers and there was a round iron *pouffe* in the middle which was referred to as '*y mul*' (the donkey). It was a cover for some sort of mechanical arrangement. This sacred spot was reserved for the Oracle of the company, usually the oldest inhabitant, always the man they reverenced the most.

67

Some of Spooner's wildest designs were never carried out, but even so the Festiniog had an exotic range of rolling-stock. Besides the ordinary slate wagons (there were over a thousand of them), there were slab wagons (flat) and slab wagons (vertical), open wagons and bolster wagons and ganger's flat wagons, a carriage wagon and a tank wagon which carried seawater to the slate tank beside the line above Plas Tan-y-Bwlch (the tank is still there today). And there were vans: gunpowder vans, and the hearse van (now on view at the Harbour station museum) and breakdown vans, covered vans and goods brake-vans, and the rail-bending trolley. Besides Spooner's famous 'boat', the Oakeley family had a twelve-seater private carriage with a brakesman, and the permanent way Inspector had a light two-seater (light enough to be conveniently lifted off the track) with very large wheels. There were several types of passenger carriages, some with the old four wheels, some with bogies. Details of Festiniog's rolling-stock, with all its innumerable permutations and combinations of different bogies, bodies, couplings and springs, are lovingly laid out in Boyd's Bible. In those days the line normally had four locomotives in steam: top and bottom shunters, and two engines to work the service between Portmadoc and Duffws. Sixty men were employed at Boston Lodge. The works maintained not only the Festiniog's own rolling-stock but locomotives for several of the Blaenau Ffestiniog quarries, as well as doing outside contracting engineering work. The works still had the capacity to build the two double Fairlies, *Merddin Emrys* and *Livingston Thompson*.

An idea of the working conditions at Boston Lodge in the late nineteenth century can be seen from the 'Rules and Regulations', published by the Company and amended from time to time. A bell was rung or a whistle sounded at six o'clock in the morning for the start of work, and at five in the evening for the end of work, except on Saturdays, when work stopped at noon. Any workman who was late at six had chances to come in at six-thirty, at eight-thirty, or at twelve-thirty, the lost time being deducted from his wages. The men worked a fifty-five-and-a-half-hour week. They had 'time tickets' which they put in the ticket boxes when they got to work – a forerunner of 'clocking on and off'. They were allowed half an hour, from eight to half past, for breakfast, and from noon to half past for dinner. They could get overtime, provided they had worked the full week of fifty-five and a half hours, at the rate of actual overtime plus half an hour for every three hours overtime.

There was a long list of fines and penalties for everything from neglecting to leave the key of one's tool drawer in the works when one went home (fine 6d.) to 'Fighting, using Offensive Language, creating Tumult or Noise in the works or writing anything on the Walls or other parts thereof' (fine 2s. 6d.). Later, fines were abolished and suspension from duty without pay instituted instead. A man was liable to be dismissed instantly for going in or out of the works by any other way than through the timekeeper's office gate, for bringing beer or spirits into the works, or for taking material belonging to the Company out. Normally, the workman was on a week's notice, either way.

The business of carrying so many passengers, tons of slates and other goods required skill and careful timing. But this, too, the railway carried off with tremendous flair and confidence. Shunting was a complex operation, involving dozens of shunting movements to prevent empty wagons accumulating in the wrong places and to have enough empty wagons available at the right places. A shunting engine normally came up from Boston Lodge first thing on Monday morning and spent the working week up at Glan-y-Pwll, going back down again at the weekend. The shunting engine, normally one of the 0–4–0 tank engines, would have a full week distributing empties to the various quarries, shunting the two exchange yards in Blaenau, and collecting and delivering wagons as required from the Cwmorthin, Rhosydd and Wrysgan quarries near Tan-y-Grisiau, the copper and granite workings on the Moelwyn and the very steep branch to the Groby Granite Quarry (though this was not opened until 1908). Loaded slate wagons from the two quarry branches (Dinas and Duffws) were marshalled in trains of up to 120 at Glan-y-Pwll, where the crews connected, greased and inspected them. Each train had two or three brakesmen who climbed on board for the trip. Sometimes the engine would have to give the train a nudge to start it, perhaps in a westerly wind it would have to push it almost to the Moelwyn Tunnel, where the steeper gradient began. At Minffordd the trains of wagons would be split up again, some wagons going down to the Cambrian sidings, others on to the wharves at Portmadoc.

The Reverend Phillips has left another of his graphic descriptions, of a Festiniog brakesman in the railway's heyday. 'This *rara avis*' (the brakesman) appeared at his best in his winter plumage, when he looked like an Esquimau in mourning. He must have been encased within layers upon layers of winter clothing, for he always looked as broad as he was long; and the process of disrobing, at the close of the day, must have resembled the continuous peeling of a Spanish Onion. And, believe me, he needed them all, for I know of no more blood-curdling, marrow freezing occupation than his anywhere this side of Siberia. He would go to work at 5.30 a.m., sitting on the ledge of the last empty truck of the long 'run' behind the workmen's train – exposed to all weathers. On reaching Blaenau, he and his mate would take charge of the loaded slate train and bring it down to Minffordd. There was no such thing as a brake-van in those days, no shelter of any kind. Watching old Griffith Jones, Bryn Nazareth, going about his business used to send a cold shiver down my spine. Seated calmly on an engineless train careering headlong in the direction of Cae Mawr where there was a drop of 100 feet; he would jump up suddenly and stand bolt upright, placing his famous brass trumpet to his lips, and sounding an alarm that would drive the fox from his lair, scatter the chickens in all directions and fling wide the gates at Corn Pickin! This solemn ritual having been duly observed, he would turn on his heel, and run, as fast as his legs could carry him, in the opposite direction – on top of the train that moved like 'The Thundering Herd' or the 'Charge of the Light Brigade' – occasionally bobbing up and down to adjust a brake, and then doing physical jerks to keep himself warm, and he would arrive at Minffordd and take his seat once more on the ledge of the last wagon going up!

With the passing of Spooner some inventive impetus drained away from the Festiniog. Things were never quite the same again. The railway still made money, and there were still many improvements and successes ahead, but it was never again to have quite that bright future, that exciting sense that anything was possible and might be introduced tomorrow. Some vital railway vitamin had gone. After Spooner, the railway jogged along into a contented middle age.

Under the Regulation of Railways Act 1889 the Company was forced to carry out a number of alterations. Locomotives and passenger stock had to be fitted with the automatic vacuum-brake system. Points had to be interlocked throughout the line. The line was converted to steel rails, at least on the main passenger sections. The engines needed refitting and new boilers. Electric lighting was fitted at Duffws in 1900. The line at Glan-y-Pwll was diverted because waste from the Oakeley quarry threatened to engulf the original route (this being the first time the word 'Deviation' was heard in the Festiniog's history).

The railway had its problems, some routine, some extraordinary. A hurricane tore off some roofs. An Eisteddfod brought some extra passengers. There were the usual railway incidents and mishaps: derailments, carriages blown off the line on the Cob in a storm, ice and snow in hard winters, slipping wheels needing sand. There were broken axles, landslides, sheep, pigs, horses or cows wandering on the permanent way. Small boys threw stones at the conductors of the telegraph poles. *Taliesin* had a cracked engine frame. *Palmerston* ran into the back of a quarrymen's train in Tyler's Cutting and wrecked its front end. There were fires in the woods caused by cinders from the engines; the Company employed boys as fire-watchers. Wires and trees fell across the track. Rotten signal-posts fell down, and walls bulged. At times the Traffic Manager, F.G. Crick, could not have known who or what was going to assail him next when he opened his morning mail. There were problems about boys riding for nothing on the slate wagons. Shunters wrote asking for more pay. There were complaints about late trains and (another very old bone of contention) about staff at Harbour station not answering the telephone promptly. Crick was accused of showing lack of respect to the station-master at Tan-y-Bwlch. The roof at Boston Lodge needed reslating. Plate-layers asked for time off. Somebody wrote an apoplectic letter about riotous chaps getting drunk on Sunday in Blaenau Ffestiniog. Crick was taken to task for not providing a proper platform to load 'three beasts' at Tan-y-Bwlch. Poor Crick never knew where the next attack was coming from. In May 1883 he had a very stiff note from the officers and members of the British Women's Temperance Association, complaining about the serious hardship and inconvenience which Temperance travellers suffered in the Company's refreshment rooms. Apparently, it was very much easier to get a glass of beer than a cup of tea or coffee. The letter was signed by a formidable-sounding trio: Margaret Bright Lucas, President, Louise Stewart, Treasurer, and Sabrina Boocock, Honorary Secretary.

Crick worked for the Festiniog from 1872 until he retired in 1916, when he was Traffic Manager and Accountant. His son A.G. Crick succeeded him as a Traffic Superintendent, and also Secretary.

A.G. Crick's working diary still survives in the Company

archives. He noted the main dramas of the year, on the railway and in Portmadoc harbour. For 1886, for example, the year of Charles Spooner's 'boat' accident (12 February), *Merddin Emrys* came off the line at points on 8 January. On Monday 1 March there was heavy snow, with drifts in the streets of Portmadoc, and snow 'blocking the trains on our line very much'. The *Fame* of Bridgewater went aground on Portmadoc Bar on 5 April and lay there for three days before getting off. On the 12th a slate train arrived at Port late, with a broken axle. Three days later, thieves broke into Duffws station and Blaenau station, and the Great Western Railway Blaenau station. However, they 'got nothing'. The same month, on the 20th, David Jones the foreman carpenter was injured at Boston Lodge, being crushed between buffers when shunting. On Friday 7 May the smack *Elizabeth Anne* caught fire. Whit Monday was a big day: the Company ran a special excursion for 500 passengers from Blackpool and Blackburn. On 14 July, however, someone called 'Fred' (possibly A.G. Crick's father F.G.) drove another 'Special' into a passenger engine and train, which could not have impressed the customers. On Tuesday 31 August there were special trains for a Grand Fireworks at Tan-y-Bwlch for the coming-of-age of Mr Oakeley's son. Thousands of people were present. Mr Crick himself went up by the 5 o'clock train. On Friday 1 October 'the Government' were 'placing telegraph poles along the streets'. On the 11th Johnny Williams (son of William Williams) left for London, and thence to India for a situation with Percy Spooner. Johnny sailed on the 14th. Crick's year ends gloomily, with death and disaster. On 25 November the engine with the one o'clock train broke down with a burst cylinder at Tan-y-Bwlch. On 5 December Miss Spooner died at Bron-y-Garth 'after a long illness'. On the 8th there was a great storm which went on for several days. Lightning destroyed Duffws ladies' waiting-room door and a train was blown over the end of the Cob. The next day many vessels were wrecked near Portmadoc Bar. Miss Spooner was buried at Ynys.

There were always personal tensions, between Samuel Holland and the railway, between the Oakeley family and the railway. There were regroupings and resignations on the Board. Animosities sometimes continued after death. The last connection with the Spooner family was severed in June 1909 when William Williams the Locomotive Superintendent (and *Scribner's* 'most trusted mechanic on the line') finally retired. He had served the railway for sixty years. He was the man who built Spooner's garden railway. Williams had disagreements with

Frederick Vaughan, then Managing Director, and he asked that when he died his coffin should not be taken past Boston Lodge on its way from Portmadoc to Minffordd lest the enmity he had incurred should follow him into the grave. It was a curious incident, showing the astonishing power the railway had over the minds of those who worked on it.

Chapter 8

In 1900 the Festiniog Railway Company shares had a public quotation on the London Exchange. This for the first time broke the private circle of men who had been concerned with the ownership and running of the railway. But it was too late. The great days had already gone. There was a succession of hard winters at the turn of the century, and some very cold winds were already blowing through the slate industry.

For more than thirty years the slate industry had undergone a hectic cycle of boom and slump – a boom in the 1860s, followed by a slump in the 1880s and another, shorter boom in the 1890s. By 1900 the industry was undercapitalized, using obsolete machinery and operating in small and unprofitable units. It was in poor state, too, with increasing competition from imports of foreign slate and a growing tile-manufacturing industry. That year a strike started in Lord Penrhyn's great Bethesda quarries which lasted for three years. In 1902 there was a strike in the Ffestiniog quarries. At the same time the shipping trade with Hamburg also went into a recession which affected the harbour of Portmadoc. Several of the smaller quarries closed, together with some of the smaller railways. The larger quarries survived, though precariously, with a drastically reduced output of slates. At the Oakeley, labour and economic troubles were aggravated by heavy stone falls at the quarry faces.

All these troubles had their due effect on the Festiniog Railway, which went into the First World War showing several ominous signs of decay, although the war concealed for some years the true, parlous state of the Company's finances. On 5 August 1914 the government took over control of the railway, and paid compensation amounting to the difference between the net receipts of the period of control and the net receipts of the corresponding period of the previous year. Translated from the official gobbledygook, this meant that the Company was given some financial stability through a form of adjustable subsidy. The Ministry of Munitions took over a section of Boston Lodge Works, which became known as a National Shell Factory. Also commandeered were the Festiniog's Locomotive Superintendent, Robert Williams, to supervise the shell factory, and some of the Boston Lodge staff.

Nevertheless, the war was a very difficult time indeed for the railway. There were still the same operational mishaps – the accidents, the occasional derailment, the obstructions across the track. The slate industry was officially listed as non-essential. There was a severe shortage of men. Many had left North Wales during the slump and the strikes, never to return. Many went to serve in the Royal Welch Fusiliers (and many of those never returned, as the war memorials in the area still show today). There was a shortage of good coal. The engines, especially the smaller ones, understandably did not perform well or reliably on poor slack. There were wartime shortages of materials, and the Company's constant shortage of money. Short of men, money and materials, the Festiniog emerged from the First World War with a huge backlog of repairs to track and rolling-stock which it could not carry out.

The war also killed much-needed plans for enlarging and improving Portmadoc harbour, which at the time was about as out-of-date as the quarries and the railway. There were also plans to extend the railway south and west to Borth Bay; the Council would sponsor the scheme, and the Festiniog would run it. These, too, were dropped. In fact, Portmadoc never recovered from the war. The bustling harbour just died. The trade with Germany, which had once provided so much Hamburg ballast for the railway, had stopped with the war and never revived. The slate ships were laid up and began to rot where they lay. The wharves which had once had ships lying three abreast waiting to load slates were all empty. Most of the offices and warehouses were shuttered and boarded up. In his book *Brief Glory*, an account of his peregrinations up and down the Welsh coast and a lament for the passing of the sailing ship, D.W. Morgan fulfilled an old ambition by sailing his sloop *Dewdrop* to Portmadoc just after the war. Snowdon looked just the same, he said, Criccieth and Harlech castles and even Borth-y-Gest were just the same –

But Portmadoc! As the current carried the 'Dewdrop' into what would have been, when I last saw it, a busy and a

crammed-full port I beheld desolation. Not a ship alongside
Madocks' erstwhile new quays, no engine puffing along the
narrow-gauge lines, no little pointsman in uniform with the
dark shadowed eyes, no ship-chandler or Puddin-rice shop.
I steered my boat over water full of shadows until my
bowsprit touched the bridge, and here I moored, feeling like
an intruder in some hallowed graveyard and wanting to
speak in whispers.

A few days only did I linger in the uncanny stillness.
After visiting a few well-remembered spots I fled, fled as fast
as wind would speed me; nor did I ever revisit the old
derelict port in any ship, large or small.

In all these gloomy records of a declining railway, it is worth
pointing out that the passenger figures never slumped as the
slate did. Whatever else might happen, people still loved to ride
on the Festiniog. They might have been temporarily deterred,
by a dull summer or a world war, but given half a chance, when
the sun and peace returned, so did they. Nor were all the
passengers tourists from outside, even in the summer. In a rural
area where roads were still few and bad, the Festiniog was a
vital outlet to the outside world for the people and district of
Blaenau and Llan Ffestiniog. By the 'Lein Bach', families could
go down to Portmadoc to visit relatives or spend a day by the
sea; choirs, musicians and dancers could attend Eisteddfodau
and concerts; agricultural shows, weddings, funerals, meetings,
chapel services with visiting preachers, fireworks displays and
county court cases could all be attended more easily.

In 1921 the Company called in a sort of 'company doctor',
an engineer called Major G.C. Spring, to examine the working
of the railway in detail and to report. Like Captain Tyler before
him (it is odd how many military men have been involved in
the Festiniog's affairs), Major Spring reported a great list of
defects, most of which one would expect to have been obvious.
Incredible though it seemed, the Company were spending 32s.
6d. for every pound they made. Although the annual tonnage of
slate carried had decreased by more than ten per cent since
before the war, and was still decreasing, the shunting mileage
worked at the top and bottom of the line had actually increased,
by very nearly half. This mileage amounted to nearly a fifth of
the total engine mileage, and accounted for nearly half the total
expenditure on engines. The Festiniog was apparently working
harder and harder to haul less and less. Much of the line's
equipment was wastefully duplicated or extravagantly super-
fluous. There were over a thousand slate wagons, far more than

76

the railway needed, which were clogging sidings and getting lost in quarries. None of the three signal-boxes or the three stations at Blaenau was fully employed. The railway had more men than it needed in some places, too few in others. While Boston Lodge works was overstaffed, there was only one inspector, one sub-ganger and nine men to look after the whole length of permanent way ('a moderate allowance of men', Spring called it). The Major had harsh things to say about the state of the permanent way, although he expressed himself in a somewhat contradictory manner. 'The track is very well maintained,' he said, 'but almost all the rails are old and worn. Ballast is poor and insufficient. Scotch fir sleepers are badly split with four holes in their short length, but larch are better. Sleepers are laid in un-creosoted.' With old and worn rails, poor and insufficient ballast and badly split sleepers one might wonder what sort of line Major Spring would have called *badly* maintained. But in fact, his remarks are not all that contradictory; the materials, the rail, ballast and sleepers, might be in a poor state, but he found the drainage, the level of the rails and other factors necessary for safety were all well maintained.

Nearly everywhere the Major's inspecting eye lighted, there was something wrong: subsidence near Boston Lodge; a wall bulging and in a state of collapse at Harbour station; poor lighting in the workshops; unbalanced winter timetables; poor slinging, poor manning and too many apprentices, who spent too much time planing by hand.

Major Spring produced a host of recommendations, some sensible, some slightly daft. ('Coal traffic might profitably be expanded,' he said. So it might, but how, and between whom?)

The Company did carry out some of Major Spring's recommendations. They closed Duffws station to passengers. They acquired a petrol shunting locomotive to work at the bottom end of each line. They readjusted the winter timetables and some of the labour rosters. They downgraded Penrhyn and Tan-y-Grisiau to 'halt' status.

They also did something that Spring had not meant at all. He had commented on the length of time that locomotives spent under repair, meaning that the repairs took too *long*. The Company took it to mean that their locomotives were being repaired too *often* and gladly cut the maintenance schedules. This, too, contributed to the disaster to come. The man who had to try and put into effect Spring's recommendations and who had to grapple with their results was yet another Festiniog military figure, Colonel Stephens.

Holman Fred Stephens, MICE, of Tonbridge, Kent (the son of F.G. Stephens, the art critic), was one of the most remarkable of all the remarkable characters who ever served – if that is the right term in his case – the Festiniog Railway.

In *Festiniog Railway Revival*, the first book to examine the post-war history of the railway in terms of the personalities on it, Pat Whitehouse says of Stephens that he

> ran an assortment of minor railways which he collected almost as other people collect books or paintings. His first was the Shropshire and Montgomeryshire, from Shrewsbury to Llanymynech, which he succeeded in re-opening in 1911 after it had lain derelict for nearly thirty years. As time went on others were added to his empire: the Kent and East Sussex, the East Kent, the Hundred of Manhood and Selsey, the Weston, Clevedon and Portishead, the Snailbeach and District, and finally, the Festiniog-Welsh Highland.

Colonel Stephens was involved in railway construction from the beginning of the century. He had the Rother Valley Railway (later the Kent & East Sussex) in 1900 and a line engineered by him, the Bere Alston and Callington section of the Plymouth, Devonport and South-Western Junction Railway, was opened in March 1908.

Colonel Stephens became Civil Engineer and Locomotive Superintendent, the first of many rolling and resonant titles the Festiniog gave him over the years, on 1 April 1923. He became a director in November, and Chairman and Managing Director in January 1925 (although still Locomotive Superintendent). The control of the railway now became extraordinarily fragmented. Stephens ran things from Kent; the chairman H.J. Jack and the general manager S.E. Tyrwhitt lived in Dolgarrog; the Secretary, Evan R. Davies, worked in Buckingham Gate in London; and Stephens's own 'man on the spot', Nevitt, actually lived in Llandudno.

Stephens, as a military man, had a military mind. He ran the Festiniog, or tried to run it, like a battalion. The tone of many of his letters to Portmadoc is of a kindly but short-tempered regimental commander attempting to control at long range an assortment of rather dim and ill-trained troops. Everything on the railway had to be just so when the Colonel did his inspections. His visits were like those of a meteor: unpredictable, and generally causing confusion. He was apt to notice if one of the troops was not on parade. 'What was labourer T. Morgan doing on Saturday 13th Ultimo,' he wrote to

Robert Williams, 'when I was on the line? I did not see him in the Works.' Like an over-fussy CO, he complained about the minutiae of barracks cleanliness – for instance, if the backs of the engine driving-wheels were dirty. He would summarily court-martial some employee and punish him with outright dismissal. On the other hand he could show generosity to those who were faithful to the railway or who acted with commend-able military speed in an emergency. Will Jones, a plate-layer under Stephens's regime and one of the few railway employees of that era to survive into the new age after the restoration, used to tell a story of the day a runaway slate train took off from Tan-y-Grisiau. Will Jones at Tan-y-Bwlch had no time to do more than divert the runaway into the sidings by the goods shed and let it pile up there. He tried to wedge over the top points with a piece of wood. The points were worked by a weighted level and, try as he would, Will Jones could not reach quite far enough to hold the lever out and drive in the wedge at the same time. He had the points nearly split when he heard the runaway coming out of Garnedd Tunnel. So he prudently retired behind the safety of the water-tank. The first wagon hit the points and left the track. The second reared up over it. The air was full of flying slates, a great cloud of dust rose into the air and there was a roar like a mighty explosion. The Colonel came up the line to inspect the damage. 'A great big upright man he was too,' says Will Jones telling the story, 'with a gruff voice. "Jones, what's this mess you've been making here?" ' A lesser official tried to curry favour by whining: 'If he had taken some sand, and run up the line, sprinkling a litt-le bit on the rail here, and a litt-le bit on the rail there he could have stopped the wagons.'

'You damn *fool*!' roared the Colonel, 'would you have liked to run up the line along the mountainside, towards the wagons, with them coming down from Glan-y-Pwll in seventeen minutes? You have done right, Jones,' the Colonel said to Will. 'Monday will be our little harvest,' he said, meaning the Bank Holiday traffic that weekend. 'You have saved us that, whatever else you have done.'

Colonel Stephens did have the virtue of giving credit where it was due. He rewarded the railwaymen who came forward as volunteers during the General Strike (though he did rather tend to treat them as gallant troops who had comported themselves beyond the line of duty in battle). He bought a mobile crane which was an embarrassment from the day it arrived. He bought various petrol-driven rail tractors, two of which, a Baldwin now called *Moelwyn* and the Simplex, survived into the restoration.

He had occasionally to beat off unrealistic suggestions from Jack and Tyrwhitt at Dolgarrog, that the railway should be equipped with a fleet of Ford Model T tractors with flanged metal wheels, or that the Festiniog and the Welsh Highland should close down completely for a month while steam engines were scrapped and replaced by Fordson tractors and rail buses.

The Cob under construction in the autumn of 1810. The view is from Tremadoc, looking across to Boston Lodge. Note the horse-drawn tramway on the embankment, and Madocks's initials on the wagon in the foreground. (*National Library of Wales*)

Port Madoc, Carnarvonshire.

The Festiniog Railway in about 1840. A gravity train of slate wagons, with an occupied horse dandy in the rear, is approaching Boston Lodge. (*National Library of Wales*)

William Alexander Madocks MP (1773–1828), whose great vision of an embankment across the Traeth Mawr eventually made the Festiniog Railway possible. (*Olive Kitson*)

Samuel Holland MP (1803–1892), one of the pioneers of the North Wales slate industry. He played an important part in the early history of the railway, and slates from his quarry were the first to travel on Festiniog rails. (*National Library of Wales*)

Robert Francis Fairlie (1831–1885), brilliant inventor and engineer. The first Fairlie 'double engine', aptly named *Little Wonder*, spread the name of the Festiniog worldwide.

One of Fairlie's locomotives, *Livingston Thompson*, at Harbour station in about 1885.

A pair of first-class observation four-wheelers in 1887. The left-hand vehicle is in its original condition (except for the tin roof); the right-hand vehicle is a rebuild of a closed carriage. (*Festiniog Railway Company*)

The Prince, without cab, in 1887. (*Photograph by R. H. Bleasdale from the Spooner Album*)

Portmadoc harbour, looking from the Garth, in about 1878. At this time, the first Festiniog Railway station was behind the ships on the right. The line ran down the quay (centre), with its zero point against the back wall of the house (the News Room) at the end of the Welsh Slate Company's wharf (foreground). (*Festiniog Railway Company*)

Little Wonder at Harbour station, with an assortment of four-wheeled passenger coaches. The picture, with masts of sailing ships in the background, was taken by J. Owen of Newtown. (*Festiniog Railway Company*)

The Princess with a down passenger train below Tan-y-Grisiau. An open quarrymen's carriage brings up the rear. The picture was taken by J. Owen of Newtown in 1871. (*Festiniog Railway Company*)

Little Wonder at the head of an up-train on the curve at Creua (just above Tan-y-Bwlch station). The train is interesting, consisting of mineral wagons, followed by passenger coaches, followed by slate wagons, with brakesmen standing stiffly to attention at intervals. (*Festiniog Railway Company*)

Charles Spooner's 'Boat', in which he suffered an accident near the Moelwyn Tunnel on 12 February 1886. (*From a drawing in* Scribner's Monthly, *August 1879*)

On the Festiniog Railway. (*From the* London & North Western Railway Official Tourist Guide, *1876*)

The Princess in difficulties. (*From* Scribner's Monthly, *August 1879*)

FESTINIOG RAILWAY

Festiniog Railway advertising between the wars: a poster by
Norman Keene showing a trainload of cheerful passengers,
despite the horrifying drop on one side and the apparently
unsecured track ahead. (*P. B. Whitehouse, Millbrook House Ltd*)

Dduallt before the First World War, probably about 1910. (*Festiniog Railway Company*)

Taliesin with a train from Portmadoc crosses the High Street on 1 August 1933.

Chapter 9

Looking back now, it is clear that Colonel Stephens had an impossible task. No man could have run the Festiniog, and later the Welsh Highland Railway in conjunction with it, efficiently and profitably. The line was already suffering from the effects of wartime neglect and from the economies suggested by Major Spring. Safety procedures were so lax that the footplatemen of the Festiniog even complained to the National Union of Railwaymen about them (they must have been extremely lax) and particularly the dangers of sanding, when the fireman had to get out onto the engine and drop sand onto the rail.

The coal used was officially described as 'soil-like'. The engines required more and more of it to pull less and less. It was nothing unusual for the Company to have to hire road transport to rescue the passengers of stranded trains. An engine incapable of going further would leave its train where it was and go on with what steam it had to the next station to send a message. (Often a motor-car was sent, being quite large enough to take the two or three passengers on board.) Even the quarrymen, who had been so faithful to the railway for so many years, now began to forsake it. They approached the Crosville Bus Company, and when they gave a minimum guarantee of passengers, the Company ran a bus for them from December 1926. Nevitt himself, who visited the line about twice a week on Stephens's behalf from Llandudno, went home via Afonwen because he could not trust his Festiniog connection at Blaenau Ffestiniog. There were complaints from headmasters and parents that pupils were late for school and late coming home. There were complaints from standard-gauge passengers at Minffordd and at Blaenau that they always missed their narrow-gauge connections. There were complaints from the locomen themselves, who naturally had their professional pride. They were tired of shovelling poor slack, hacking out clinker, leaving trains standing. They were all local men and did not relish leaving trains full of their own relations and friends stranded in the woods while they went for help. One mishap led to another, a series of misfortunes would establish itself, and before anyone could stop it the line would fall into a state of chaos and paralysis.

The Colonel blamed the men on the spot – Robert Williams in charge of locomotives, and Robert Evans, the Traffic Manager. He bombarded them with letters and sometimes with telegrams. He wrote on most days. Sometimes he wrote three letters in a day. The detached reader, even sixty years later, feels a growing surge of exasperation. Stephens must have been the most infuriating employer. Robert Evans must have had the patience of a saint. Stephens wrote about everything and anything. He complained that there were no labels on first- and third-class carriages; he complained about sandboxes, and coal consumption; he complained about faulty magnetos on the Simplex and cushions for the carriages, and the way to turn up truck wheels on a lathe. He peppered his text with words like 'Urgent' or 'Required Now'. Words were often strenuously underlined, 'as an order' 'at once'. There was one interminable correspondence about carriage lights and roof lamps. 'Try the lights in the tunnel,' wrote Stephens, 'and only in the tunnel, and let me know whether one bulb in each compartment is enough. Urgent, without further delay, reply early please.' Another correspondence, about the vacuum brakes on the quarrymen's trains, went on, to and fro, for nearly a year. An exchange about the length of time an engine-driver took to recover and return to work after having a wart on his face removed took six months. 'I confess,' wrote Stephens plaintively, 'I do not like going to all this trouble and then not getting local support. IT WILL NOT DO.'

Still the letters came in a steady, maddening stream. There was more trouble about the vacuum brakes. The man who usually looked after the situation was away, at his wife's funeral. Fireman Thomas had an accident: he had fractured a finger lifting a clinker paddle out of a firebox on the Fairlie. A small boy got his foot caught in the turntable at Glan-y-Pwll. 'Put a lock on it,' Stephens ordered curtly. 'Why was labourer T. Morgan not in the works? Why was there no steam in the engine at Minffordd?' Why? Why? Why?

Stephens dealt out dismissals with a draconic hand. There

was a boiler attendant for the twenty-two-horse-power heavy oil engine at Boston Lodge. Colonel Stephens had bought it himself and arranged for the Company to repay him by instalments for the money they were saving by not having to buy coal for the former steam engine that used to drive the works machinery. The engine was sometimes worked by an 'old hand' and sometimes by T. Morgan (obviously something of a *bête noire* for Stephens) 'who was in the stores but now assists the painter'. In successive letters, Stephens commanded that the heavy-engine attendant should be given a week's notice, that the heavy-engine attendant's week's notice should be withdrawn and Morgan given a week's notice, and finally that neither of them was to be given a week's notice.

Stephens sometimes made the fatal mistake of descending to sarcasm. Concerning a report that there was the smell of a dead animal in the carriage pit, Stephens indulged himself in a little elephantine humour. 'Possibly it is some of the "energy" which might have been applied in turning the work out, buried in the pit. This may account for the slow output.' Such an attitude, from a distant Englishman to Welshmen on the spot naturally gave rise to disloyalty and disobedience. The staff submitted to the new instructions, obeyed them while the Colonel was there, and when he left quietly went on as they were. He tried to catch people out but the staff had a warning code: the driver and the guard of any train carrying the Colonel used to stroke their chins and beards to warn people by the line of danger. Only occasionally did Stephens admit some linguistic inadequacy, only rarely did he seem to appreciate that Tonbridge was many miles away and across a major ethnic frontier from Portmadoc. 'Can you tell me,' he once wrote, 'what the Welsh is for "Trespassers will be prosecuted, by Order"? Have you any stencils for this in English and Welsh?'

And still the letters came – about timetable boards, the water-level in Quellyn Lake, the brushing of platforms to stop the railway 'looking draggle-tailed', repairs to Minffordd warehouse, broken lamps on Portmadoc station, and apprentices' working hours. 'It is rather tiresome,' he wrote, 'this small line giving all this trouble. I am glad the rest of my lines do not give me so much.'

Colonel Stephens was not helped by the frequent changes of personnel in the boardroom and on the line. Stephens himself remained, under various titles, but under him all was in a state of flux. S.E. Tyrwhitt, the General Manager, retired and was followed for a short time by Captain John May. He in his turn was succeeded by E.H.R. Nicholls in 1924, who left in early 1925. Stephens was General Manager, in fact, whatever his current title might have been. At Boston Lodge Robert Williams was Locomotive Superintendent. When the Colonel took over that title, Williams stayed on but allowed the rolling-stock to fall into an appalling state of neglect. The railway had an able man, Hugh Hughes, who might have replaced him but unfortunately, on 8 May 1926, when Hughes was travelling in a special train to the scene of one of the many derailments of the time, he stepped from the train prematurely thinking it had entered Penrhyn station. In fact the train, still moving, had not reached the level-crossing. Hughes fell and later died of his injuries. He was replaced by Morris Jones, who had once been a Boston Lodge apprentice, and who happened to be home on leave from his ship. He went to work for the Festiniog and was to have an important part to play in the restoration.

'The tiresome small line giving all this trouble' was actually not the Festiniog but the Welsh Highland. 'Welsh Highland Railway' is a name which even now is capable of arousing strong emotions – of nostalgia, regret, rage and frustration. The Welsh Highland was one of those romantic concepts which grew out of the tangled complex of schemes for little railways that had been projected for North Wales at various times and in various places in the previous half-century. With all that mineral wealth known to be waiting to be tapped in the hills, and with the example of the Festiniog as a proven commercial success, it seemed to many people that narrow-gauge railways would improve communications and be the best way of exploiting the mineral wealth of the area.

Amongst several little railways that became involved with the Festiniog was a concern called the North Wales Narrow Gauge Railway (NWNGR). Charles Spooner had once helped to promote it. It was formed in 1872 to build a network of two-foot gauge lines over much of Caernarvonshire. The Company did actually build the first section of a proposed line from Dinas Junction, three miles south of Caernarvon, up to South Snowdon-Rhyd-Ddu, but then went bankrupt after one year in existence. However, the Company somehow struggled on for the next forty years, until its passenger services were suspended in 1916. The intention had been to build a further stretch of line from South Snowdon, south and west to Beddgelert, through the Aberglaslyn Pass, and so finally down the Traeth Mawr to Portmadoc.

The project would have been a very considerable civil

84

engineering feat, involving dozens of bridges, cuttings, loops and embankments and, since the line was to be electrified, a very stiff gradient up to one in twenty-eight. In 1906 another company, the Portmadoc, Beddgelert and South Snowdon Railway Company (PBSSR) started to build the line. But in 1908, when the section was almost complete, they too ran out of money.

There matters rested, for over a decade. But expectations locally continued to run high. There was much local feeling that a railway would open up the countryside, bring extra employment and prove to be a general boon. Public meetings were held. Letters were written to local newspapers. Such local enthusiasm was generated that when the government agreed to pay half the costs, local authorities almost competed amongst themselves to contribute the other half. Some councils were almost over-enthusiastic; the Glaslyn Rural District Council, for example, approved an astonishing general rate increase of 4s. 5d. in the pound to pay their share of the Welsh Highland Railway.

So, in 1921, work began again. By that time the track of the old NWNGR was in a deplorable state. But it was repaired, and by the spring of 1923 it was ready for traffic. A new Light Railway Order had been obtained, a new company had been formed and by the summer of 1923 trial runs were being held. A new track through the streets of Portmadoc was laid, from the harbour to the new station on the south side of the Cambrian line. The new station had a loop with platforms, name-boards and a refreshment room.

The route ran from Portmadoc along the north side of the Traeth Mawr following the line of the old horse-drawn Croesor Tramway for four miles to Croesor Junction. There, it swung northwards up the Glaslyn river valley to Nantmor. Here, it started to climb, passed through a half-mile tunnel to the Aberglaslyn Pass and thence to Beddgelert. Various wider loops and deviations were built to lessen the gradient to about one in forty (the notion of electrification had been dropped). From Beddgelert the line climbed north and west to its highest point at Pitts Head, eleven miles from Portmadoc. The line then ran across the moor to join the old NWNGR at South Snowdon and from there followed the NWNGR route downhill, past Lake Quellyn and down the Gwyfrai valley to Dinas.

It was a most romantic railway route, passing through some of the most gorgeous scenery in Wales – and in the world. But it made no sort of commercial sense at all. Even at the time the Welsh Highland opened, the quarries it was supposed to service were declining, some of them near to closing. The freight traffic could quite comfortably be carried by two trains a week from Dinas to Bryngwyn, and one a week down to Portmadoc. The Croesor Tramway gave a little business at the Portmadoc end until 1930 when the Croesor quarries had all closed. Passenger traffic never came anywhere near expectations. Having hungered and thirsted after a railway for so long, the local populace than ignored it when they had it. There were practical snags, too: the train did not even take passengers into Caernarvon town as the buses did, but dropped them three miles short at Dinas. The winter passenger service was soon withdrawn for lack of custom. The summer tourist traffic was brisk but it was never enough to stop the Welsh Highland losing money.

Lost money on the Welsh Highland affected the Festiniog. The two railways were closely connected from the beginning. H.J. Jack, chairman of the Festiniog, was also Managing Director of the North Wales Power and Electric Traction Company which owned a controlling interest in the Festiniog, and also owned the old Portmadoc, Beddgelert and South Snowdon Railway. The two railways issued joint tickets and timetables, shared rolling-stock, office stationery, staff and Colonel Stephens.

Colonel Stephens made strenuous attempts to 'tailor' the Welsh Highland engines to fit the narrower Festiniog clearances – especially in the Moelwyn Tunnel. The couplings between the Festiniog and Welsh Highland stock did not match properly, nor were all the Festiniog staff properly taught how to couple them up. In one famous episode, on 1 July 1924, a train of Welsh Highland and Festiniog coaches, double-headed by the Festiniog *Palmerston* and the Welsh Highland Fairlie *Moel Tryfan*, broke in two in the middle of the Moelwyn Tunnel. Pat Whitehouse gives a good description of the incident:

> *Palmerston*'s driver was then overcome by smoke, so his
> fireman uncoupled their engine and drove away to summon
> help leaving *Moel Tryfan* on her own. Her driver, who must
> have been a lightly-built man, had meanwhile managed to
> crawl between coaches and tunnel side, survey the broken
> coupling and then squeeze himself back to the engine to
> bring the coaches together. Having done this, he crawled
> back again to the break, repaired the coupling, but was
> unable to return to the footplate and had to walk out of the
> tunnel over the top of the hill and into the other end before

he could reach the engine and finally drive the train out into the open. It must have been a gruesome experience for the passengers who were trapped in the smoky dark for over an hour.

The Welsh Highland was always a financial invalid. Receivers were appointed as early as 1927. Nevertheless, hopes still ran high, particularly for summer tourist traffic on what was known as the 'Five Valleys' tour. Holiday-makers from the North Wales resorts could take an observation car on the LNWR and come through the long Crimea Pass Tunnel to Blaenau Ffestiniog. There they would leave the standard-gauge train, cross the road to the Festiniog station and catch the narrow-gauge down to Portmadoc, through the streets of the town to the Cambrian Line where passengers had to get out and cross the Cambrian rails on foot before taking the Welsh Highland to Dinas, where they changed yet again for a Bangor or Llandudno train. And so home to bed, no doubt feeling as though they had been to Birmingham by way of Beachy Head.

But people must have enjoyed the tour because the Welsh Highland had a moderately good year for passengers in 1933. The Company showed a profit and actually paid a small dividend. This promoted the Festiniog Railway Company to the disastrous step of taking a forty-two year lease on the Welsh Highland on 1 July 1934, for a nominal rent of twenty shillings.

It was a case of the halt leading the lame. Any hopes of survival the Festiniog may have had were now doomed. In practice the lease meant that any funds the Festiniog might earn were used to prop up the Welsh Highland, which made a loss for the last six months of 1934, and another for 1935 – in fact 1933 was the only year the Welsh Highland ever showed a profit or paid a dividend. Nobody who put money in the Company ever got it back, or any more return than that single, tiny dividend. Passenger services on the Welsh Highland ended in September 1936. The rails were lifted and sold for scrap in 1941.

Colonel Stephens died on 23 October 1931, probably not much lamented by the Festiniog Railway. He was an honest, upright and sincere man, who had done his best according to his lights. The railway staff probably annoyed him as much as he annoyed them. His place as Chairman and Managing Director was taken by Evan R. Davies.

Evan Davies could have been the Festiniog's saviour had he not died prematurely in 1934. He realised how much money could be made out of tourists. The Five Valleys Tour was his idea (and he was largely responsible for the Welsh Highland's

87

one and only dividend). When he took over, Davies faced a steadily dwindling slate trade, fewer passengers from the quarrymen and local residents, very little goods carriage except for local merchants' stores, coal and milk deliveries to people living along the line, and occasional business such as the mussel trade when, for some reason, for a short time the railway carried consignments of mussels from Portmadoc up to Blaenau.

Evan Davies concentrated upon the tourist trade. Under him the railway did a brisk business in tours and also began a profitable sideline in special trains for school outings, football matches, agricultural and flower shows and fairs in Portmadoc, with special rates of daily return tickets. For the second time in its history, the Festiniog Railway entered into the guidebooks of North Wales as the 'Toy' railway. The guides stressed the natural beauties of the line, its uniqueness and charm, its 'Fairy Glens'. The Company commissioned one striking coloured advertising poster by Norman Keene which still survives: a Festiniog Fairlie is pulling a train along a very narrow mountain ledge through Tyrolean-looking scenery. The carriages are full of smiling, cheerful passengers, all evidently quite unconcerned at the precipice on one side or the apparently unsecured state of the track in front of the engine.

In October 1930 ordinary winter passenger services were suspended for good. Henceforth only tourist trains ran, from May or June until September each year. There was a steady retrenchment in other ways. Duffws station was finally closed, along with the Groby Granite branch line, and some of the signal-boxes. In 1936, the centenary year, the Llechwedd stopped sending their slates on the Festiniog. However, the BBC struck a more cheerful note with a centenary programme on the Festiniog on the evening of Saturday 13 December. Recording vans had been up to Blaenau, Minffordd and Portmadoc the previous October to record sounds of working trains and 'crewling'. Those taking part in the studio were Mr Seaborne, manager of the Votty quarry, Bessie Jones of Tan-y-Bwlch (wife of Will), the engine-driver Tom Davies and Robert Evans the manager. It all went very well. Several people wrote to say they had listened and enjoyed it. Robert Evans enjoyed himself too: 'I felt quite at home in the studios,' he wrote to the BBC, 'and would not mind being called to broadcast again.'

Chapter 10

The summer of 1939, the last summer of the old world, was a good one for weather and for passengers. The sun shone, Wally Hammond made a hundred against the West Indies at the Oval, and England won the series. Lord Rosebery's Blue Peter won the Derby. The Festiniog ran its usual cheap day excursions on August Bank Holiday, taking passengers down for the athletic sports and bicycle races at Portmadoc, with a grand display of fireworks and the Portmadoc Horticultural Show. Third-class return fare from Blaenau was two shillings.

Meanwhile, ominous events were happening at home and abroad, like distant rumblings of thunder beyond the Rhinogs. Conscription was introduced in April, and the first ARP exercises were held in the cities. The first evacuees were packed off to the country, to be followed by civil servants in government departments. The nation's art treasures were moved from the galleries and stored in Manod slate quarries for the duration, where, in conditions of steady temperature and humidity, they never had it so good. They were quickly followed by wealthy old ladies from England and anyone else who could afford a 'funk-hole'. They all settled down to knit, play backgammon, criticize the Welsh and their weather and generally see the war out in hotels and boarding-houses all over North Wales.

For the Festiniog, this was to be a different war. This time there was no special compensation, no financial guarantee. Slate was not officially classified as a strategically important material (although, in view of the Blitz damage to come, it arguably should have been). Possibly, there was an element of personal animosity in Whitehall's attitude towards the Festiniog. It was suggested that favours done in the First World War were the result of personal influence by the Festiniog's directors. There was, too, the matter of two new boilers, so confidently ordered by the Company on the assumption that the government would pay; government investigators had come to Portmadoc to enquire about them. The Welsh Office and the Ministry had long memories.

Passenger services were suspended on 15 September 1939. On the same day the directors of the Company met some of the quarries' directors and the slate merchants at the harbour offices. It was decided that the railway would work a three-day week, closing down completely the rest of the time. *Princess* or *Merddin Emrys*, then the only engines still serviceable, would take the empty slate wagons up to Blaenau from Minffordd while a tractor ran between Minffordd and Portmadoc (the rails on the Cob were thought, even then, unsafe for steam locomotive running).

The war hardly touched the railway physically – there was no bomb damage – but it undoubtedly hastened the end. Members of the staff were called up, or just left. Gravity working ceased in 1940. The Welsh Highland was then in its death throes. Negotiations in 1941 were taking place to sell its track to scrap merchants. The Festiniog finally divested itself of that lease in December 1942.

The track had already begun to look decrepit even before the war. Now it simply got worse. There were the usual derailments, trees across the line, weeds everywhere and abandoned wagons choking the sidings. Although slate was to be badly needed later to repair roofs, the quarries were all on short time. The slate wharves were used as vehicle parks. The Resident Naval Officer, who must have been anticipating a German landing, asked the railway to clear slate wagons from the harbour. The Home Guard used the station buildings, and built anti-tank blocks across roads and the line. One of their pill-boxes at Pen Cob was still in existence long after the war. Dutch troops were billeted in the Harbour station for a time in 1942 and 1943. The Air Ministry wanted to store ammunition on the Welsh Highland. They were refused, but the Festiniog did sell the War Office about twenty old slate wagons for £30 each. These were at the top end of the Welsh Highland between Pitts Head and Hafod Rhufydd, where the line was still laid. They were rolled down the track and used as targets for anti-tank gun practice. Bits of shattered wagons are still there today.

Ironically, at this time of deepest depression for the Festiniog, there was a call for its services. As the war went on, petrol was short and the bus service was cut. Local residents asked for a passenger service (other than the unofficial passengers who had always continued to travel free in the brake vans of the slate trains). Portmadoc Council asked for a service to be resumed but they got a dusty answer. The Company replied, and one can hardly blame them for a certain gleeful satisfaction, that the local people had never shown much interest in the railway when they had it. It was their lack of support that had caused the railway to close down its passenger service in the first place. 'No complaints were ever made to us,' they wrote to the Council, 'by the public of the discomfort of travelling on crowded buses when they could have travelled in our trains with their ample accommodation.' The Company then suggested that if the local authorities really wanted a passenger service so badly, they might like to contribute to the cost of it. But the skeletons of the Welsh Highland were still rattling vigorously and the local authorities declined. And here the matter rested. The railway and its remaining staff waited for the war to end.

On VJ Day, August 1945, when intoxicated revellers were turning cartwheels in Trafalgar Square, the Festiniog Railway was facing its last crisis. Almost all disposable land in Portmadoc had been sold, including the site intended for the new station in the brave, hopeful old days of the Welsh Highland. The scrap dealers were still hovering around. There was an overdraft of £400 at the bank (who, understandably, were much more worried about it than about the railway). The National Farmers' Union were complaining on behalf of their members that stock was wandering all over the line and being killed. The amount of slate carried had shrunk to about fifty tons a day on the three-day working week. There was just Robert Evans, the Manager, at Portmadoc. Boston Lodge was run by Morris Jones, with one apprentice and an old-age pensioner to do some cleaning and brew the tea. There were four men on the traffic staff, to act as shunters, pointsmen and brakesmen, and only two engine-drivers, the brothers Will and Thomas Davies. There were three men on the permanent way, which had now passed out of any semblance of order.

In February 1946 the situation was so desperate that the Company asked for charity. A circular was sent round the quarries, setting out the position and appealing for money. The railway could keep going only if contributions were made. The Oakeley quarry was then sending slate by its own outlet line to the LNWR station in Blaenau, and nothing at all to Minffordd. The Maenofferen, the Llechwedd and the Wrysgan sent fifty tons a day to Minffordd. The Votty travelled about a quarter of a mile from their incline to the LNWR yard. In fact by 1946 the quarries were hardly using the Festiniog Railway at all. Not surprisingly, in view of their historical attitude towards the railway, they refused to contribute anything. The railway appealed to the Ministry of Transport for a grant, but Portmadoc is a long way from Whitehall. The Ministry evidently did not realise the need for urgency and it was June before a man from the Ministry arrived, having (he said) been delayed by repairs to his car. By then the bank overdraft had risen to £800. That same month a ship (which must have been captained by the Ancient Mariner) astounded everybody by calling at Portmadoc for slate.

In July the Company appealed once more to the quarries, and once more there was no support. The request for a grant had also been refused. The Ministry told the Company to make arrangements to give the quarries an outlet along their metals to the standard gauge. This could be done without running the Festiniog's own services. In August the quarries and the railway would be closing for the summer holiday. There was no more money, no more suggestions, no more to be done. Some 600 yards of Festiniog track were leased to the Maenofferen and Votty, to connect their inclines with the LNWR standard gauge. The quarries were responsible for maintaining their own stock. The last train ran between Minffordd and Duffws on Thursday 1 August 1946. Thereafter Robert Evans remained at Portmadoc, Morris Jones at Boston Lodge. The rest were sent letters of dismissal.

And that, finally, after 110 years, was that.

Chapter 11

Although the Festiniog Railway had been officially told to lie down, it simply refused to die. There were no trains running, but people still insisted on coming to see where they used to run. Some came to pay (as they thought) their last respects to a dear departed friend, still fondly remembered from many pre-war holidays in North Wales. Some came to wallow in their nostalgia, and to point out to their children the scenes of their former triumphs. 'Of course, I remember this when . . .' and 'Of course, it's all gone to pot now.' Some came frankly to steal whatever they could lay their hands on and made no bones about their intentions. A few came as 'souvenir-hunters', which is just another name for a thief.

A few came with ideas about reopening the railway. There was only a trickle of such people, but it never really dried up. Eventually, Robert Evans tired of them and his conducted tours grew shorter, as did his temper. He did all he could to magnify the difficulties, although those who went round with him could see that he grieved for the railway. He remembered it in better days. The difficulties spoke for themselves and needed no emphasis from Robert Evans. The would-be entrepreneurs retired, appalled by the size of the task.

Robert Evans was quick to point out that the railway was still in a workable condition, whenever there was anything to be gained by it. He became adept at 'opening' and 'closing' the railway, depending upon who was asking. When there was a question of paying rates or settling outstanding bills, Robert Evans said firmly the railway was closed. On the other hand, when there was a legal requirement to prove the railway was open (or the land might revert to its original owners after a lapse of four years), Robert Evans argued that occupants of various railway property at Blaenau, Dduallt, Coed-y-Bleiddiau and the Moelwyn Tunnel cottage were all using trolleys on the line and therefore were keeping it 'open'. At the same time, he did not hesitate to write to the same occupant of the Tunnel cottage and warn him that he was trespassing by using his own private trolley on the line.

In March 1947 Morris Jones's employment was 'terminated', leaving Robert Evans at Portmadoc as the Company's sole resident employee. The Chairman, W. Cradoc Davies, lived at Pwllheli. The Secretary, Evan Davies, the Chairman's nephew, lived in London.

One of the earliest genuine attempts to reopen the line was made by Bill Broadbent, who was to play a major role in the restoration of the railway (though not through his original scheme). He later became a director and was for over twenty years Chairman of the Festiniog Railway Society Limited; representative director of the Society on the board of the Festiniog Railway Company; a trustee of the Festiniog Railway Trust, and a director of the Festiniog Railway (Sales) Limited. He had travelled on the railway often during family holidays as a child in the 1930s. He and a friend R.C.S. (Michael) Low, both in their early twenties and both professional railwaymen (Broadbent having started as an apprentice at Crewe in 1942) came back to North Wales on a climbing expedition at Whitsun in 1947.

On the Friday after dinner they walked up from the Oakeley Arms Hotel to Tan-y-Bwlch, and had a look at the line as far as Whistling Curve. Their interest aroused by what they had seen, Broadbent and Low went down to Portmadoc to see Robert Evans.

At that time, the line was not nearly as overgrown as it was to become. Broadbent 'could see a year's work for a gang of three'. The pair had plenty of ideas: they would engage as many paid staff as were needed to run the freight service; reinforce the permanent staff with volunteers during the tourist season; have a restaurant car serving meals on a comparatively leisurely journey up the hillside; and they even thought of a hotel at Dduallt, accessible only by rail. Broadbent and Low would themselves provide the full-time administration, as well as carrying out the rolling-stock maintenance. Hopefully, the pair took measurements and stock of what they thought they would need and began to search 'war-torn, ration-ridden England' for materials, especially wooden sleepers and sixty-pound-per-yard rail.

Something might have come of it. Looking back, Broadbent

himself thinks they very probably over-estimated the difficulties. But it was 1947. Everything was in short supply. It took them six months to disentangle red tape, before they could even get round to ordering anything. However, they went to London to see Evan Davies and found him a willing seller. But, in the end, as Bill Broadbent now says, 'time and the bureaucratic maze' defeated them. They both had their careers as railwaymen; although Broadbent joined an oil company in 1950, Low went on to become Managing Director of British Rail Engineering.

Another determined effort to revive the railway was made by a body of business and professional men known, very loosely, as the '1949 Group'. A leading member was J.I.C. Boyd, whose book *Narrow Gauge Rails to Portmadoc* was published in 1949 and did much to focus interest in the Festiniog. The group went as far as a public meeting at Portmadoc Town Hall on 20 April 1950, to explore and explain the situation. A committee was formed which had representatives from the quarries, from local government, and from the group – but not, oddly, from the Railway Company. It was made clear that the quarries did not intend to send any slate down the railway again. The local authorities were haunted by the spectre of the Welsh Highland. The best, indeed the only solution, as the group realised, would be to run passenger trains for tourists in the summer, and reopen the railway, stage by stage, as money became available.

The group had intended to lease the railway. The Company refused. They had information of the Portmadoc meeting only from press reports and hearsay, but evidently they did not consider the group as satisfactory lessees. The Company replied that part of the line was already leased (as it was, up at Blaenau) and they were not allowed to lease the rest of the line. They refused to send circulars to their shareholders or to take any action on behalf of the group.

The Company already had ideas of their own for the future of the railway. Rumours began to circulate in Portmadoc that the railway was about to be formally abandoned. Scrap merchants gathered in flocks again, some of them, it was said, offering five figure sums for the railway just as it stood. The rumours, for once, were true. At an extraordinary general meeting held on 9 November 1950, the Company decided to apply to the Ministry of Transport for an Abandonment Order, so that they could realize the Company's assets, such as they were.

Here, events took an ironic turn. The Ministry's reply, when it came, was something of a bombshell. They said they had no powers to grant an Abandonment Order for a railway, or any part of a railway, after it had once been opened for public traffic. The Festiniog Railway had been embodied in an Act of Parliament. Another Act of Parliament would be needed to disembody it.

The Company were thus caught in the grip of an impasse which would have made old Samuel Holland chuckle. The railway could not be bought or sold, and it could not be leased. Those who owned it did not want it, but could not get rid of it. Those who wanted it could not afford to buy it. It was not a commercial proposition, and never would be. Nobody would take on the task of running it, because it was worth more as scrap than as a railway. But it could not be sold for scrap.

However, in spite of this seemingly deadlocked situation, in spite of the Company's cool attitude and in spite of the obvious difficulties, the hope of reviving the railway would not die away. People still canvassed opinions, still exchanged letters and ideas, still called at Harbour station to see for themselves. All that latent enthusiasm needed just one spark to ignite it. It came, with a letter in the *Railway Gazette* of 27 July 1951. In its own modest way the letter was an historic document in the Festiniog's story. It was headed 'Proposed Festiniog Railway Preservation Scheme':

Sir,
The Festiniog Railway, one of the few existing un-nationalized railways which operated during the war, but unfortunately closed shortly after it, is, it is hoped, to have a new lease of life. An organized attempt is to be made to save it from being abandoned and its priceless historical relics lost to the scrap-iron dealer.

The Festiniog railway is possibly the world's first narrow-gauge public railway. Locomotives introduced by Charles Spooner still exist after 83 years of hard work. In 1873 Spooner introduced the first bogie carriage to Britain. This still exists at the railway's famous Boston Lodge Works and is now 78 years old.

The warrant of abandonment applied for by the railway company has been refused by the Ministry of Transport. A preliminary inspection of locomotives, and so on, is to take place, and it is hoped that a meeting will be arranged in the near future. I shall be pleased to hear from anybody interested in the scheme especially if they are in a position to help financially or professionally.

This seminal letter was signed by Leonard A. Heath Humphrys, who was then only seventeen years old. He was the 'extremely young man' already referred to in the Company's correspondence, who had asked to look round the railway on the day of the Portmadoc meeting. He was young and inexperienced, but he was exactly what the railway needed. Plenty of older and more experienced men had already looked at the railway and retired, appalled by the difficulties. What the railway needed at that moment was the blissfulness of ignorance.

Heath Humphrys had first become interested in the Festiniog in 1949 and thought of what he called 'a rehabilitation fund' early the following year. But when he suggested the idea to a 'well known railway magazine' in March 1950 it was, he says 'not greeted with enthusiasm'. He first contacted the Company in July that year, and in October visited the slate quarry railways of Penrhyn and Padarn, the Talyllyn Railway – and the Festiniog. At the end of the year he wrote to people he knew were interested in a Festiniog revival, and again to the Company. The replies he had were curiously at odds. While the Company offered every co-operation, everybody else said 'there is no hope of re-opening the Railway – the Company will not co-operate'.

The first published reference to Heath Humphrys's activities was in the Journal of the British Locomotive Society, in January 1951. It drew two replies. A short editorial comment appeared in the March *Trains Illustrated*, which brought twenty-two replies, and, by its inaccuracy, provoked a magisterial correction from J.I.C. Boyd. By this time Heath Humphrys realised that he needed the help of professional railwaymen and engineers, rather than of ordinary railways enthusiasts. His letters appeared in the *Railway Gazette*, *The Engineer* and *Engineering*. These produced forty-eight more replies.

Today, when industrial archaeology is a thriving academic discipline and railway preservation societies and groups are two a penny, appeals to restore a line or part of a line, or a single locomotive, or even a single carriage, are no longer newsworthy. But in the 1950s, Heath Humphrys's was a remarkably far-sighted and original initiative and it is curious that he thought of a Festiniog restoration before he had ever heard of the Talyllyn Preservation Society.

Disappointed by the Portmadoc meeting, and having decided that nothing was likely to come of it, Heath Humphrys called his own meeting, the now famous (in Festiniog mythology) 'Bristol Meeting', in the Club Rooms (actually an empty cellar) of the Bristol Railway Circle on 8th September 1951. Amongst the dozen or so people who attended were several who were to become well known in Festiniog affairs: J. L. H. Bate, A.G.W. Garraway, F. Gilbert, H. Holcroft, J.C.V. Mitchell and R. Winter. Also present was the Ministry's Inspecting Officer for Railways, Lieutenant Colonel E. Woodhouse.

The idea of restoring the Festiniog was discussed in general terms. Heath Humphrys rather damped the rest by talking of the five-figure sums he thought would be needed to bring the railway back to life. But others felt it could be done for much less. A committee was formed, called for some reason the 'Bath Committee', but nothing much else seems to have happened until a second meeting on 8 October, at the Old Bull Inn, at Barnet, in north London, when what Heath Humphrys called a 'legal committee' was formed.

Heath Humphrys now had to do his National Service. He turned over his duties as Secretary to his own nominee, a Mr Rear of Waenfawr, a shadowy figure in Festiniog history, who was to acquire a degree of notoriety for what he did not do: he did not answer enquiries, or correspondence, or indeed take any action or play any part in any further proceedings whatsoever.

As a result of Mr Rear's inactivity, the organisation set up at Bristol, in Gilbert's words, 'died completely'. Mr F. Gilbert himself, who was to be a very important figure in Festiniog history, became Secretary at another meeting called at the Stephenson Locomotive Society's premises in Kensington, London, on 20 April 1952. There was an attendance of about thirty, and a Chairman, a Vice Chairman and a committee were appointed. It was from this meeting, not the Bristol Meeting, that the body calling itself The (Proposed) Festiniog Railway Preservation Society first appeared and provided the real impetus to reopen the railway. Heath Humphrys had supplied the first spark, but it was Mr F. Gilbert and the others at the Stephenson Meeting who kept it alive in the disheartening times to come. (Nobody ever knew Mr Gilbert's christian name; as Pegler said, 'he was such an elder statesman, nothing other than "Mr Gilbert" ever seemed appropriate'.)

Different people have different recollections now of what happened. When anything becomes a success, it is a very human tendency to exaggerate one's own part in it when reminiscing about it all years later. The main thing was that the will to restore the Festiniog Railway had now been given some sort of corporate shape. There was now a core of people, a focus to which all inquiries could be directed. Many of them were also involved in the restoration of the Talyllyn Railway at

Towyn, which was the first of all the post-war railway restorations, under the leadership of L.T.C. Rolt (and fascinatingly written up by him in *Railway Adventure*). But to many, it was the Festiniog that gradually began to seem the more attractive.

The Festiniog Railway has always attracted a very wide range of personalities and professions. The men who were to play major roles were already assembling; a survey showed that, of the first 500 members of the Society, half were still members in 1970. Those who formed that first embryo society, or who arrived very shortly afterwards, when it became the Society Limited, were from all walks of life: Gilbert, who was to play a main part in the sometimes very delicate negotiations with the Railway Company, was a builder at Potters Bar, who later became a newsagent in Basingstoke. W.K. Nelson, the Treasurer, was a local government officer with accountancy and finance experience. L. Taylor Harris was a solicitor (actually Gilbert's) from Essex. Tom King was Deputy Engineer and Surveyor to the Borough Council of Finchley in north London (the 'London connection' was very strong in the Festiniog's early days). Vic Mitchell was a dental surgeon, Allan Garraway and his father Ron were both professional railwaymen with British Rail. Trevor Bailey's firm dealt in medical supplies.

The early Society also had connections with men who had technical resources in engineering and construction companies in a wide swathe of the country, from Birmingham and Coventry across to Leicester and Nottingham, down to Northampton and up to Manchester. Bob Smallman worked in his father's firm in West Bromwich, supplying builders' requirements. Ian Smart ran the transport side of his family's textile business. Norman Pearce was a director of a Northampton firm of leather manufacturers, and was an expert on telephones and communications. Bob Hunter was assistant in charge at the Railway Museum, York. John White worked for the Westminster Bank and was Honorary Secretary of their Railway Society. Norman Gurley was a 'buying progress chaser' with Scammell Lorries Limited.

But whoever these new men were and whatever their skills, at first they could do little more than carry on trying to interest people in the idea of restoring the railway. The old Company were for a time extremely suspicious. They would not allow the words 'Festiniog Railway' to be used in any title other than their own. However, the Company gradually began to warm to the new Society (Mr F. Gilbert worked up a particularly close relationship with Evan Davies, the Secretary) and eventually even looked favourably on their never-ceasing efforts to obtain control of the shares of the Company.

In financing the Welsh Highland Railway the Company had had a loan from the National Provincial Bank and as security the bank held a large number of debenture shares. Interest of about £600 was due on this loan and on a bank overdraft. With the Manager's salary, expenditure was about £1,100 a year. The Company received an income for rents on property, the lease of the line between the quarries and Duffws Station, and the hire of about 250 slate wagons, of just under £1,000 a year. After much discussion the Aluminium Company of Dolgarrog, which owned the bulk of the shares, agreed to transfer its holding for nothing if others agreed to do the same. The bank was (eventually) prepared to sell its debentures for £2,000. To wipe off all debts and overdrafts the further sum of about £1,000 was needed. So, to get complete control of the railway, the Society needed about £3,000 in cash. It seems dirt cheap now, but it was a sum beyond their members at the time.

The Society Committee thought they would also need another £2,500 to start some form of service going. They felt they could probably raise this by appealing to the public. But they wanted to own the railway first before they appealed for money to rehabilitate it. To buy the railway, they needed a patron. The situation was more than usually difficult because the Society did not have an orthodox commercial proposition to offer. The Company were still in a highly sensitive state. They had been fooled too often, had shown too many idlers and charlatans round, there had been too much empty talk, too many rumours, too many hopes had been raised and dashed. This time the idea had to be good and it had to be solid. The trouble was that what the Society needed was a benefactor who would buy the railway and then run it for its own sake, as a hobby, or a charity, or as a rich man's toy, but *not* as a business proposition expecting a satisfactory return on his capital investment. What the Society needed was, in fact, a Fairy Godmother.

Alan Pegler may not have looked much like a Fairy Godmother, but he worked the charm for the Festiniog Railway. He was one of several men who were attracted to the Festiniog through links of circumstances: a shared interest in railways, family ties, attendance at the same school or university, shared service in the armed forces, colleagues in the same office, chance meetings and conversations in trains – all played their parts at various times in bringing together the right personalities, of whom Alan Pegler was to be the most important.

Alan Pegler was a part-time member of the board of British Railways, Eastern Region, and by the middle-management, middle-income standards of most Society members he was a comparatively rich man. He first heard of the Festiniog's sad state from Lord Northesk, then involved with the restoration of the Talyllyn Railway, in 1950, on one of the special trains Pegler and two friends, Trevor Bailey and Les Smith, used to organise to celebrate centenaries or anniversaries in railway history.

Alan Pegler and Trevor Bailey had been undergraduates together. When Bailey joined the forces in 1940 he found himself occupying the next bunk in barracks to Les Smith, who after the war was a Planning Officer with Finchley Town Council – whose Deputy Engineer and Surveyor was Tom King. Mr F. Gilbert had co-opted Tom King to be Civil Engineering Adviser to the Society. Tom King it was who mentioned the Festiniog to Les Smith, who in his turn interested Alan Pegler and Trevor Bailey.

The crucial 'special', jointly organised by Pegler, Bailey and Smith, was in 1952 – the *Centenaries Express*, to celebrate the centenary of the opening of the Town Line of the Great Northern Railway – the modern east-coast route from Peterborough to Doncaster. In Alan Pegler's words, 'At the end of a highly successful day out on the east-coast main line and much time spent either on the footplate or in propping up the bar of the buffet car, Trevor, Les and I were quite convinced we had a mission in life, namely, to do something about the Festiniog.'

Pegler and his friends attended a meeting (another of those famous meetings which still reverberate in Festiniog history) with King and members of the embryo Society at the Great Northern Hotel, King's Cross. In January 1953, Pegler, Smith and Bailey visited the railway. They spent 'a rather dreary morning' at Boston Lodge, 'to the accompaniment of heavy drops of rain through the roof and the doleful prognostications of dear old Robert Evans'. They then went up to Blaenau, walked to Tan-y-Grisiau where they hired a trolley from a farmer for 2s. 6d., and bowled down by gravity to the Moelwyn Tunnel. They had shot some way inside before they were able to discover how to stop the trolley. Water was pouring down their necks and lay several inches deep on the tunnel floor. But, somehow, the Festiniog had worked its magic, because 'despite getting very wet and having had a full morning of prophecies of doom, we were all tremendously excited by what we had seen and when, next day, the Welsh weather did one of its incredible rapid changes and turned on positively spring-like sunshine we were well and truly hooked.'

In June 1953 Trevor Bailey and Mr F. Gilbert went to Llandudno to try to find another solution: an interview with the liquidator of the Welsh Highland Railway, which still held powers to *lease* the Festiniog. But nothing came of this either. Meanwhile, fresh personalities were gathering on the scene. Trevor Bailey's brother-in-law, having married his sister, was John Routly, a solicitor. Routly had served in the RAFVR, was a director of Rootes, a county councillor and later Vice Chairman of Buckinghamshire County Council and High Sheriff of Buckinghamshire. He had the legal knowledge and the negotiating skills to be able to deal with Ministry and local government civil servants on their own ground and in their own language. He was especially interested in the fact that the Festiniog Railway Company was a rare surviving Parliamentary Company. He and a Rootes colleague, E.D. Nicholson, set out on an enjoyable eighteen months unravelling of the complicated legal knots. Routly and Nicholson called on the National Provincial Bank, who still held a £12,000 Debenture, and obtained the release of the Debenture for £2,000. (On the way back in the taxi from this meeting, Routly and Nicholson calculated that they 'had knocked the Bank down at the rate of £50 per minute, by showing them photographs of their ruined assets'.)

It was probably at this point that some members of the embryonic Society began to grow suspicious. They had assumed that the Society would own most of the shares and ultimately would have control. But here were Pegler and his friends apparently muscling in and taking the (perfectly reasonable) view that those who were going to pay the piper should also call the tune.

To Alan Pegler's 'great astonishment', his father said he would let him have the necessary amount as an interest-free loan. Pegler Senior 'had bad hang-ups about Wales and the Welsh which stemmed from his not getting on with one of his brothers-in-law who was a Welshman: he made it absolutely clear that he had no intention of having anything to do with the railway once I got control. He was as good as his word and never did!'

With Routly having the legal side well under way and with the promise of the necessary finance from Pegler Senior, Alan Pegler's representatives, Trevor Bailey and Les Smith, met

Tom King, Bill Broadbent and Mr F. Gilbert one raw wintry day in January 1954 at Finchley Baths. Tom King was told that Alan Pegler agreed to negotiate for the control of the moribund Festiniog Railway on condition that he, Pegler, appointed the directors of the new Board of the Company; that the Society could see their way to raising a minimum of £2,500; and that the Company and the Society work together. Bailey and Smith said that they quite understood that this was not what the Society's Committee intended, so they would quite understand if these proposals were not acceptable.

'Not what the Society's Committee intended' was the understatement of the railway's long history. Tom King reported to a stunned Committee. However, some members of the Committee thought they still had some cards to play. Many of the shares had been provisionally offered to the Society, not to any individual.

But Pegler's terms were clear and unequivocal: no agreement, no money. The Committee discussed and argued long and earnestly. They had no money, and no chance of getting any. If there was no money, there might be no railway for anybody. Reluctantly, the whole Committee agreed to accept Pegler's terms. But there were some very disappointed men amongst them, and very disappointed men do not make the best of collaborators.

There were more negotiations. There was a meeting in Birmingham to discuss the position and to take advice from the Talyllyn Railway (which has always been as firmly orientated to the Midlands as the Festiniog has to London). Finally, at a ceremony at the Hyde Park Hotel, London, in May 1954, Mr Pegler Senior handed over a cheque for £2,000.

Armed with this money, on 24 June John Routly and Bill Bellamy attended a meeting of the old Board, who resigned in favour of Alan Pegler as Chairman, John Routly as Deputy Chairman, with Trevor Bailey and Les Smith as Directors, and Bill Broadbent as a Director nominated by the Society (the Act creating the Company prescribed that there should be no more than five directors.) Bill Bellamy was Secretary and E.D. Nicholson Registrar.

There were four types of stock and shares in the Company: four per cent Debenture Stock, four and a half and five per cent Preference Shares, and Ordinary Stock, with one vote for each Share and for every twenty-five of Ordinary Stock. There had been upwards of 200 stock and share holders, but many of them were dead or untraceable. Alan Pegler held a majority holding

103

in both Preference Shares and the Ordinary Stock. All Alan Pegler's Ordinary Stock were vested in a trust, with trustees John Routly and Trevor Bailey, shortly joined by Colonel Rudgard and Ron Garraway, representing both Company and Society. The object of the Trust was the same as that of the Society Limited; the Railway could not pass into 'undesirable hands' and if the Company ever again paid dividends on its shares, a majority of the money would be ploughed back into the railway. Alan Pegler would not be able to sell the shares and gain from their enhanced value, because the shares were held by the Trust. (In fact, as Pegler says, the shares passed into the Trust at once and he never actually owned the railway.)

In October 1954 the Society was given formal permission by the Company to use the name Festiniog Railway in its title. The Society had been mounting a recruiting campaign all that summer. Bill Broadbent had three cardboard files containing twenty-six folders, boldly and optimistically marked in alphabetical order, with some 350 names and addresses. The Society had assured Alan Pegler they would have 2,000 members within a couple of years. And so they did.

Bill Broadbent represented the Society on the Company Board. The Society itself underwent a legal change that year, attaining legal status by becoming the Society *Limited*, being first registered (No. 542449) on 24 December 1954, with a capital of £49. 12s. 6d., subscribed by L. Taylor Harris, (14. 12s. 6d), with Broadbent, A.G.W. Garraway, Gilbert, Heath Humphrys, King, Nelson and Winter all stumping up £5 each. These eight became founder Directors. But as soon as legal status had been established, Taylor Harris relinquished his directorship, remaining as legal adviser but taking no further part. Ron Garraway took the vacancy. The Society's first Board meeting was held on 10 February 1955, its first General meeting, at Porthmadog, on 8 October 1955. The Chairman was Lieutenant Colonel R.H. Rudgard, with Trevor Bailey (representing the Company), and Norman Pearce also becoming directors. The Society has always had twelve directors.

The Society Limited undertook to acquire subscriptions and donations, and turn these over to the Company, who would use them to resuscitate the railway. It was a peculiar situation, in that those who raised the money did not actually administer it, because they did not own the railway for which they were raising money.

Thus from the first days there were these two distinct bodies, the Company and the Society, both concerned with the

104

running of the railway. On the one hand, there was Alan Pegler and his associates in the Company; on the other hand there were the Garraways, Gilbert, and all the others in the Society. For years this division resulted in a state of what might tactfully be called creative tension. For years the Society fought to gain more control over the running of the railway. Some prominent members of the Society resigned over the years when they discovered that control still lay inexorably in Company hands. Annual General Meetings were times of mutual suspicion, when both sides prowled around each other like strange dogs in another's backyard. Both sides have somewhat mellowed over the years, but the fires smoulder on and occasionally burst out, showing that they are only banked, not extinguished.

The Society has never had any control over the Company. Quite to the contrary: the Society often proposes but the Company still firmly disposes. One Society member said 'as Winston Churchill once said of Soviet Russia, the Festiniog Railway Company are an enigma wrapped up in a puzzle hidden in a riddle'. The Company now give a great deal of prior information about their intentions, through the magazine, through Group Information Memoranda (known always as GIMs), and by word of mouth on Directors' visits to the line. The Society has a nominee Director on the Company board. Otherwise, the Company claim the need for a degree of secrecy, and there is some force in their argument. 'If you are just about to approach somebody for x thousand pounds, with precious little hope of any return on his money,' they say, 'it does not help matters much if he reads all about his own generosity first in the Railway's publicity material.'

However, some would say that the Festiniog's organization was admirable, in that it removed control from the wilder and woollier elements of the romantics and preservationists. There was, in Gerry Fiennes's phrase, a singularly low 'twit-ratio' in the Company and the Society which meant that the Railway had an usually sound commercial expertise in its management. The Earl of Lindsay, formerly Lord Garnock, has been its Commercial Director since 1962.

Thus, at the end of 1954, there was a Railway Company and a Railway Society, both legally constituted. They had bought with Pegler's money just under fourteen miles of finely-engineered railway, now in a state varying from fair to shocking. Many of the double-headed rails were rusted or worn away. Sleepers had rotted. Keys were missing. Drains were blocked. Cuttings were overgrown. Above Tan-y-Bwlch the line was clear and was being used by residents with 'private wagons'.

By 1946, of the locomotives, *Welsh Pony* had been pensioned off (in 1936); *Palmerston* had been relegated to a stationary boiler providing steam for a hammer; *Princess* needed re-tubing – the tubes were in the works; the chassis of *Prince* was partially refitted and re-erected, in the erecting shop, and there was a new boiler; one Fairlie, *Taliesin*, was partly stripped, being re-tubed and overhauled; *Merddin Emrys* also required re-tubing and general overhaul. The carriages were mostly under cover and in fairly good condition. There were also several hundred wagons of various kinds. The last of the Welsh Highland engines, *Moel Tryfan*, also required major repairs which involved almost a complete rebuilding.

Boston Lodge was an excellent but decayed example of a nineteenth-century engineering works. Doors, windows and roofs were in a poor state, but there was an iron foundry and a brass foundry, a smithy and an old carpenters' shop. There was even a large paddle-wheel for removing sawdust. There were some cottages, a boiler-house and engine-house, and some carriage sheds. In the machine shop there was a Bolinders single-cylinder marine engine. The railway also owned property up and down the line – stations and sheds, cottages and warehouses (but not, oddly enough, Harbour station which was leased, until the freehold was bought for £15,000 in 1978).

Chapter 12

Having bought a railway, the first thing to do was to run something on it. Allan Garraway, already a prominent figure amongst the Society volunteers and a frequent visitor to the line, walked the whole line on 7 August 1954. There had been rumours that the Ministry of Transport were not keen to allow trains to run, especially because of the tightness of the clearance in Moelwyn Tunnel.

A local contractor was engaged at a cost of £165, paid by the Company, to clear at least a walking path through the jungliest stretches from Tan-y-Bwlch down to Penrhyn. The Ministry's Inspector Colonel McMullen visited the line on 18 August. August is traditionally a wet month in Snowdonia and that day was one of the wettest. The inspecting party travelled by trolley down from Blaenau to Tan-y-Bwlch where they ate a packed lunch. They had to abandon the trolley at Whistling Curve and walk the length to Minffordd. From there they made detours through the fields to Boston Lodge, because of obstructions on the line. The inspection was a wet and thoroughly exhausting business, but the party went to the Oakeley Arms to dry out and have dinner, while the Colonel reported his conclusions.

The Colonel's report was both good and bad news. It had, he said, been a first class railway. Although the responsibility for the restoration was the Company's, not the Ministry's, the Ministry would do all they could to help if they decided to go ahead. But the Colonel said he was appalled by the railway's condition. He wondered if those present had any idea of what was involved. He himself thought they would have to spend some £40,000. He warned that they should not cut any corners over safety precautions. It was a gigantic task, but he wished them all luck.

Many people thought as Colonel McMullen did. They applied to the Festiniog the standards of British Rail. Actually, although it certainly was a gigantic task, nothing like as much as the Colonel's forecast was needed to get the Festiniog working again.

There had been some sporadic publicity in various railway newspapers and periodicals and a small but reassuring number of volunteers had been offering their services. They had not yet been organised in any way, but on Garraway's advice the Company began to write to volunteers through Robert Evans at Harbour station. By the end of September volunteer work was well under way. The first ever was a party of boys from St Paul's School who were especially energetic, and the line was cleared, partly at least, to a point well past Minffordd cemetery.

None of the engines was capable of steaming and some of them never would be, but Garraway remembered that Morris Jones had said that the Simplex tractor (a relic of Colonel Stephen's regime) had been running when the railway closed down. Morris Jones, the last employee at Boston Lodge, had been working three days a week at the Talyllyn Railway but now returned to the Festiniog on condition that the Festiniog would help out on any mechanical emergency on the Talyllyn.

One day in late September Garraway and Bill Harvey checked and repaired the Simplex, rewiring plug leads, repairing the water-pump drive, cleaning plugs, carburettor and petrol line.

When Garraway swung the handle, the Simplex fired and ran quite easily. They cleared sand away from the yard rails, poled away two carriages fouling the track, and on the afternoon of Tuesday 21 September 1954 rolling-stock once again moved on the Festiniog. The Simplex set off across the Cob. Understandably, it was a moment to remember. 'I shall never forget the feeling of elation on that run', Garraway wrote later.

> The tractor is virtually unsprung yet it simply glided across (the Cob) with only one or two slight bumps. After getting more pairs of points to work at Portmadoc we proceeded along beside the main road. Here we had our first derailment, the tarmac being too hard for the flanges, but we soon got the tractor rerailed, hacked a flangeway and proceeded as far as the town side of the bridge, where a length of rail was missing. From there it was not far to carry petrol from a garage.

The most pressing need was to bring some money in somehow, from somewhere. The next day Garraway signed a contract with some scrap dealers at Portmadoc. Amongst the remains scrapped was the old Welsh Highland engine *Moel Tryfan*, which was taken across to Portmadoc to be cut up. The loss of this engine caused a deal of heartburning, then and since. In Garraway's opinion, in his memories of the time, *Moel Tryfan* was 'so completely stripped and so much was either missing or rusted away that it would have been a considerable job even to restore it sufficiently to be worth keeping as a museum piece. As for working again, it would have meant a very considerable expense, in fact, nearly a new engine.'

Two days after the first venture, the first passenger journey took place under the new management. This, too, was an historic occasion. It was a train of two bogie coaches, No. 2 (now renumbered No. 10) and No. 17 – even their numbers have been recorded with care – hauled by the Simplex. The passengers were Herbert Thomas, a local Portmadoc reporter and a good friend of the railway for many years both before and after the war, Mrs Thomas, Robert Evans and a handful of volunteers. Garraway drove. The train ran across the Cob to Portmadoc and back again to Boston Lodge. It was from Boston Lodge that the first trains ran, and from there that the first important steps to restore the railway were taken.

One of the earliest 'clearing' trips, in October 1954, is described by Trevor Bailey:

> The undergrowth and brambles completely covered the line from outside Boston Lodge works to Minffordd and after taking stock of some wagons for disposal for scrap we collected the Simplex and set about the destruction of the undergrowth by charging into it until the loco was about to stall, backing up, and then removing the uprooted gorse and brambles by hand – an unpleasant task, but a rewarding one. By nightfall we had reached the upper end of Boston Lodge Halt area, where there was a nasty bank slip over which the track was suspended for about half its width. We had an early night (we'd set off that day at 3.30 a.m.) and returned to our labours at 6.00 a.m. By breakfast time we had jacked up the track, shored it with sleepers and taken the Simplex across the gap – known for some time afterwards as *Bailey's Gap.*

On 6 November there was another small personal milestone. A special train was run from Portmadoc to Minffordd and back, drawn by the Simplex, to mark Robert Evans's sixty years of

109

service with the Company. He had started as a booking-office clerk in 1894. The Directors of the Company, Society members and friends were present. There was tea at the Queen's Hotel, Portmadoc, and Robert Evans was presented with a clock. It was a nostalgic occasion. Robert Evans was one of the few living links with the railway's past.

What were Robert Evans's thoughts that day, as he looked around him at all those new unfamiliar faces, all saying that *they* were going to run the Festiniog? Ten years later the Society's magazine wrote of Evans:

> We remember him, later, as a solitary figure, sad in carpet slippers amid the sparrows and green ruination of the Harbour Station, murmuring unhappily: 'I am afraid . . . it has gone too far . . . the track . . . trains cannot now be run.' To speak plainly, this was not the sort of stuff we wanted to hear, and after a short interval this humble old man who had given his life to our line was eased off the stage – gently and honourably, to be sure, but off the stage.
>
> Mr Evans's big trouble was, of course, that he knew too much; he had seen the Festiniog run properly. Railway preservation is rather like marriage in that the bitter knowledge of sordid truths essential to make it work is inimical to the zest and optimism with which it must be entered into. In those two wobbly lines of wet rust across the Cob, Robert Evans saw the raddled husk of a 60–year liaison; we saw them twinkle with the beckoning promise of a new life, and, starry-eyed, blundered into the unknown.

Alan Pegler himself had vivid memories of that particular trip. 'I must say, I well remember that train! Goodness knows how the two passenger coaches had been got up to Minffordd, but going down there were branches of trees bashing against the windows and one or two actually broke. This was all the more embarrassing as I had invited our first guests, Sir Osmond and Lady Williams and their two small daughters, to join me as passengers; the little girls took a very dim view of the breaking glass and screamed their heads off!'

The first officially advertised working party of volunteers arrived in December and the line was cleared as far as milepost five and a half (about to Cutting Gwlyb). Morris Jones and his apprentice Arwyn Morgan started full-time work at Boston Lodge and soon had the Crossley diesel generator running so that machinery could be used. They also started to rebuild *Prince*. In January more volunteers were at work, and again, the mass media were present. On 8 and 9 January BBC television cameras recorded the spectacle of gangs of volunteers clearing trees and undergrowth, and dragging stumps out of the line beyond Minffordd. The workers afterwards looked for themselves on the national TV news, confident they would be the 'lead' story. Hence most of them missed their own appearances, earlier in the evening, on children's television.

By the end of that year of 1954 the restoration had begun to gain momentum. In November the first public appeal had been made for subscriptions to the new Society. It brought in about £300. A little more dribbled in for some time afterwards. It also brought in the names of more volunteers ready to help in various ways.

Personalities amongst the volunteers were beginning to emerge and to make their individual marks. Ian Smart, for example, who was a Director of the Society, had a family firm, Arthur Smart and Sons Limited. His first introduction to the Festiniog was in 1945, 'when he broke into the works in the approved fashion'. That January of 1955, he took away on his lorry an ex-Welsh Highland plate-layers' trolley which had been on a siding outside the erecting shop. It had a reversible two-stroke engine. It came back as a horizontally-opposed four-stroke. It had two speeds, 'Fast' and 'Very Fast', and was a most useful if somewhat erratic locomotive, known as *Busta* (nicknamed by a friend of Garraway's, Bill Hoole, a King's Cross engine-driver). On 22 January, despite some clutch trouble, *Busta* took a plate-layers' trolley of people up as far as the Long Tunnel.

It was the first 'train' of any kind under the restoration to get as far as the Long Tunnel and it began a year of 'firsts'. On 5 February the first mains electricity was installed at Boston Lodge, through the efforts of Mr Salmon from South Wales. On the 10th, there was the first official Society Board meeting and on 5 March the first engine and coach ran into Blaenau Ffestiniog.

Runs had already been made as far as Glan-y-Pwll with the Simplex running light, and, on 5 February, with the Simplex and No. 1 van to Tan-y-Grisiau (Allan Garraway driving, with Les Smith and his brother 'Jinks') to meet British Electricity Authority officials; that was an important meeting, when it had been decided that for the sake of creating an impression the Festiniog Railway men would arrive by train.

The intention was to recover wagons from Blaenau. The track was still in very poor condition. Trees banged against carriage windows, often breaking the glass. The train that day in March 1955 was once again the Simplex with No. 17 and No.

1 van. The driver was Allan Garraway. Another of those early trips to Blaenau was made by Keith Catchpole, a London schoolmaster and a qualified engine-driver. Because of the state of the track it took Catchpole until three in the afternoon to reach the Moelwyn Tunnel. The tunnel was in a highly dangerous state, with rockfalls inside, and water cascading down through the ventilation shafts. At one point Catchpole and Ian Smart, who was with him, had to leave the Simplex and clear the blocked track by hand. At the time, Catchpole reflected that he was 'probably the only engine-driver in the world who has ever gone into a tunnel with his right hand on the throttle and his left on the Ordnance Survey map to find out where the tunnel comes out the other end'.

Their wives had a picnic at Tan-y-Grisiau, while Keith Catchpole, Ian Smart and two boys pushed on into Blaenau. Catchpole's story was recorded by Jack Owen, for many years the railway's Electrical Manager, on one of several tapes he made of Festiniog Railway reminiscences. It is an odd sensation, to hear from the great wooden Voigt-horn speaker in the corner of Jack Owen's living room, these voices from the Railway's past:

> As the line gets into the outskirts of Blaenau we had to use spades to dig off the refuse which the inhabitants had been showering onto the track, I suppose, for many years. The noises of the Simplex, of course, heralded our approach. People started looking out behind curtains, and behind doors, and from behind windows. Not very friendly-looking people. We finally arrived at Glan-y-Pwll crossing where we produced a bunch of keys and proceeded to unlock the level-crossing gates. This, of course, caused some consternation because the County Council had tarred over the rails and, again, drivers hadn't been stopped there for many, many years and so when they came round the corner and found the gates shut, a traffic block soon began to accumulate. We, meanwhile, with picks and shovels, were digging out the tarmac on the road. Finally, we managed to go over the crossing and shut the gates, which were very badly broken.

At Duffws, these intrepid strangers set about the job of collecting thirty or forty slate wagons.

> Quite a crowd gathered by this time, locals, miners, children, but they were rather a peculiar crowd because they were completely silent. I thought at the time one could almost feel the hostility in the air, which later turned out to be right. But they watched us struggle, there were four of us, we had to force over the blades of catch-points which hadn't

112

worked for years and by the time it was getting dusk we
had only succeeded in freeing five slate wagons. Meanwhile
the crowd had continued to grow and I suppose that there
were two or three hundred people standing at the side just
watching us. We finally got them coupled up and we were
rather glad to get away. We felt rather like the tale of the old
mariner who had killed the albatross. You could almost cut
the atmosphere with a knife. We coupled up, we let the
clutch in and we bounced back under the bridge.

The Company intended to run a passenger service of some kind
that summer of 1955. Work was very slow, and by the time the
services started what Garraway later called 'only the absolute
minimum' had been done. Nevertheless it was a great deal. A
landslide near Boston Lodge had been filled in, and the track
above replaced. The curve near Boston Lodge had been
repaired. Work had begun to improve the track on the Cob,
which was in about the worst condition of the whole line,
through the actions of salt air, sea and wind, and constant
vandalism by pedestrians.

The railway had a stroke of luck when Will Jones, the
former permanent-way ganger, returned to work on the line.
The new Festiniog had the benefit of his long experience, wit
and tall stories of the old Festiniog. When trains eventually
began to run to Tan-y-Bwlch once more, Will's wife Bessie met
them in her Welsh national costume. It was a spontaneous
gesture, but a brilliant publicity stroke which no professional
PRO could have bettered.

The site of Boston Lodge Halt was cleared, sign-posts for it
and for Portmadoc painted and put up. The yard at Minffordd
was, literally, dug out and scores of lost slate wagons recovered
from under the general debris and undergrowth. Fencing along
the line was restored to its best state for nearly twenty years. In
charge of 'anything to do with wood' was Fred Boughey,
another schoolmaster (from Birkenhead), and another stalwart
volunteer of the early days who has survived into the modern
era. Fred Boughey became head of the Festiniog 'carriage trade',
responsible for rebuilding and restoring passenger coaches.
The first carriage back into regular service was an ex-Welsh
Highland third-class, No. 23, followed by No. 12. Fred Boughey
and his volunteer working party turned them out with a
marvellously bright livery of green, with ivory upper panels,
red ends and grey seats.

Allan Garraway had by now long since abandoned the
Talyllyn in favour of what he called the 'proper railway'. In

113

June 1955 the Company appointed him Manager and Engineer, the first full-time railway employee of the restoration. Robert Evans retired but unfortunately his wife died the very next day, which, as Allan Garraway said, 'made the turnover period a little more difficult', but Garraway was soon firmly in the 'hot seat' he occupied until Dick Wollan's appointment as Chief Executive in April 1979.

Garraway's appointment, in several ways, gathered together a number of traditional Festiniog threads. Like Charles Spooner, he was a railwayman and the son of a railwayman. Like Holland, he was an engineer, and like Colonel Stephens he was a military man, with a military cast of mind and turn of phrase. His father Ron Garraway was District Motive Power Superintendent at Lincoln from 1941 until his retirement in 1955 and his move to the south of England, when Allan persuaded him onto the Society Board to add some practical railway experience. He had been a very early Society member and for some time was Financial and Membership Secretary; at his death he was a Vice-President of the Society.

Allan Garraway was born in Cambridge, went to the Leys School and to Cambridge University. Like Spooner, he also had a model railway in his garden. When he joined the Army he was still involved with railways, first at the Longmoor Military Railway and then in Germany, where he was Locomotive Superintendent of the Detmold Military Railway. He joined British Railways when it was not usual for graduates to do so: 'the University Appointments Board laughed at anyone who wanted to go to BR'. But he eventually joined as a Grade 3 fitter earning 99s. 6d. a week. He travelled around – as people do when working for railways – to Doncaster, Leeds and York, then Stratford-atte-Bowe, King's Cross and Liverpool Street. He was assistant to the Motive Power Superintendent at Liverpool Street when he was offered the job as General Manager on the Festiniog. It was a professional risk, to leave a secure appointment and join a railway which might be anything, or nothing.

With his moustache and his oilskins, what the Society magazine calls his 'Cod War gear', he was, as they say, the 'very distillation of all those once bowler-hatted men who have laid down the law in brown offices with engines hissing outside'. He was not just a manager. He drove an engine in the regular daily timetable: *Linda*, one of the two Hunslet 'ladies' bought from Penrhyn Quarry in 1962.

In October 1965 Allan married Moyra MacMillan, a local Portmadoc girl of Scots descent, at St Mary's, Tremadoc. A

114

special train hauled by white-ribboned *Prince* took the couple to Minffordd on the first stage of their honeymoon in Scotland. Amongst the wedding telegrams was one saying, 'Come back, all is forgiven, Linda.' For some years the Garraways lived 'above the shop' in the flat at Harbour station, where the books, the ornaments, the small model trains chugging eternally across the mantelpiece – all suggested that the owner might in some way be connected with railways.

Like Stephens before him, Garraway admits he was not an easy man to work for, and he had Stephens' vocabulary. One of the subjects which made him react violently was 'the railway enthusiast'. He did not trouble to conceal his contempt for him. 'This railway,' he used to say firmly, 'is run by enthusiastic railwaymen. *Not* by railway enthusiasts. The enthusiastic railwayman is keen on railways for their own sake. The railway enthusiast is a bit of a crank, a fanatic, intensely interested but he won't do a damned thing for a railway. He'll travel miles to track down the last steam engine of a certain class. But he will travel himself by car or coach.'

Enthusiasts of the worst type Garraway called 'gricers'. What is a 'gricer'? 'He wears a beret on top of his head, a blue gaberdine mac, long greasy hair, pimples, glasses, and he has cameras strung all about him.' So strong were Garraway's views on the 'gricers' that the very phrase 'railway enthusiast' acquired pejorative overtones at Portmadoc and nobody dared use it.

About the 'preservationists', too, Garraway had unconcealed views. 'I'm here to run a major tourist attraction, not to preserve a railway. This leads to all sorts of trouble with people who want to keep things as they are. Oil-firing, for example. We turned over from coal to oil because it was cheaper, easier and cleaner. And that's that. But there are those who get very incensed about it.'

The Company hoped to start the passenger service in July 1955. Colonel McMullen made another inspection. He authorized a maximum speed of eight mph and advised the track be slewed round the pillbox on Pen Cob (however, it was demolished – all but a stubborn bit of the roof which was still there for some years afterwards). Morris Jones and Arwyn Morgan laboured overtime, assisted by volunteers working, as they said, 'all the hours God gave', to get *Prince* on the road again. They failed, just, and the Simplex had to take over. It had been very expensive to run on petrol and had been converted to TVO.

For a week before the opening day Les Smith worked in Harbour station, clearing, cleaning and painting the booking

115

office. Brother Jinks read about the intended opening, on the day, in the *Daily Telegraph,* and drove from Surrey in time to act as booking-clerk, using the record book last used before the war.

On the great day, 23 July, one of the volunteers there was Mike Seymour, yet another schoolmaster, and for years now the Festiniog's archivist. 'We started with track work,' he wrote in his diary that day,

> but for the operation of passenger trains I was promoted to shunter and guard; permanent way working clothes had to suffice as uniform. The first train was at 2.30 p.m. and posters were already up to announce the fact. The station was invaded by all sorts of Very Important Company Officials, and the first issue of tickets was made, to be impounded for posterity before public booking began. From issuing tickets I then proceeded to join Driver Allan Garraway on the Simplex, and we made the historic first passenger journey all the way to Boston Lodge Halt. Before the return journey the carriage doors were locked and the train was backed cautiously down to the works turnout, where the Simplex was uncoupled and did a chain shunt round the carriages, which were then propelled back to Boston Lodge Halt for the return journey to Portmadoc.

The Official Opening Day was Friday 29 July 1955, when the Welsh Tourist Queen, Miss Janet Jones, travelled on the Festiniog from Boston Lodge to Portmadoc. The service then was two morning and four afternoon trains a day, hauled by the Simplex. Michael Seymour records that there were 281 bookings on 23 July, 309 on 29 July, and the railway took £10. 11s. 10d. in fares both days. *Prince* was in steam and on display outside the works, but not yet fit to haul a train.

On the evening of 2 August, nine years to the very day since *Princess* had last run on Festiniog rails, *Prince* steamed across the Cob. After trials to test its behaviour on the track, *Prince* went into regular service on Friday 5, and worked every passenger train from then on until September 1956, when *Taliesin* appeared. There was no passing loop at Boston Lodge and, as Michael Seymour records, the engine had to run round with a chain shunt, a tricky operation in which an engine on one line uses a chain stretched across so that it can draw carriages along the next-door rails.

That first primitive service ran until 24 September, when over 10,000 passengers had travelled on the line (or, over 20,000 passenger journeys, as the Festiniog, like all railways, always prefers to record them).

116

Chapter 13

Nobody who knew Alan Pegler could be in any doubt about his bona fides towards the railway. He and his Board of Directors intended to restore the line up to Blaenau Ffestiniog as soon as possible. That was, is, and always has been Company policy. But in those early days, suspicions grew overnight and the advent of the pumped storage scheme, by which the top end of the line was to be flooded, and all the argument and debate about compensation, made it easy for people to spread the slander that Alan Pegler had only bought the railway to feather his own nest. Such suspicions were encouraged, though with the best of motives, by personalities such as Bill Bellamy, who coined the phrase 'Festiniog Lente', and who was so tight-lipped about the Company's financial affairs as to make a Trappist monk seem garrulous by comparison. Eventually, the Society called upon Mr Pegler to declare that he had 'no intention, nor is there any prospect of his "lining his own pocket" as a result of the operations of the Railway Company'.

After the original Trust had been formed, the next step was to draw up a formal agreement between the Company and the Society. This was signed by both in 1956. The 1956 Agreement, as it was known, could be ended by the Society at any time, under the signature of its then Secretary, or by the Company if in the opinion of the Company the Society failed to perform any of its obligations. The Society, the Company, the Trustees, and Alan Pegler were all stipulated in the Agreement's clauses. The Society undertook to enlist as much volunteer help as possible, to work on the resuscitation and running of the railway, under the instruction of the Company's staff. The Company, for its part, agreed that the Society might use the name Festiniog Railway in its title so long as the Agreement was in force; undertook to devote such funds as it received from the Society

117

for the purpose of the railway; and agreed to give privileged travel on the railway to Society members, on such terms as the Company decided from time to time.

Under the Agreement the Trustees had power 'at their absolute discretion' to convey shares for any future Directors of the Company on whatever terms they thought fit, and if necessary, for nothing. (One would have expected this clause to have been in the original Trust deed.) Alan Pegler, for his part, undertook to give the Society the first opportunity of acquiring any of his holding of Preference Shares or Debentures of the Company if at any time he wished to sell them. (In fact, in 1961, the Society became a shareholder in its own right, being the possessor of a hundred £10 five per cent Preference Shares).

In the winter of 1956–7 much of the volunteer effort was spent in recovering wagons for scrap. The sunken road and submerged yard at Minffordd were dug out, the undergrowth was mostly cleared and about fifty extra wagons were discovered down there. Most of them were scrapped. A coal chute was also uncovered, which made loading coal very much easier. British Rail suddenly announced that they had decided to take up most of their track in the sidings, as they had planned to do when the Festiniog seemed dead. They were reminded of old agreements between the two railways, that alterations to the yard would be carried out by mutual consent. British Rail agreed to a realignment scheme which suited the Festiniog very well, placing all the facilities they needed in one long siding. Meanwhile the great scrap drive went on. Two or three more trips were made to Blaenau to fetch wagons. At Christmas the flat-bottomed track at the Dinas branch was taken up and sold to the ever-ready Cohens, some of it being resold to the Talyllyn. (The cast iron Blaenau station building was sold to the local football team, who still use it.)

At the same time, many much needed improvements were being made to the line and the facilities. The curve at Harbour station was relaid, and the awkward passing loop shortened. (It has subsequently had to be lengthened again.) The carriage pit at Boston Lodge, which was in a dangerous state, was dug out and a new pit constructed of reinforced concrete. A new water supply was put in at Boston Lodge, and a new tank at Portmadoc. Jack Owen, who was to become the Festiniog (Honorary but very much Acting) Electrical Engineer, began the task of installing an improved electrical system at Boston Lodge.

The electrical staff system was also restored. Even today

uninitiated passengers look out wonderingly as the fireman leaps off his still-rolling engine at Minffordd or Tan-y-Bwlch or Dduallt and disappears behind a door, re-emerging a moment later brandishing a metal staff like a relay runner's baton. The staff is the engine-driver's authority to proceed along the next section of track. It is a safety device to ensure that two trains do not accidentally enter the same stretch of single line.

Improvements were made to *Prince*'s tender to make the engine ride more easily. But clearly the main requirement for the new season of 1956 was another engine. It was decided to restore *Taliesin*. This engine, named after a famous Welsh poet, was historic. She was the double Fairlie originally built at Boston Lodge and completed in 1886 under the name of *Livingston Thompson* (and in 1961, re-named again *Earl of Merioneth*, by kind permission of HRH Prince Philip, one of whose titles it is). The portable parts of the engine were sent to the Vulcan Foundry, but the main work was carried out by Vulcan Foundry employees with Festiniog assistance at Boston Lodge in the summer of 1956. The engine was in steam for the first time on 1 September, ran trials on the evening of Sunday the 2nd, drew the passenger train on the evening of the 4th and entered full passenger service the next day. This was, as Garraway felt then and wrote later, 'an occasion for much rejoicing'. If there had ever been any remaining doubts that the Festiniog was in the process of being properly restored, the spectacle of a double-engined Fairlie called *Taliesin* once more steaming across the Cob must have put them to flight.

Passenger services that year began on 19 May with the line opened as far as Minffordd. Through the winter Fred Boughey and his team had converted a 'pseudo' first-class compartment on carriage No. 11. This was good sales psychology. It was found that people were only too ready to pay the fifty per cent higher fare to travel first class on the Festiniog across the Cob. In July No. 17 went into service, with its first-class compartment in all its genuine Victorian splendour, with seat cushions from the Llandudno and Colwyn Bay Tramway. When the season ended on 22 September, there had been 21,000 bookings, or nearly 39,000 passenger journeys, as they will have it. Not one train had been missed through mechanical failure and until September, when *Taliesin* arrived, *Prince* had not missed a train.

On 12 November some grandees of the Western Region of British Rail, headed by K.W.C. Grand, the General Manager, came to see how their smaller cousin was getting on. Grand and his party, in four coaches hauled by *Taliesin*, were in the first

119

steam-hauled passenger train to Penrhyn since 1939. *Taliesin* had been fitted with an 'elephant whistle' which roused the echoes. After lunch the party drove to Tan-y-Bwlch where Bessie Jones greeted them in her Welsh costume. The *Baldwin*, with four-wheeled brake and a bogie brake composite, took the visitors up to the mouth of the Moelwyn Tunnel.

The rock-bottom essence of volunteering on the Festiniog was hard physical work: shovelling, digging, wheeling a barrow, hauling out tree-trunks, cutting down branches, pulling out nettles and brambles by hand, tipping out loads of ballast, carrying heavy rails and sleepers. Often it was not immediately rewarding work. Restoring the railway was like the children's game of 'Grandmother's Footsteps', played out along several miles and over several years. Nothing much happened while you watched, but if you looked away and then back, you saw that things had changed ever so slightly. The volunteers for the Festiniog, as in every volunteer organization, fell into two categories – those who talked a lot and did a little, and those who talked less and did a lot; there were a great many who came a few times, and a few who came a great many times.

Volunteers were organized in regional groups almost from the very first days. The longest-standing is now the Lancashire and Cheshire, closely followed by groups in the Midlands and London. There are separate Groups in Bristol, Dee and Mersey, East Anglia, East Midlands, Gloucestershire, Hampshire and Sussex, Leicester, Milton Keynes, North Staffordshire, Northumbria, North Wales, Sheffield, South Wales, (recently formed), Upper Thames, a White Rose Group from Yorkshire and a Heritage Group. Groups took up individual projects, which was psychologically a shrewd move, because while a volunteer might grandly say he was 'restoring a railway', it was difficult for him to grasp the meaning of it. But he could much more easily point to something on the line and say, we painted those signs, we rehung that door, our group refitted that coach or those wagons. Sometimes groups did work at home: it was called, literally, 'home work'. The pedestrian cross-over bridge at Tan-y-Bwlch station was the work of several groups who prefabricated the structure, brought it to the site and erected it. The Midland Group built No. 1 van, and rebuilt one of the old open 'knifeboard' coaches as a museum piece. East Anglian Group rebuilt an ex-Welshpool and Llanfair Railway luggage and stores van and built a new transportable plate-layers' hut, complete with hot and cold running water and calor gas. This was mainly the work of Geoffrey Johnson. All the Festiniog's permanent way staff needed to do was to move in. Groups arrange their own working weekend timetables, staying in digs, or in caravans, or latterly in the hostel imaginatively converted (by volunteers) from the old station building at Penrhyn. The groups often have their newsletters, their own group meetings, outings and annual general meetings.

Only the toughest survived the early volunteering days. The London Area Group, for instance, used to meet at Baker Street at ten p.m. on Friday evenings and drive up the interminable miles of the A5, stopping at an overnight cafe at Dordon en route. In those days there was no motorway and the Bala road had not been improved; in fact the only practicable road in from Bala, through Llan Ffestiniog, had only recently ceased to be gated. (The first LAG Working Party Officer, Derek Guard-Day, suffered badly from car-sickness and used to *cycle* the 500 miles to join the working parties!) After braving cold and blizzards, engine breakdowns, and running out of petrol in the wilds of Wales, the LAGs arrived at Boston Lodge for a pre-breakfast 'prowl around'. Many volunteers stayed at the Commercial Hotel in Portmadoc (known always as the 'Comical' in Festiniog sagas of the day).

In spite of these rigours, LAG membership rose under the chairmanship of Roy Cunningham to over 200 in the late 1950s and to 300 in the early 1960s. The group sent regular monthly working parties of a dozen or more from the autumn through to the spring. They worked all Saturday, clearing the track, laying lines, or helping to run trains, and until about midday on Sunday when it was time to leave, so as to arrive back in London in time for buses and trains home. Many prominent Festiniog personalities, such as Arthur Lambert, Norman Gurley, Fred Howes and Dan Wilson, started their connection with the railway through the London Area Group.

Various parties of volunteers came just by themselves, unconnected with the area groups. Some of them had tribal nicknames on the railway – the Brambles, the Weirdies, the Egyptians. The first and greatest of these parties were Keith Catchpole's boys from Chace School, Enfield, in North London. They were given the Boston Lodge nickname 'Tadpoles', partly because of their high work/weight ratio and partly a pun on Catchpole's name. Keith Catchpole was one of the first volunteer engine-drivers on the Festiniog and for years he brought parties of boys to work on the line. During the year before they started work the boys were briefed, with talks and reminiscences from those who had been before. When they got back they made up scrap-books and wrote up logs of their experiences.

The volunteers soon produced their own manual, edited by Roy Cunningham and published by the London Area Group in September 1960. Later expanded and completely revised, it is now virtually a plain man's guide to railways. It gives advice on safety and first aid, on how the volunteer should comport himself, what to do and what not to do, how *not* to lift heavy objects, how *not* to use tools, how to dig ditches, and how to build a stone wall. It dips into the more arcane depths of railway lore, with details of telephone ringing codes, the difference between bull-headed and double-headed rail, hand gestures for marshalling rolling-stock, signalling-lamp colours, the mysteries of permanent way ballast and sleepers, rules for firemen, advice for guards, and hints for buffet-car attendants. It makes good reading even for non-railway enthusiasts, and in its own modest way gives a more accurate and detailed picture of the Festiniog and its working than any other publication.

Restoring the railway was a dual process, of lopping off as well as grafting on. While some volunteers were hard at work batting down the weeds on the way up to Penrhyn, others were busy taking up the line in Portmadoc where it crossed the Britannia Bridge, for use on the Cob. It was just like cutting out old wood, allowing new to grow.

There were those who opposed this way of doing things. The battle between the 'preservationists' and, for want of a better definition, the 'progressivists' was hard fought and, though it has now subsided, it might flare up at any time. Preservation was so large a part of the motivation of those early volunteers that it deserves respect. There were those who wished to seal the railway in a kind of technological aspic, perhaps as it was in 1939, or in 1889, or even 1839. The problem is to decide at what point, in what form, the railway should be preserved. Exactly when should we stop the clock? At any point in its history the railway had anachronisms and innovations side by side. There is no such thing as an absolute historical shape of the railway. As the progressivists argue, and their argument too is a compelling one, the railway has always been changing. It has changed every year since it was first built. It needs change, like all living things. Thus the disagreement between the preservationists and the progressivists is a further source of tension in the railway, with both sides, to a certain extent, acting as a check on each other.

In the event, as the railway progressed, changing and

pushing out fresh growth like a living organism, it had something for everybody – for those who loved its history and those who wanted to push on into the future, for those who liked to build and those who liked to knock down.

There were many changes for the new season of 1957. Part of Glan-y-Mor carriage shed, which was in a dangerous state, was pulled down. A new passing loop had been put in at Penrhyn and trains ran regularly to Penrhyn that year. Passengers now got a trip of three and a quarter miles for their fare money. Traffic rose by forty per cent to over 50,000 passenger journeys. A special fund was opened to pay for the refitting of a second double Fairlie, *Merddin Emrys*. A *Festiniog Railway Guide Book* was on sale at Harbour station, with photographs and a brief history of the railway. It was the first of a stream of publications over the years, accompanied by lapel badges, calendars, pennants, postcards, posters, slides, books, model kits, tea towels, plaques and souvenirs of all shapes and sizes and prices; the Company realised very early on the potential combined purchasing power of holidaymakers and railway enthusiasts. Thomas Spooner Lascelles, a descendant of Charles, presented the railway with the *Spooner Album*, a book of Festiniog Railway photographs collected by his ancester taken by R.H. Bleasdale in the summer of 1887. A museum was started at Harbour station, with Michael Seymour as its curator, which included such curiosities as the hearse van. The first edition of Boyd's Bible, *The Festiniog Railway*, was published, and the railway's technical history was given lapidary form.

In April a special Society train, the first of many over the years, brought members from London and the Midlands to the Annual General Meeting in Portmadoc. From Wolverhampton to Ruabon, it was drawn by the veteran *City of Truro*, which once clocked 102.3 mph on the Plymouth mail run in 1904, and had been specially brought out of retirement in the York Railway Museum for the trip.

Punch sent along Charles Reid. He treated it all as a tremendous lark. He was, he said, wearing his 'Rare Railways Waistcoat', 'in peasoup satin, with motifs of forget-me-nots, fog detonators, viaduct arches and Hudson the Railway King's profile, the whole furbished with a set of Stephenson's Rocket buttons'. He was fascinated by the hearse wagon, or 'Corpse Car', as he called it, and by the first-class carriages which, he said,

> are quaint, shamelessly so. Strong stern men – wholesale
> hardware factors and electricity board attorneys, for example

123

– have been known to giggle and collapse with gratification at the sight of them. Designed apparently for trick circus midgets they have monogrammed antimacassars on blue upholstery, sepia photographs of deer glens, small tarnished mirrors and a strong feeling of crinolines and stovepipe hats.

Charles Reid met one of the Company Directors, 'a politely nurtured and sedentary person – he collects Picasso pots and carved auks' eggs and is wild about Webern' (one is left wondering who on earth Reid was referring to), who had scarred palms from lifting eight-yard-long steel rails at fifty pounds weight the yard and packing slate chippings under new sleepers, which, he said, 'left one feeling gay, important, and slightly shredded'.

But, like everybody else, Charles Reid seemed to have had a good time.

> And suddenly there we were at Minffordd, halted amid rhetorical mountains, with gleams afar of estuary and sea and clouds the colour of butter piling the sky. Over the big railway line ran the little Festiniog one. A row of dolls coaches awaited us, sunlight making the most of their new cream and green paint. They were hitched to one of the nicest and silliest engines anybody ever saw, an engine with two boilers, a driving cab in the middle and two chimneys, one at each end. The thing was obviously capable of staging a stiff tug of war with itself. The name-plate on her crupper said *Taliesin*. As soon as *Taliesin* saw us she whooped.
>
> Then, genially swaying and bumbling, she hauled us up and down the three and a half rehabilitated miles between Portmadoc and Penrhyndeudraeth. All the hamlets had done themselves over with bunting and put on their Sunday suits. At level crossings there were respectful, handwaving knots. It was in all respects a journey worthy of a railway with a Corpse Car.

The piece was entitled 'Branch-Line Fever'. It makes very amusing reading, even now. But it was an easy and predictable first response to the railway. It took up a favourite stance of the media (a few days later, *Picture Post* published a piece under the headline 'The Barristers' "Toy" Train: The Only "Pro" is the Engine-Driver'). The impression, amusing though it is, of a railway line run by faintly eccentric moneyed amateurs and enthusiasts is only partly true. It is only part of the story and the least important aspect of it. The 'wealthy Home Counties stockbroker playing trains' image is not fitting for the Festiniog and it is one they have always strenuously tried to avoid, just as the Company, undoubtedly a commercial success, has always been extremely careful to point out that its 'profits' have all been ploughed back into capital expenditure. At the slightest whisper that anybody is making money out of them, volunteer labour would disappear overnight.

Much more representative of the Festiniog in those days was the massive physical effort of Keith Catchpole and his schoolboys in the summer of 1957, which helped so much to make it possible for services to run to Tan-y-Bwlch for the new season which opened on 23 May 1958. There were then seven and a half miles of track in use, and traffic figures took another leap upwards, so much so that extra effort was required of the volunteers: half a dozen of them, including John Halsall, John Alexander and Fred Boughey, worked through Sunday night before August Bank Holiday to make serviceable three of the old four-wheeler carriages. They made up a train known as the *Flying Flea*.

The following year, on 26 April 1958, *City of Truro* again hauled the Festiniog Railway Society Special, this time all the way from Paddington. Trevor Bailey and J.B. ('Blanco') White, by then the Company and Society's Public Relations Officer, had 'all the right contacts' and the eight-car train included four new British Rail prototype coaches, all different, the famous Great Western Long Bar, and a kitchen buffet car. Tickets were 57s. 6d. (£2.87½p) second class return, 84s. 0d. (£4.20p) first class return and all seats were sold long before. *City of Truro* arrived at Minffordd after what Ross Gregory, a former Vice Chairman of LAG called a 'joy of joys' – 'the lovely meander from Ruabon, through Llangollen, Corwen, Bala Junction, Dolgelly, Barmouth Junction and over the estuary to Barmouth . . . ' From Minffordd many members had their first trip that day up over the newly-opened extension to Tan-y-Bwlch.

From the first, the Festiniog has always put itself in such a position as to be able to accept gifts. To make oneself amenable to giving is an art. At the same time, members showed a fine flair for scavenging and for picking up bargains, obtaining everything from surplus telephones and telephone equipment from the London Midland Region to what was the biggest scavenging operation of the old days, 'Operation Snapper': the recovery in 1959 of a derelict carriage of the defunct Lynton and Barnstaple line which was lying in a field near what had been Snapper Halt in Devon. It had been used as wartime accommodation for evacuees and, latterly, as a hen-shed. Dismantled into conveniently sized bits, it was loaded into Ian Smart's lorry and taken to Boston Lodge, where it was refitted and emerged in 1963 as the present No.14 buffet car, named 'The Snapper Bar' and later 'William Madocks'. (Another FR coach, the ex-Welsh Highland No. 26, was once a hen-house on a farm at Groeslon, near Caernarvon.) But scavenging for coaches in this manner is no longer Company policy (although scavenging generally still is). It is cheaper and better, in the end, to build a new carriage. But in those days, Operation Snapper made good use of willing volunteer labour, which was then the railway's only ready resource.

Over the years, Company and Society have both found out that first enthusiasms often fade. Much of that early 'Work Done' so proudly recorded, had to be quietly and surreptitiously done again later. In the long run, cheap sleepers were not an economy. Good ballast did not just look right, it was an essential part of the railway's long-term capital. Ultimately, there were no substitutes for proper methods and materials – which both demand money.

In 1964 the original Trust of 1954 was amended so that it could be registered as a charity. The Trust owns the majority of the shares in the Company. Alan Pegler appointed the Trustees, limited to five, and he has the power to fill vacancies. After his death the Trustees inherit the powers themselves. The Trust therefore controls the Festiniog Railway Company, which by its Act of Parliament is limited to five Directors (one nominated by the Society).

The Festiniog Railway Society Limited, with its (traditionally) twelve Directors, one nominated by the Company, exists solely to support the railway by providing volunteer labour, professional expertise, and cash. It also publishes the Society magazine and, working with the Company, undertakes press relations and publicity.

There are also some seventeen (the number varies over the years) Festiniog Railway Society Groups, spread around the country. These exist to co-ordinate regional volunteer effort, to 'channel' labour, materials and expertise, to motivate volunteers' enthusiasm towards the railway (and prevent a group becoming just another 'railway group'). Their morale and 'sense of belonging' are encouraged by visits, lectures and film shows organised by Company and Society Directors and members of the permanent staff. The groups have no legal connection with the Society, which gives guidance and instruction where necessary, but the Society has in the past paid off debts

126

incurred by wayward groups, so as to uphold the Festiniog's good name.

The triumvirate of Trust, Company and Society has proved a very strong structure over the years. Although it came about almost fortuitously, it is the only way in which the Festiniog could have survived and prospered as it has. The Company could never have revived the railway without the massive Society volunteer effort over the years, and the steady flow of materials made available free or at low cost by Society members. But the Society, who were not able to raise the money to buy the railway, very probably could not have run it as efficiently without the steady flow of management skill, useful contacts and, in some cases, capital, organised for the railway by the Company's Board.

The Trust, with its tax advantages which accrue from being a registered charity, gives an unusual amount of financial flexibility. In fact, the Festiniog Railway can be a charitable trust, a company, a society, a society limited, or even (for a time) a society (sales) limited, whichever is preferred. Using Light Railway Orders and some determined lobbying, the Festiniog can open and shut stations, route and reroute tracks, change and rechange signalling arrangements, timetables and operating schedules with an ease which British Rail can only envy.

Some Society members have always been slightly uneasy about these trusts and limited companies and fast financial footwork. They take an almost puritanical attitude towards some of the Company's commercial enterprises. There is undoubtedly a feeling that it is faintly *infra dig* for the railway to be mixed up in 'trade', to get down and slug it out in the grubby market place, and that it hardly suits the image of a gentleman railway preservationist that his railway should actually be seen to make any money.

The 1960s were years of steady advance for the Festiniog. The railway took one commercial step forward after another. In 1967 there was what Allan Garraway called a 'traffic explosion'. Passenger journeys rose by twenty-six per cent to well over 220,000. Volunteer effort over a number of years was concentrated upon replacing the old and spent double-head rails between Tan-y-Bwlch and Dduallt with bull-head rails bought from the Penrhyn Quarry. By the spring of 1968 the line was ready for the opening on 6 April. Some ten miles of track were now in regular use and at once passenger figures took another upward leap, by a further thirty-three per cent to nearly 300,000 in the year. A shuttle known as the 'Dduallt Diddy' ran between

Tan-y-Bwlch and Dduallt.

There were those who objected to the Dduallt extension. They seemed to hanker after a 'Tan-y-Bwlch Railway'. Dduallt has no road access of any kind, only footpaths up from the valley floor or across the Moelwyns. Only hikers and mountain goats can get there other than by train. The objectors had a point. There is a stage beyond which extra mileage becomes uneconomical. The average holidaymaker does not worry about distance. He will pay as much, or almost as much, to travel five miles as ten. For years the Festiniog has been, in a sense, a one-ended railway, with one foot firmly in Portmadoc and the other left in the air at 'Unpronounceable' in Welsh. The return to Blaenau has restored the other base. If pre-war traffic patterns are re-established, more passengers will embark at Blaenau than at Portmadoc.

In 1971 the Company took another step which offended the traditionalists – changing from coal to oil burning. It was probably a decision which Spooner himself would have approved. There was no reason, except tradition, for keeping on burning coal. Oil was cheaper, more consistent in quality, and much easier to handle, and made it possible to turn trains around more quickly; but above all it virtually removed the fire risk in the woodland stretches of the line.

The Welsh Highland Railway still casts a long shadow locally. Although, in 1963, the chairman of Portmadoc Urban District Council had steeled himself as far as to propose a pro-Festiniog resolution and although, by 1973, the railway had become one of the largest employers in the district and the Member of Parliament for Merionethshire was asking for assurances that the railway really did intend to return to Blaenau, local people in general have still been slow to support it wholeheartedly. Some of the railway's permanent staff have been puzzled and hurt over the years by what they think of as an astonishing lapse in local appreciation. The Railway's own public relations exercises – special train trips for councillors, landladies and the press, public meetings at Blaenau, dances at Tan-y-Grisiau – are slowly changing the local climate of opinion. Even more potent in Welsh eyes are the huge sums of money the railway earns in a year (although there is a great deal of local misunderstanding about the difference between turn-over and profit).

One shining exception to the rule that in general local people are lukewarm towards the railway was the late Reverend Timothy Phillips. He was himself the son of a Boston Lodge fitter, and he lived in retirement at Boston Lodge for many years. He was an army chaplain in the First World War and a parish priest in England until his retirement. He was an expert on dogs and judged them at many shows. He was as much at home mending the foundry bellows in Boston Lodge as in translating the classical Welsh of the 'Rhybudd' ('warning') posters. Just after the war he stopped scrap merchants from virtually looting the works by threatening to call the police. He had his own anti-vandal campaign, keeping the running sheds and the works securely nailed and boarded up – so stoutly that the new and rightful owners themselves had difficulty in getting in later. He was an expert on the Festiniog Railway and its history. The articles he wrote for Herbert Thomas's *South Caernarvon Leader* in 1946 are still some of the most informative and affectionate ever written about the railway.

Of all the hundreds of volunteers who have come to work on the Festiniog, only a few score have graduated to the footplate, and of those few only a minute and exclusive company are qualified to drive a double engine. But one of them is Fred Boughey:

> On arrival at Harbour Station there is shunting to be done, and a final topping-up with water. There are two pitfalls for the unwary here. First, certain controls on a double engine are somewhat different to those on a conventional machine. The bogies, 'Top' and 'bottom' swivel; following the curves like the bogies on a carriage, whilst the boiler/firebox/cab, rides like the carriage body. Thus any controls which are fixed in the cab, and yet must, at the other end, move with the bogie, tend to alter fractionally on curves. This means that adjustment of the engine brakes are critical; over or under-adjust, move round a curve, and the brakes lose some effectiveness. While running light engine one must always be prepared, in case stopping seems doubtful, to stop in the old fashioned way – reverser over, and give a little steam! Second, the double engine carries water for one trip; start with a low tank or waste water/steam by leaks, incorrect ejector settings or too free use of blower and the trip can be disastrous. Waiting for the 'rightaway' can be a finger-chewing exercise; watching the steam pressure rising – will we get away before it blows? Once on the move one heaves a sigh of relief, and then realises that some troubles are over – others are about to begin. Are we late? Should one open the regulator main valve? If we do, will we pick up speed too quickly, and have to shut off again? It should be remembered that the poor unfortunate fireman has to deal

with two atomising steam valves and two oil control valves; to 'play tunes' on the regulator means adjustment to the four controls, and there are enough 'slacks' due to curvature and so on on the Festiniog to suit a railway three times as long, without adding to his troubles. For the driver, when running under steam, it is most necessary to be certain that both engines are doing their share of the work commensurate with their state of mechanical health at the time. The experienced driver merely listens to the exhaust from both ends; the makes learn runs from one end of his footplate to other, cocking ears at each end.

People are a problem, particularly at stations. The prevailing impression seems to be 'it's only a little train, I'm well clear of it'. You can whistle at them, but remember, the 'bottom-end' whistle drowns the fireman in condensate! At Tan-y-Bwlch, water is taken, and the splashing sounds mean no more water worries for the rest of the trip. The driver can assess the condition of the bearings here by the extremely scientific system of placing the back of his hand against them. Tan-y-Bwlch can be a nasty place sometimes, to get away from. There is the curve out of the station and the railheads are wet from spillage from the water 'bag'. No sooner have you got back to normal running than it's time to ease off again for Tunnel Fach – a very tight hole for the train to fit through. Arrival at Dduallt, after nearly an hour on a double engine, the cab of which, although well ventilated, can be intensely hot – particularly on the fireman's side – leaves the crew in a very dry state. A few minutes to grab a drink of some sort is welcome. The drink must be non-alcoholic; and the crews' lips get nearly licked off watching the passengers supping their great frothy-headed pots of ale! Then back to the engine for the run down; on the double engine a reasonably pleasant prospect as the vacuum brake controls are at the downhill end of the cab. There is a snag for the driver who is not so familiar with the double engine. One gets a beautiful smooth ride so that one can easily creep over the speed limits. It is however, not so simple for the fireman; if he leaves his burners high he wastes valuable oil, creates steam nobody wants, with consequent eruptions from the safety valves! But if burners are turned down too low, certain combinations of the lie of the land and wind, can put the fires out. Some places cause much head swivelling to see both chimneys on the part of the fireman, and of course, they always wait until you're not looking to go out. Passengers must be watched in Tunnel Fach, as steam from the safety valves can, in the confines of the tunnel, cause alarm and despondency among the passengers, to say nothing of the soot and muck of ages disturbed from the tunnel roof.

130

One of the very first volunteers on the Festiniog was Bill Hoole, who began his working railway life as a dock messenger boy in Liverpool for the Midland Railway in 1913. He worked his way up to become a mainline driver at King's Cross where his feats at the regulators of A4s and their contemporaries became almost legendary during a career which lasted thirty-two years. He used to drive *The Elizabethan* and other crack expresses. His top recorded speed was 113 mph. He retired from British Rail in 1959 and came to drive on the Festiniog, becoming especially associated with *Prince*. When at 10.30 on 27 July 1964, his seventieth birthday, he drove *Prince* past Boston Lodge he was serenaded by a memorable steel band. He retired at Easter 1967, after suffering two strokes. He and his wife Dolly lived in the Boston Lodge cottage nearest to the works for seventeen years. After Dolly's death in 1976 Bill Hoole went to live with his daughter in Birmingham. He himself died in June 1979, amidst all the festivities to celebrate the Festiniog's Silver Jubilee, which he would have thoroughly enjoyed, and was buried at Minffordd, beside the line. He inspired many stories and at least one book, *Engineman Extraordinary*, by P.W.B. Semmens.

Bill Hoole used to tell very well the story of the frustrated-looking man at Portmadoc whom Bill saw peering for some time under the double Fairlie *Earl of Merioneth*. When Bill eventually asked what he was looking for, the man straightened up, with a cheated expression on his face. 'You made a pretty good job of this, mate,' he said to Bill. 'Good job of what?' asked Bill. 'Joining these two engines together.'

That story, one of many about double engines (for instance, that they use one half to pull uphill, and the other half downhill) comes from a great reservoir of what are known in the Festiniog vernacular as 'passenger plums'. The remaining human element, not so far mentioned in the Festiniog Railway story, is the great travelling public, who provide the staff and the volunteers with a constant source of amusement and irritation, being entertaining and exasperating in about equal measure. I myself, from my brief experience as buffet car attendant and 'assistant guard', can vouch for the fact that people can be good-tempered or ill-mannered, witty or morose, appreciative or critical. Some of them sit back, obviously awed by the sheer wonder of it all. Others are carping and critical. 'Why do you have this hill on one side of the train all the time?' they ask.)

The staff hug their sides in glee over 'passenger plums'. Passengers are often bewildered. They need constant reassurance. 'Is it *safe*?' they ask. 'Will it bring us back all right?' 'Today?' 'Is it run by clockwork?' 'Is this railway finished?' (Unanswerable). 'Is it run official-like?' (Meaning, is it nationalized?) They regard the timetable with disbelief. 'What time does the 2.15 go?' they ask, and seem absolutely thunderstruck when told, '2.15'. At 3.30 they ask, 'Are we too early for the 4.30?' 'Is this hotel finished yet?' 'What is the best connection for the Isle of Man/Paris/Monte Carlo?' 'It's not a very *small* railway, is it?' said probably the most disappointed passenger of all. 'How much is it?' one small boy asked, at the booking-office window. 'Three and fourpence to you, sonny.' 'No,' he said, with withering scorn, 'I don't mean the whole train, I mean just the engine.' The buffet car attendants, with perhaps the closest and longest contact with the travelling public, come in for the most comment. If they ever get ideas above their station, chance remarks puncture their self-esteem. 'My dear,' said one woman of an attendant, 'he sounded as if he'd been to university. You'd think he'd get a better job than *that*.' And always the same unanswerable questions, each one composed by Lewis Carroll. 'Can we board the next train now, or do we have to wait until it arrives?' 'Can I go back from here if I haven't come?' (A hiker at Dduallt without a ticket). 'Are the trains at different places at different times during the day?' And the surrealist dialogues, each one surely lifted verbatim from *Through the Looking Glass*: 'Is this the train that goes up the mountain?' 'No, madam, this is the one that goes up the valley.' Often the last word was with the Deviationists. At Dduallt: 'How do we get to Blaenau Ffestiniog from here?' 'Start shovelling, mate.'

Chapter 14

The case of *Festiniog v. Electricity Authority* lasted for over fifteen years. As it went on, the great law case took on all the epic proportions of an heroic saga. It was David versus Goliath, the ordinary citizen, in this case the railway enthusiast, against the faceless ones in their Whitehall fastnesses. There were overtones in it of the Crichel Down affair of the 1950s, when a government servant behaved in a quite indefensible manner to a private citizen. There were resemblances, too, to the great battles between Manchester Corporation and the Lake District in the 1960s, and to the successful struggles by the people of Wing, Cublington and Stansted over the third London airport in the 1970s. In its own way, the 'Great Festiniog Law Case' demonstrated that it always pays to persevere.

The affair first began in November 1951, two months after the 'Bristol Meeting', when the old Railway Board were informed that part of their property between the top of the Moelwyn Tunnel and Tan-y-Grisiau station was to be acquired by compulsory purchase in order to provide a reservoir for a hydroelectric scheme. In those days, the railway was moribund and the old Railway Board do not seem to have reacted in any way. Certainly they did not object. If anything, they probably hoped that the scheme might give them some extra leverage to have the railway abandoned. Nothing would have pleased them more than to have officially abandoned the railway and accepted what compensation they could get from the Electricity Authority.

This early scheme was dropped in 1953, but it was replaced by another, a pumped storage scheme, then the first of its kind in the world. The scheme, as it was finally approved in the North Wales Hydro-Electric Act of 1955, called for an upper and a lower reservoir with a pumping and generating station.

The station and the lower reservoir would occupy roughly the same stretch of countryside above the Moelwyn Tunnel as the first scheme. In short, it meant flooding part of the top end of the Festiniog Railway.

When the new Board, Alan Pegler's Board, heard of this threat they of course objected, and made it clear they were going to go on objecting. But their requests for information were ignored. Their letters were unanswered. Such information as they could get came from Merioneth County Council and from the jungle drums of local rumour. But they had undertaken to restore the railway and that was what they were about to do, come hell or pumped storage scheme water.

For many years, the Electricity Authority seemed quite unable to grasp this attitude. At first, the Authority's representatives seemed suspicious of the Festiniog Railway Company's sincerity when it said it intended to restore the railway, the whole way, as far up as Blaenau Ffestiniog. The Authority seemed convinced that Pegler and his colleagues had bought the railway for the sole reason of holding the Authority to ransom for a large sum in compensation. It therefore saw itself as doing battle on behalf of the taxpayer. Alan Pegler, for his part, saw himself as a David of a private citizen, doing battle against the Goliath of a bureaucratic monolith.

Both attitudes surfaced at a meeting in November 1954, at the Electricity Authority's headquarters. While waiting in an ante-room, Alan Pegler and John Routly happened to find some papers, apparently prepared as a 'brief' for Lord Citrine and left accidentally-on-purpose, which effectively described them both as pirates and stated that 'horse-dealing' would be necessary to arrive at a settlement. When they got inside, Pegler and Routly found they were outnumbered by fifteen to one – the thirty Electricity Authority's men being ranged all along the opposite side of a long table. On their objection, twenty-eight of the Authority's men left, leaving only the Chairman (Lord Citrine) and Deputy of the Authority, who hinted that Pegler and his Board were solely out for personal gain, whereupon the pair got up to leave. They were persuaded to stay and, as Brian Hollingsworth's account of the affairs says, 'a useful exchange of views resulted, but the matter was not really set right for 17 years, when John Routly (then Festiniog Railway Chairman) was invited to a placatory lunch at CEGB HQ.'

Les Smith, his brother and Garraway had gone to that Tan-y-Grisiau meeting in February 1955 to discuss possible deviation schemes by Simplex, under the touching and quite

134

misplaced belief that it would somehow help their case if they arrived by rail. Nobody in the Authority appeared to believe that the Board meant what they said.

The local people of Blaenau Ffestiniog thought the same. They believed that their best hope of getting more jobs locally lay with the Electricity Authority. These outsiders, these Englishmen, who had bought the railway and said they were going to restore it, were only saying that, it was believed, so that they could screw the maximum compensation money out of the Electricity Authority. Blaenau jobs were going to be jeopardized for the sake of money paid to knaves from over the border. This was the reason why those early Simplex trips up to Blaenau met with such hostility. Anti-Festiniog Railway resolutions were adopted by the local council. Anti-Festiniog Railway editorials and letters appeared in the local paper. Anti-Festiniog Railway sermons were preached in local pulpits. The railway work was hindered and obstructed in every possible way. Sleepers and keys were plundered for firewood. Tools were stolen, walls were pulled down, equipment was damaged and wagons were derailed.

Looking back now, of course, one can see that the people of Blaenau would have done much better to have backed the railway. The storage scheme only offered any number of local jobs while it was being built. Long since completed, it now provides very little local employment. Most of its personnel have come from outside, bringing specialist qualifications and highly skilled technical expertise which are very thin on the ground in Blaenau. Now, ironically, it is the railway which is the town's best hope for the future, bringing the prospect of a tourist boom to equal the great slate bonanza of the nineteenth century. But this is to be wise after the event.

The Great Law Case makes knotty reading, even for a lawyer. For a layman it is fiendishly difficult. Briefly, it seems that the British Electricity Authority, later the Central Electricity Authority, and later still the Central Electricity Generating Board, were very ill-advised to ignore the presence of the Festiniog Railway's new management in the first place. But, having committed that initial error, they then compounded it and made things much worse by sticking to it, and thus putting themselves and everybody else to a great deal of extra trouble and expense. It was not that anyone in the Electricity Authority ever behaved incorrectly. It would be going much too far even to say that the Electricity Authority were in fact against the Festiniog Railway. It was just that nobody was for it. Nobody made it their business to consider seriously whether or not the Railway had a case, and if they had, whether they might not take it to court and win. As so often happens in these battles with bureaucracy, the bureaucrats began by treating the other side as irrelevant nuisances, and ended by being taught a painful lesson. And again, the bureaucrats began by trying to save the taxpayer money, and ended by spending far more in the long run.

The main conclusion, after reading the history of the case, is not that the law was wrongly applied. The law itself was wrong. It did not sufficiently cater for this aspect of compensation. And yet one is still left with an uneasy feeling, very well expressed by Francis Wayne, for many years secretary of the Railway Company and one of its main protagonists: 'If, without malice or deliberate maladministration, and with the safeguard of a patient hearing by an impartial tribunal, this sort of thing can still happen, it is terrifying to think what chance the citizen would have if there were any deliberate misuse of power.'

The North Wales Hydro-Electric Act was a politically non-controversial bill, debated in detail before a Select Committee of the House of Lords in March and April 1955 (during a national newspaper strike, so there was no publicity). The Festiniog Railway Company was one of the objectors. The others were what are now known as 'conservation and amenities groups', such as the Council for the Preservation of Rural Wales. The Ffestiniog Urban District Council supported the scheme and opposed the Railway Company.

The Railway Company had what now seems a very reasonable amendment to propose. They wanted the works altered so as to avoid flooding, or, if flooding was unavoidable, a clause inserted in the bill for a deviation to be built at public expense. For the opposition, the Electricity Authority maintained that if the Railway Company failed public money would have been wasted. Considering that no passenger had at that time paid for a trip on the line this was a reasonable argument. But counsel for the Authority went further and indulged himself in some quite unjustifiable ridicule. 'My personal view,' he said, 'is that your railway is just a hobby for elderly gentlemen and young men. It is playing trains. I may be wrong in this, but you asked for my personal views.' The counsel for the railway was interrupted and rudely told to 'go and play with your trains'. The Authority said that there was no evidence that the public wished to use the railway (which at the time was true enough) and the people of Blaenau Ffestiniog had said they already had 'a perfectly good bus' (which was not quite so true).

In the event, the Select Committee rejected the railway's amendment, but the chairman went so far as to say they had done so 'after great searching of heart and with very great regret and on the ground of expense that would be involved in that deviation'.

Once they had their Parliamentary approval, the Authority evidently reckoned that the battle was over. They were not going to waste time or effort in being polite to the Festiniog Railway. They gave formal Notice to Treat on 2 February 1956, and Notice to Enter the next day. The inference was quite clear. There was nothing more to say. The Railway Company were irrelevant nuisances who had now been properly swept out of the way. The Authority began to build access roads and other works, but because of financial 'stop-goes' there were delays, and Notice of Entry to the Tunnel was not given until 4 July 1958, by which time the scheme was well under way. The scheme was finished and the Queen officially opened it on 10 August 1963.

But in the meantime the railway had not given up. Clearly a line with a break in it was of no use. They therefore set about surveying a new route to bypass the flooded section. In this, as in so many matters, the Festiniog showed its amazing ability to produce the men for the moment. John Routly and Les Smith were both then on the Board and were both accustomed to moving in the paper jungles of bureaucracy. As early as September 1956 Les Smith was appealing in the railway's newsletter for members of the Society with surveying experience to come forward and help.

One promising route, called the Goode route, after one of its originators (others involved were Les Smith and John Bate) was to run the railway west of the reservoir, as it now is, through a 600-yard tunnel to Tan-y-Grisiau. This plan was vetted by Livesey & Henderson, consulting engineers, who advised the Festiniog free of charge for many years. It was estimated to cost £80,000. No other route was discussed by either side. In June 1957 the railway reminded the Authority of their intentions for this route. Early in 1958 the railway had completed a survey, with the knowledge of the Electricity Authority.

The Authority replied that the plan for the pump storage had been changed. Without consulting the railway, they had moved a switching-station site to a position where it would prevent the line running along the west side of the reservoir. By this time, 1958, a passenger service had been restored as far as Tan-y-Bwlch and it must have been obvious to everybody that the railway really meant business. Once again, it appears that the Authority were not acting maliciously or tyrannically, but insensitively – stupidly, in fact. They seemed to have had no idea of the calibre of the people they were dealing with.

The railway set to again and surveyed another route, known as the Livesey and Henderson route. This one ran to the east of the reservoir, past Brooke's Quarry, through a tunnel, crossing the reservoir dam, going through a sharp curve and a cutting to Tan-y-Grisiau. The main works on this route were the tunnel, and the reservoir spillway viaduct. The route would cost £180,000, more than twice as much as the previous one. The higher figure was important, because in the negotiations to come it would be the figure used as the basis for negotiation.

The Railway Company now had to apply for compensation through the normal processes of law. The law that applied was called the Acquisition of Land (Assessment of Compensation) Act of 1919. Since another Act of 1949, cases under this law were heard before what were known as 'Lands Tribunals'.

The 1919 Act had six 'Rules' under which the arbitrator could award compensation. Number 2 was 'disturbance'. Number 6 related to the value of the land and the installations on it. Number 5 read,

> Where land is, and but for the compulsory acquisition would continue to be, devoted to a purpose of such a nature that there is no general demand or market for land for that purpose, the compensation may, if the official arbitrator is satisfied that reinstatement in some other place is intended, be assessed on the basis of reasonable cost of equivalent reinstatement.

On legal advice, the Company decided to go for Rule 5. 'Equivalent reinstatement' was to be the great battle-cry.

The case came before the Lands Tribunal on 11 and 13 May 1960. The Company's argument was that they were a poor struggling organization, set upon and robbed of their full opportunity to make good by a rich and enormous concern – the Electricity Authority. The Tribunal had to decide whether Rule 5 was applicable in this case. If not, then the two parties agreed that compensation would be paid under Rules 2 and 6. The Company's counsel argued that the word 'may' meant that the Tribunal had powers to go back to the old principle of reinstatement. In other words 'may' meant 'must', or at least 'should'.

138

As it turned out, this line of argument suited the other side very well. They were able to allege that, according to present estimates, the cost of replacing the last missing bit of railway was more than the whole of the rest of the railway was worth! To award the cost of reinstatement would be a wholly unreasonable charge on public funds. The President of the Tribunal, Sir William Fitzgerald, ought to exercise his statutory discretion; in other words, the word 'may' meant 'may'.

Here, there arose a certain amount of debate about how much the railway was actually worth. At that time the Railway Company were still forced, by law, to present their accounts in a form which dated back to the nineteenth century. This put the Company at a disadvantage because they were unable to give any evidence about the value of the railway. For that reason the Secretary, Francis Wayne, refused to estimate the capital value of the line in evidence, saying that to do so would be unrealistic and even misleading. (For the same reason, the Company did not publish its accounts in the early days, thereby generating a good deal of heat between the Company and the Society.) Wayne said he was a chartered accountant and not a valuer. The President showed surprise at his attitude, but did not comment on it in his decision.

The President inspected the line and on 18 July gave his decision. Compensation was *not* payable on the basis of reinstatement. He could not apply Rule 5 if, as in this case, the cost of reinstatement exceeded the value of the business. On that basis, reinstatement could only be justified if the restoration would increase the Company's profit by £30,000 a year, including depreciation. As this would require another 120,000 extra passengers a year, Sir William said that he could not 'believe that anything like this increase is within the bounds of the possible'. In fact the Railway went on to smash Sir William's figure, and every other record in sight; but nobody was to know that.

The Electricity Authority had conducted their side very well. The increase in the cost of reinstatement, from £80,000 to £180,000 had worked in their favour. At the old figure, the Tribunal might just have been convinced that restoration was justifiable. But at the new figure they decided it was more than the railway was worth. The Authority's objections had raised the cost of deviation from £80,000 to £180,000, which the Tribunal had decided was not a reasonable cost of reinstatement. Thus, by jacking up the cost by another £100,000, the Authority escaped paying the original £80,000. It was not magnificent, but it was the law.

The Railway Company could not appeal on matters of fact, only on legal points raised. It appealed on the ground that the President had no discretion, in other words 'may' meant 'shall', and, if he had discretion, he had exercised it unreasonably. The case went before the three Lord Justices at the Court of Appeal on 11 December 1961. According to an eyewitness the proceedings were surprisingly informal. Arthur Lambert, a Society Director who was there, was surprised by 'the frequency with which their Lordships gave voice during the hearing. Only one of the three ever gave the impression, beloved of court stories, that he was asleep.'

Asleep or awake, Their Lordships threw the Railway case out. One of them said that Francis Wayne's attitude was tantamount to contempt of court. Lord Justice Harman said that the appeal was an endeavour to reverse a decision of Parliament. He also said that there was no evidence that reinstatement was possible if the case were not won, even if the intent were there. Lord Justice Harman thus joined the growing ranks of those who were proved utterly wrong by the Festiniog Railway.

The long and the short of it, announced in February 1962, was that the appeal was dismissed.

There is no blinking the fact that this was a major defeat for the Company. However, the railway had lost a battle, as they say, not the war. Having been defeated at the Lands Tribunal, the Company could have given up and it could have been argued (it probably was by the CEGB) that they should be content with what they had. After all, they had some lovely scenery, some interesting old engines and rolling-stock, about ten miles of possible track up to the bottom end of the Moelwyn Tunnel, and what seemed like a horde of enthusiastic volunteers to play trains with. Could they not be satisfied with all that?

The answer was no, and there were several reasons for this, which are worth setting out again. The Festiniog Railway was a 'proper' railway, with a serious transport role to play: it was a rail link between a remote part of the Welsh hinterland and the sea. The Company had a statutory duty to maintain the whole service over the whole of the line, and this could not be changed except by Act of Parliament. The Company had given undertakings to their members and to various interested parties at both ends that the line would be restored. The railway was fast becoming a major tourist attraction. People flocked to it from its earliest days. In 1964 it was awarded a Certificate of Merit by the Welsh Tourist Board. Furthermore, the Festiniog was an outstanding example of nineteenth-century industrial archaeology. Lastly, but very importantly, it provided a great many people with a chance to do some rewarding voluntary manual work for the public good in the open air. The Company decided to try again, basing their case this time on 'loss of profits'.

But first there were several things that had to be done. The railway's accounting system had to be overhauled. The railway's first accountant was the late Bill Bellamy, whose methods laid the foundations for the Company's success. But, as Arthur Lambert has said, Bill Bellamy was an accountant of the old school, an uncompromising character; 'the contemporary Russian *"Niet"* in the Security Council was a great compromise compared with the Bellamy "No!" He coined the phrase "Ffestiniog lente", "Festiniog slowly", which could equally well be spelt with one or two fs. Bill Bellamy believed that the less fewer people knew about company accounts the better.'

After some consultations with the Ministry of Transport, to see how the accounting system could best be changed, the old Revenue and Expenditure Account was replaced by a new Operating Account and a Revenue Appropriation Account. In the winter of 1962–3 the magazine published monetary information on the Company for the first time, going back to the date when services restarted in 1955. As the years went by, the magazine published more and more information. Today, the accounts are given in full.

The new Revenue Appropriation Account needs some explaining, because the Company later had to justify it in court. Briefly, it meant that the Company divided money spent on maintenance into two: 'current' maintenance, for the normal running of the line, and 'deferred' maintenance, for restoring the line and its equipment to a 'standard' condition before it had been allowed to run down. Arthur Lambert gives the most succinct explanation:

> Whereas current maintenance was put on the expenditure
> side of the Revenue and Expenditure Account and was thus
> deducted before the operating profit was declared, this
> profit became the 'income' side of the Revenue
> Appropriation account and, taking one year with another,
> was all put to deferred maintenance. The allocation of the
> two forms of maintenance, from the total sum of money
> available, was not done very exactly, but reasonably, having
> regard to what was going on on the line.

At the time, the Trust consolidated its share position, particularly in Debentures, so that eventually the Trust were assured that

141

they were in an impregnable position, even in the most unlikely event of all remaining shareholders (many of whom have never yet been traced) banding together.

This was the situation as the Company shaped up for the next round. In the spring 1962 magazine they published a policy statement. The line was to be consolidated below Tan-y-Bwlch, and work was to begin towards Dduallt. The severed link was going to be completed. The line was to be restored above Tan-y-Grisiau. The push to Dduallt was delayed for a time because the work might have to be redone, depending on what route the new link took, but the other proposals were always Company policy.

Negotiations had been opened with the new CEGB, in 1962 to try and find a basis for settlement. The CEGB decided that the Railway wanted too much in compensation and said that the law must be allowed to take its course. However, the two sides did reach agreement on the value of the line and materials under Rule 6. The Company published a document, read by very few, called 'The Festiniog Case', updated by Francis Wayne. This commented bitterly on the state of the law of compensation and the treatment the railway had received.

At this point a new figure stepped on to the scene, an ex-schoolboy railway volunteer called Gerald Fox, who was then a civil engineering student at Cambridge. He conceived the startlingly original idea that if a spiral loop was constructed at Dduallt to gain about thirty feet in height, the original gradient or something very like it could be maintained on a route past Brooke's Quarry and across the dam along the east side of Llyn Ystradau. Gerald Fox and a number of fellow students carried out a survey in the terrible winter of 1962–3 to show that the route was feasible. Later, it transpired that Gerald Fox had asked the CEGB about a route west of the lake, and had been refused point blank.

In all, some fifty people contributed their time, skill and effort to the survey and design work. They spent ten weekends in Wales, some eight to twelve people at a time, surveying the sites, taking measurements with levels and theodolites. Each visit to the site meant many hours work at home preparing a series of contoured survey sheets, to a scale of fifty inches to the mile. Eventually they produced over fifty large and complicated scale drawings, each to full professional surveying standards. Even at modest consultancy rates and at 1960s prices, the cost of this survey would have been thousands of pounds. The value to the railway was incalculable and the names of those who played a principal part, with Gerald Fox himself, should be recorded: Mike Elvy, A.F. Farthing, R.A.B. Hall, Peter Jamieson, G.J. Keleher, G.A. Pinfold, D.A.H. Richmond, Mike Schumann and A.B. Stainer. They all deserve the gratitude of the railway for a tremendous technical achievement and a marvellously generous contribution.

As sometimes happens in sagas of this kind, a change came over the atmosphere. Although settlement was still a decade away, daily the tide began to run for the railway. Fox's route was officially adopted although nobody (not even the CEGB's engineers) was really happy about the east side route. Planning permission was obtained for work to begin. The Company survived an inquiry at Blaenau Ffestiniog. They applied for, and got a Light Railway Order. One landowner referred to the Lands Tribunal for an assessment of compensation. The Tribunal's value of the land taken was paid by the Company to the landowner's solicitors and, as the legal jargon has it, 'occupation proceeded'.

At Easter 1968 the line was opened for passenger traffic to Dduallt. Traffic figures soared. Even the CEGB had to concede that the Railway meant real business. Besides, the line was now running 'only just over the hill' from the pumped storage scheme. It seemed time to have another try for compensation.

In October 1968 the Company wrote to the CEGB about a west side route. The Board did not reply for almost a year, but their letter when it came did not slam the door, although it was hedged about with precautions. The railway must now have seemed irresistible, and the CEGB's own engineers had never wanted a line across the dam. There was further correspondence. The CEGB were weakening. Perhaps they were sick of the whole subject. They must have sworn a great oath that never again would they touch a railway, even if it looked dead. Another west side survey was done in the summer of 1970, and this became the official one. In September 1971 the CEGB considered, but did not yet formally approve, a west side route which was very similar to the one they had rejected out of hand over ten years earlier. In October the two parties faced each other in court again.

The Company claimed £154,000, made up of £139,000 for loss of profits, £8,000 for the additional capital value of the new route and £7,000 for what were known as Crawley costs (from an earlier case establishing them) for such items as Light Railway Orders and acquisition of land. Loss of profits was

143

projected forward to 1977, when the railway was expected to be open to Blaenau.

On the second day of the hearing, the CEGB approved the west side route. This they did under pressure, when the Company told them that if they insisted on the east side route the sum to be paid in compensation was likely to be much more. So, at last, the CEGB gave in, with not too good a grace. It was ironical that the Electricity Authority, who had manipulated evidence about money so brilliantly in the earlier stages, should now have to succumb to the same threat themselves.

The President gave his decision on 19 November 1971. He awarded the Crawley costs. He found the principle of deferred maintenance fair. Finally, after some legal balancing and hair-splitting, he awarded the Company £65,000, subject to interest from 1956, giving a net sum, after allowance for corporation tax and timing of the award, of £107,000. Costs were also awarded to the Company. Afterwards the CEGB 'made noises' about an appeal but the time limit expired without any further action.

It was, in its own way, a famous victory. But although the Company liked to present itself as a David faced by a monolithic Goliath, the Company's Board were not above some stratagems of their own. Routly writes: 'If we had sued for Loss of Profits in the first place we would have been lucky to get £5,000! We could not have proved profitability.

'In the mid 1960s a most relevant case affecting us decided that in Loss of Profit cases it was possible to bring evidence arising *after* the cause of action, i.e. we therefore *could* bring in evidence of profitability right up to the time of hearing. As a matter of strategy therefore, we kept the case alive but managed to delay the hearing for *years* while building up our profit record. I had to placate those impatient for progress, e.g. at Society Annual General Meetings, without making public what our strategy was!'

Boston Lodge workshops and sheds, abandoned, in the early 1950s, with the Cob in the background. (*Geoff Charles*)

An historic occasion: the first passenger train of the new era at Boston Lodge on 23 September 1954. On the Simplex, left to right, are Allan Garraway, Robert Evans and Morris Jones. (*Herbert Thomas*)

A party of volunteers in the mid-1960s on board *Mary Ann*, built by Simplex of Bedford in 1917.

Part of the 'Bog Railway' on the Deviation, with (centre) Tunnel Mess, Dduallt.

Going home at the end of a day's work on the Festiniog Deviation.

Work on the Deviation: looking down from the Coed Dduallt at Dduallt station. (*Norman Gurley, Festiniog Railway Company*)

Mountaineer, the first steam locomotive through the tunnel, on 28 May 1977. Note also the profile gauge with feelers fully extended, the BEV battery electric locomotive used throughout the boring, and *Moelwyn*. (*Festiniog Railway Company*)

The 'Spiral' on the Deviation, with *Blanche* and a down-train. Dduallt station is in the centre, and the Trawsfynydd power station on the horizon. (*Norman Gurley, Festiniog Railway Company*)

Earl of Merioneth, pulling the special train past the site of Stesion Fain (left) on the resumption of services to Blaenau Ffestiniog on 25 May 1982. (*Author*)

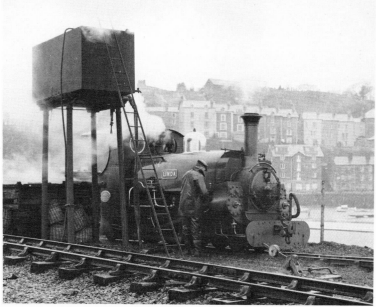

Linda at Portmadoc, with Allan Garraway (wearing his 'Cod War gear') oiling round. (*E. N. Kneale*)

On the open weekend to celebrate the twenty-fifth anniversary of the Festiniog Railway Society on 15 September 1979, *Merddin Emrys*, pulling a service train, approaches the summit of the new line behind the power station.

The Prince, newly-restored, near Tan-y-Bwlch, 1980. (*Peter Johnson*)

The new double Fairlie engine, *Earl of Merioneth*, built at Boston Lodge, entered service on 19 July 1979, exactly a hundred years after Boston Lodge completed its last new steam locomotive. (*Norman Gurley, Festiniog Railway Company*)

Late afternoon sunshine at Minffordd. *Merddin Emrys*, with an assortment of coaches, leaves for Portmadoc. (*Norman Gurley, Festiniog Railway Company*)

Two double Fairlie engines at Portmadoc – *Merddin Emrys* (right) and *Earl of Merioneth* – to celebrate the centenary of the death of Robert Fairlie, 30 July 1985. (*Festiniog Railway Comany*)

Autumn on the Festiniog Railway: *Linda* at Hafod-y-Llyn on 6 November 1971, with sunlight glinting through the trees. (*E. N. Kneale*)

Chapter 15

Just as a pruned tree often grows ever more furiously to compensate for its loss, so the drastic lopping-off of the upper section of the railway stimulated the Festiniog volunteers to their most spectacular and sustained effort to date. The new motto was 'Building Back to Blaenau'. The method was announced in a Company press statement of March 1964. The railway was going to return to Blaenau Ffestiniog by means of what was called the 'Llyn Ystradau Deviation'. This was the route as surveyed by Gerald Fox, and later modified. In its final form, it meant the spiral at Dduallt, a long stretch across the side of the hill at Gelliwiog, to a new short Moelwyn tunnel, passing behind the power station building, to join the old line just before Tan-y-Grisiau station. The tunnel, and parts of the line near the power station, would be built by engineering contractors, but the greater part of the new route would be built by a new sort of Festiniog volunteer – the Civil Engineering Groups, or, more simply, the 'Deviationists'.

The Deviationists were something completely different. Very few of them were Festiniog Society members. Most of them were not railway enthusiasts; in fact some of them were not in the least bit interested in railways. They were as wide a social mix as the orthodox Festiniog volunteer, but they were much more concerned in the civil engineering aspect of the work. They included rather more architects and civil engineers, and a great many people who simply liked shovelling. They formed a group within a group, a specialized society alongside the already specialized society of the railway, with their own methods, their own working, travelling and accommodation arrangements.

Although in that spring of 1964 many things (including two more Light Railway (Amendment) Orders, of 1968 and

1975) had still to be settled about the new route, although many letters had still to be written and hours of legal testimony still had to be heard, at least some work could begin at Dduallt, whatever final route was decided. As so often on the Festiniog the hour produced just the right man, Mr Evershed, a member of the Festiniog Railway Society, who arranged for the Economic Forestry Group to present the Festiniog Railway Company with just the right piece of land for the first 400 yards of the Deviation. Led by the slave-driving, porridge-eating Gerald Fox, the Deviationists cut the first sod of the new stretch of line on 2 January 1965. "Cutting the Sod" is a ceremony still commemorated with almost religious fervour every year, on the 'sod-cutting' weekend nearest to that golden date of 2 January.

From the first, the Deviationists had their own routine. They used to arrive at Tan-y-Bwlch in the middle of Friday night. They loaded their belongings and their food for the weekend onto a trolley and pushed it up to Dduallt Manor, where one of the outbuildings was converted into a hostel. At first, conditions in the hostel were very primitive, but in time the Deviationists made improvements; using willing muscles and scaffolding of empty fruit-juice tins, they installed a fireplace and a mantelpiece, put in a hot water and shower system, brought beds, chairs, tables and cooking apparatus. The Deviationists relied then, and for years afterwards, on the generosity and hospitality of Colonel Andrew Campbell and his wife Mary, of Dduallt Manor. Until 1973, the railway was the only means of access to the house, apart from goat-tracks. The Colonel, an ex-Black Watch soldier, solicitor for the County of Merioneth, a qualified shot-firer and demolition expert, was himself one of the best-known personalities on the line.

On Saturday mornings the Deviationists went down to Tan-y-Bwlch to load a supply train with fencing materials, lengths of rail, an excavator loaned by Taylor Woodrow, an air compressor loaned by Colonel Campbell, tools and other stores and took it back up to Dduallt to start work. Later the Deviationists could call upon a range of quite sophisticated earth-moving machinery, but in the early days the Hudson wagons, called 'skips', were loaded by hand, pushed along temporary rails to the end of the embankment formation, and tipped over. It was very hard manual labour, with picks, shovels, wheelbarrows, pushing and pulling, drilling and blasting, lifting and shovelling; except for the horses, it was a working scene very like the building of the Cob.

The Deviationists had no Society, in any formal meaning

of the word. They did not have to join, or pay any subscription. They were organized in four main regional groups, London A and London B, Western and Northern, each group contributing about the same totals of annual working 'man-days'. But many Deviationists came simply as themselves: in parties from universities, youth clubs and schools, regular working teams of boys from the Crusaders and Christian Fellowship (known aptly as the 'Godsquads').

The variety and temperaments of the working parties is shown by the log kept by the Deviationists. One marvellously terse entry merely says 'Slept, dug, ate, slept, dug, and went home.' Another, by the Edinburgh University Officers Training Corps, recorded that they 'paraded 1105 hrs. at site 3 with picks, mattocks and shovels general service other ranks for the use of. In action 1110 hrs. Withdrew 1600 hrs. Rations. Counter-attacked 1800 hrs. – rain – mud. Last post 2300 hrs. mess orderly absconded. Sunday re-engaged enemy after short church parade. Weather poor. Fox keeps on complaining. Lunch 1400. Rain. Severe casualties, many skips lost. 2100 hrs Fox AWOL.'

The Deviation was directed, if that is not too precise a word, by a group known as the 'Junta'. Its membership varied over the years, but in the beginning it consisted of Gerald Fox himself, with Paul Bradshaw, a solicitor and Cambridge graduate, Roger Simons, a civil engineer, and two more Cambridge men (the Cantab flavour was very pronounced) Mike Schumann, a civil engineer, and Peter Jamieson, an architect.

The Junta were careful to distance themselves from anything that smacked of 'railway enthusiasm'. They took up a markedly anti-railway-enthusiast posture. Up in the clear air and quietness beside the Moelwyns, the Junta tended to become impatient and even intolerant of the dwellers in the plains, and especially the dwellers at Harbour station, and more especially one in particular, Allan Garraway.

The position is best put by Brian Hollingsworth:

The Deviationists to a man cast Allan Garraway as the villain of the piece, and *vice versa*, of course. The scars of their battles still, even now, ache and keep them awake at night. But, objectively speaking, the General Manager of the Festiniog Railway had a duty to give priority to things that directly affected the running of the trains. From his point of view, the cancellation of one train was a major disaster, while a wasted weekend on the 15–year project of the Deviation was not even a flea-bite. He had all the traumas of a major expansion (33 per cent in passenger journeys and 25 per cent in miles of road open as between 1967 and 1968) and of having museum-piece equipment in intensive use; to cope he had only a shoe-string budget and a tiny staff. Of Allan, it should simply be said that he kept his eye on the ball and, as a result, turned – with a little help from his friends – the ruin of 1955 into what is now regarded fairly generally as the premier tourist line of the world. A well-earned MBE came to him in 1979.

The Junta also had problems with the Company Board. As David Currant, chairman of the London Junta once wrote to the Board, 'It is sometimes extremely difficult to believe that the Deviation is being built with the Company's blessing let alone its guidance.' The Junta complained of lack of decisions, lack of money, lack of determination to see that the Deviation was built, a lack of leadership, in fact.

The Company eventually responded to this prodding, somewhat in the manner of present-day politicians, by appointing Gerard Fiennes who, rather like a minister with special portfolio for the inner cities, would act as advocate for the Deviationists on the Board. He was a notable figure in the railway world who once might, and many people thought should, have been Chairman of British Rail. (He was sacked from BR by Barbara Castle one day, and recruited by the Festiniog Railway the next.) Communications between Company and Junta took several turns for the better. Gerard Fiennes won the Deviation a budget and some machinery, and was a persuasive and experienced voice at Board meetings.

In 1967 the Deviationists outgrew Dduallt and built the Tunnel Mess – a famous building made of prefabricated sectional timbers, sixty feet by twenty, on a foundation of parallel rails laid on sleepers, standing across the old line of the railway, below the Moelwyn Tunnel entrance. It had a work-room, mess-room, showers, lavatories, a water-tank with a gravity system, and its own power generator. Chairs, tables, crockery, cutlery, pots and pans were all made or donated. The Tunnel Mess also had draught keg beer on tap. The building cost £400, which the Company could not afford to pay back to the Deviationists until the following year.

With its communal life, its songs, its shared menial tasks, its wall decorations of railway notices, posters, cartoons and newspaper cuttings, and its general air of workaday dishevel-ment, the Tunnel Mess had an unmistakably pioneering atmosphere about it. One thinks of the logging camps of Canadian colonial days, or the cowhands' bunkhouses of the old Wild West. Many of the Deviationists said, with some justification, that the Deviation was the only place on the railway where the original pioneer spirit still survived in its purest form.

One entry in the log, in a feminine hand, records how some (male) Deviationists succeeded in carelessly derailing a loaded skip just before packing-up time and how 'the dear, good, clever, kind, strong, handsome men got it back on in only just over an hour . . . ' From the very earliest days, many of the Deviation parties included a fair proportion of girls. Deviationists were always firmly, almost determinedly, free of sexual discrimination. Obviously young men could not be entirely dissuaded from showing off their muscles occasionally, and the girls often left work at the site early so as to prepare meals. When the Deviation later became more mechanised, the girls tended to drive the various bits of machinery. The girls certainly improved the standard of cooking, hygiene and general comfort. As always, their presence had a civilising effect on language and dress in what, in all-male circumstances, might have become a barrack-room atmosphere.

But there was never any special allocation of bunks in Tunnel Mess – no 'girls only' annex, or 'men only' bar. A few, a *very* few, girls complained, and one or two mummy's boys said their mummies wouldn't like it. But, in fact, Tunnel Mess did not lend itself to prurience. The general ambience was, if anything, mildly puritan rather than orgiastic. The true Deviationist frowned on any expenditure of energy on anything other than the Deviation and, besides, few had excess energy to expend. Many were students, or normally led fairly sedentary office lives. The mountain air, the hard, grinding physical exercise, the unaccustomed surroundings, meant that when they went to their bunks, they slept as though poleaxed.

However, there were a number of Deviation marriages, although nobody is quite sure how many resulted between people who first met each other on the Deviation. Also, it is arguable, at this distance of time, whether it was the Wild Men chasing the Gorgeous Girls, or vice versa. Certainly when Colonel Campbell, with his wife and daughter, visited the working site one day in 1966, he made a remark which, in Brian Hollingsworth's words, 'still rings in the annals of the Deviation'. He was asked, as all sightseers are always asked, whether the ladies would like to give a hand. He replied 'I don't think so, they have their husbands already . . . '

Perhaps the most famous of all those marriages was that of

149

the Deviationist Jane Ayres to Bunny Lewis, the first member of the permanent Festioniog Railway Company staff appointed to the Deviation. With the high annual rainfall of the Blaenau and Moelwyn area, and the generally wet working conditions on much of the Deviation, it was entirely appropriate that the Company should appoint to supervise the work a professional amphibian, a Royal Marine sergeant and landing craft skipper, fully accustomed to operating *per mare* as well as *per terram*.

After working for some time as a Deviation volunteer, Bunny Lewis was officially appointed on 16 May 1970, and at once the whole railway, even the wooded slopes below, became constantly aware of a restless mountain spirit, somewhere 'up there', like an elemental force of nature, with bushy beard and raucous voice, ever urging his troops onwards and over the top. Those on the quieter, lower reaches of the railway lived in constant trepidation that they might be visited by Bunny Lewis and his amazing machinery. Meanwhile, up among the Moelwyns, it was clear to all, man, beast and Deviationist, that there were only two ways of proceeding: Bunny's Way and the Wrong Way.

An evocative account of what it was like to work on the Deviation was written by a prominent Deviationist and Junta member, John Grimshaw, for the 'newspaper' *Moelwyn Express*. He, Bunny Lewis, and two more well known Deviationists, Chris Chitty and Rosalind Newburger, attended First Sod Day in January 1969 and stayed on to work, with eight boys from Westminster School, on erecting the concrete piers for the new Rhoslyn bridge, just below Dduallt station. The design had just been completed by Roger Simons in December and the bridge was needed for the opening of the new season traffic. With what Grimshaw called a 'Chorus of concreters, scaffolders and steel-fixers' the work was accomplished in time.

The bridge building was not only a very fine engineering achievement, but something of an emotional experience. 'No clear picture remains of the building, only isolated flashes of memory . . .

- of trollying down Moelwyn with lanterns in the morning.
- of rain, more rain, dripping macs and cold slippery scaffolding.
- of John Harrison fighting diesel and tobacco fumes in the winch engine.
- of Dougal [Campbell] the scaffolder with red woollen cap and spanners in his belt.

- of the Colonel fretting ill in bed in the Manor, longing to be up on the mountain.
- of more concrete, concrete being winched up through the birdcage of scaffolding, dribbling grout on Hugh [Watkins] and John below.
- of Bunny's language deteriorating to the barrack-room floor as the week progressed and he kept us laughing – laughing so much we had to rope Dave [Somervell] to the Tubes.
- of the fantastic food produced by Ros.
- of beautiful clear skies with horizons tipped up over Manod.
- of complete freedom to work as hard and as long as one wanted away from the petty regulations on site and knowing that we were all in it together.
- of the Manager and his hound and their frequent visits.
- of concrete and yet more concrete and the hurrying to have all the scaffolding and shutters ready.
- of floodlights far into the night with this little world, this little patch of brightness isolated so high on Moelwyn.
- of warm bags in the mess and the alarm clock ringing us awake.

'It is a patchy record of a time we enjoyed and our thanks to all who make it possible and our apologies to those who would have liked to be there but did not know, or were unable to come.' John Grimshaw later married Rosalind.

The feelings and the frustrations of many young volunteers are described by Charles Wilson, a student accountant, a Deviationist who in 1971 was taking examinations for the Association of Certified Accountants by correspondence course.

On the Friday before I was due to go on the Deviation weekend I arrived home to find my exam results. On a pre-printed, impersonal piece of paper, a computer had printed out the word FAIL. I couldn't believe it and looking at it in detail I saw that the computor had failed me for not sitting a paper from which I had been exempted! Ignoring the note saying that 'further correspondence concerning the above results cannot be entered into', I wrote a letter to the Association pointing out their error, and as I returned from posting it, my mind was full of anger at computers, accountants, exams – in fact most modern society.

Charles Wilson went to the Deviation to work off his frustration.

The job in front of us was removing a tree-stump that was overhanging the shelf at Coed Dduallt – and a most intractable object that tree-stump turned out to be. We spent the morning trying to dig round it, so that it could drop to the formation where we could tip it over the edge towards the lake below. Having dug round it so that we couldn't see how it was still suspended, we gave up and went for lunch. As we were walking away we heard a crunch behind us, turned round, and there was the tree – on the ground.

All we had to do was move this stump about six feet so that it could drop off the shelf, and it took us the rest of Saturday and most of Sunday. We attacked that stump with mattocks, shovels, and an axe, and used a winch to try and pull it over, but it refused to budge until Sunday afternoon when we finally managed to roll it over. Well, I think as I attacked that stump I worked off most of my frustration and anger that I had felt on Friday – and put it to good purpose – even if we were no nearer Blaenau, and had only a fallen tree-stump to show for our pains, I really felt that I had done something worthwhile.

On Sunday evening, we caught the evening 'beer' train down to Harbour station. I will never forget that journey, out of the countless times I have travelled on the line. It was a nine-coach train, hauled by double engine *Merddin Emrys*, with buffet car No. 14, reserved for volunteers, near the end of the train. I sat in the corner, supping my pint and listening to 78 records on a wind-up record player. When the train stopped at Minffordd I looked out of the window and the sight of *Merddin Emrys* gently steaming at the far end of the train was really beautiful. Even more beautiful, and making a really fine climax to the weekend, was the sight of the engine, drifting round Boston Lodge curve, silhouetted against the orange-pink sky, with the dark shape of Moel-y-Gest in the background.

Although much of the work was manual (some of it highly skilled: dry-stone walling, for example) the Deviationists became increasingly mechanized, with various locos, and such machines as the Massey-Ferguson crawler-loader. But even the mechanisation had a kind of unbeatable innocence about it, well illustrated by the Great Smalley Saga.

A Smalley is a giant yellow excavating machine, fitted with a huge grab, standing on its own great stalk-like legs and looking like something out of *The War of the Worlds*. The Deviationists decided that they needed one, to work particularly on the site at the northern end of the new tunnel. But a Smalley costs thousands of pounds. Undeterred, the Deviationists set out to buy one – with trading stamps.

A special fund was opened, a Smalley Appeal, masterminded by Mike Schumann, who had assumed Gerald Fox's mantle as project engineer. Cash, postal orders, and a truly astronomical number of books of trading stamps were assembled. Even so, the Smalley still looked a long way off until, by another of those *deus ex machina* strokes which do happen on the Festiniog, a Smalley appeared. Mr Youell of the Sterling Plant Hire Company of Coventry heard about the appeal and presented a Smalley machine, complete, with the provisos that his company's name should be painted on the side, and the Smalley itself returned when the work was finished. A grateful Festiniog Society made Mr Youell a life member, and nobody has ever deserved it more.

Obtaining the Smalley, though it appeared a near miracle at the time, began to seem only a minute problem as the work of tunnelling got under way. The new Moelwyn Tunnel, as finally decided, was to be 284 metres (931.5 feet) long, 4.5 metres (14.76 feet) high and 3.5 metres (11.375 feet) wide. It was to be a do-it-yourself tunnel, built by men directly employed by the Company (a rare occurrence in railway history) at a cost of £50,000, for which there would be a grant from the Wales Tourist Board. As so often in the past, the job of estimating the work, preparing the budget, obtaining machinery and generally overseeing progress fell to Mike Schumann, as project engineer.

A great many new buildings, including a standard steel explosive store fitted with a lightning conductor, were required, and a great deal of new machinery, including a larger capacity air compressor, a battery-driven locomotive for use inside the tunnel and a self-propelled, air-driven mucker-out, or 'Over the Shoulder Boulder Thrower'; this loaded up its own shovel from the floor of the tunnel, lifted it over and round, and deposited it into a skip.

Once again, in the Festiniog tradition, the hour produced the tunnelling men – Bob Le Marchant, Peter Hughes and Robin Daniels, three Cornish tin miners. They were specifically engaged (and their precise task was set down in an agreement) to bore the main tunnel to the stated profile, building it true to line and level; making the walls and roof safe from loose rocks; pressure grouting or rock-bolting unstable areas; enlarging the cross-section at intervals to provide refuges; excavating a drainage channel on either side of the floor; and clearing the floor of all loose rocks and debris. Mike Schumann decided that the tunnel would not need lining with cement. After all, the old Moelwyn tunnel had done perfectly well for over a hundred years in a state of nature inside.

153

By the end of August 1975, the miners were on site and ready, the equipment had been obtained, and the Wales Tourist Board grant approved. Work began to build a pilot heading, the full width but only some eight feet in height. The tunnellers knew their business and the rest of the railway were staggered by the progress they made. Their routine was: first to muck out and load up the rock and debris from the previous day's blasting; then, to extend and adjust the track inwards for the next blasting; drill holes for the explosive; blast; and await the dispersal of fumes. Blasting was normally done last thing, so that the fumes could disperse overnight. Then, in the morning, the routine began again with the clearing away of the debris.

The miners were backed up by a considerable team who ran the empty skips up to the face and the loaded skips back out into the daylight, as well as sundry jobs such as working the machinery and breaking up stones which were too large or awkward to be handled normally. Bunny Lewis, David Payne, Norman Gurley and Martin Duncan (Bunny Lewis' second in command, who incidentally, also married a Deviationist, Alison Cooper) bore the brunt of the manual work, which was extremely hard going.

Despite some extra pressure – of four shifts in two days – the 'breakthrough' happened as planned, in front of the BBC television cameras, early on Saturday 1 May 1976. It really did seem that the tunnel might be ready for the booked start of train services, which was Easter 1977.

However, the best-laid plans are often bedevilled – by bureaucratic intervention from the Health and Safety Inspectorate at Work, amongst other things, which seemed more than usually unnecessary, even allowing for normal bureaucratic stupidity and bloody-mindedness. The first train passed through in February 1977, the first test train under steam on 28 May, when some clearances were found wanting. The first inspection by Major Olver RE was on the following day.

The official opening took place on 25 June 1977, when a special train with invited guests steamed (with *Merddin Emrys*) through the tunnel and along as far as the temporary halt at Llyn Ystradau, which was to be the Festiniog terminus for about a year.

Much of the tunnel had been rock-bolted inside, with the bolts sealed in place with resin cement. But Mike Schumann's hopes that the tunnel would not need sealing were dashed. Modern safety standards had risen enormously since the days of the old Moelwyn tunnel. The rock itself proved to have many more veins, and to be much less stable, than expected; it also seemed that modern high explosive, in a curious way, shattered and 'injured' the hillside more than the old gunpowder had done.

Shot-creting began in January 1978 and a long, exasperating and frustrating business it proved to be. There were many snags, with the equipment and with the technique. Again, it was a do-it-yourself operation, because there was no money to engage professional shot-creters. New machinery was required and, in one case, designed on site (by Andy Putnam, who made a do-it-yourself drum wagon).

The technique was to spray concrete over the inside of the tunnel with a gun which atomised the liquid concrete with a jet of compressed air; special ingredients were added as the concrete passed the nozzle, to make it set instantaneously when it hit the rock. But if there was any delay (such as any stone more than half an inch in size, which would jam the nozzle aperture) the ready-mix concrete at the site had to be used quickly before it set. Similarly, the next load of ready-mix, on its way up from Minffordd would also be wasted if it were not used at once. However, the Festiniog team did so well that they held a Shot-creting Open Day in March, which was attended by civil engineers (including interested shot-creters) from all over the country, and the shot-creting was finished in June 1978.

The Deviation has evolved its own terminology and folk customs. There is the 'Ffestergraph', showing the number of skips unloaded during the years. There is the 'Golden Spade' (now in the Museum) presented to the group which dug the hardest and filled the most skips. The working sites have acquired their own names, some of them most romantically inspired. 'Dragon' is where a wagon fell through a hole, obviously to be devoured there by dragons. And there is 'Spooner's Hollow', 'New Moon', 'Rosary' (named after two girls, Rosalind and Hilary) and, less poetically, 'Midge' and 'Barn'.

The opening of the tunnel in June 1977 was only one of a number of anniversaries and events which the Deviation celebrated in its thirteen-year history. A special train, with visitors, ran to Barn Cutting in July 1973. In May 1975, a small diesel shuttle service started between Dduallt and Gelliwiog.

In 1978, McAlpine's (using Manpower Services Commission labour) completed the formation behind the CEGB power station and the Deviationists erected the new Afon Cwmorthin bridge, near Tan-y-Grisiau station. At exactly 12.06

155

p.m. on 24 June 1978, *Blanche*, drawing a train full of Deviationists, came off the Deviation and ran on to the original Festiniog line, north of Tan-y-Grisiau. More VIPs arrived thirty minutes later on another special train, drawn by *Merddin Emrys*. Mr Dewi Rees, Director of the Manpower Services Commission, drove in a Golden Spike, while typical Deviation rain fell in torrents.

Like a great many long-awaited parties, the final end of the Deviation was something of an anti-climax. As the first train packed with Deviationists neared Tan-y-Grisiau that morning, Dick Davies, who as a polytechnic student had taken part in the west side survey back in 1970, turned to Chris Chitty and said 'I didn't enjoy that, let's go and build a railway somewhere else!' In Brian Hollingsworth's words, 'the whole carriage fell about laughing. When all was said and done, they had worked sixteen months for every minute of train ride!'

The Deviation was, of course, not finished. As Andy Putnam, now Plant Engineer up at Blaenau said, 'there's about five years' work there.' But, in the old sense, the Deviation was finished. Tunnel Mess has gone and sheep now graze over the site. The bog railway tracks became just marks among the bracken. But if anybody is bold enough to stand on the Deviation at Rosary, say, late on a winter's night, when the wind is soughing through the tree-tops of Coed Dduallt, there may come to him the rumbling of wheels, the gleam of lights, a laugh, a great voice roaring 'What *Are* You Doing?', with volleys of oaths, as the Deviationists go by.

Chapter 16

As the Festiniog climbed in a series of extensions back up the hills towards Blaenau again, the name and date of each fresh terminus eventually made a roll rather like a warship's battle honours: MINFFORDD 19 May 1956, PENRHYN 20 April 1957, TAN-Y-BWLCH 5 April 1958, DDUALLT 6 April 1968, LLYN YSTRADAU 25 June 1977, and TAN-Y-GRISIAU 24 June 1978. The later extensions, certainly from Tan-y-Bwlch onwards, had their critics, who argued that there was an optimum economic length for any restored railway and Tan-y-Bwlch had reached it, that a longer railway would impose impossible strains on the railway's resources in rolling stock, track maintenance, and manpower. The traffic figures, at least until the mid-1970s, proved the fainthearts wrong.

The opening dates were all in the spring – April, May, or June, comparatively early in the operating season. For practical reasons, the Festiniog has always taken note of the seasons. The bulk of track work, by staff and volunteers, is done in the winter and a spring opening date makes a good psychological target. No matter which terminus was in use, the timetable has settled down over the years into a familiar seasonal pattern: two daily trains over the Christmas period, until New Year's Day, followed by an almost complete shut-down, except for works trains, until mid-February, when a two-train service resumes, on Saturdays and Sundays. A daily system, normally of three trains, begins again sometime towards the end of March. This is stepped up to some eight trains a day from the Spring Bank Holiday in late May until the end of the main operating season in mid-September. In the high holiday, the peak of the railway's annual effort, from mid July until the end of August, there are as many as eleven trains a day, running from half past eight in the morning until well after nine o'clock at night. In mid-September, the timetable reverts to three trains a day, until the beginning of November, when once again the railway shuts down completely until the Christmas trains.

It is an awkward fact of the Festiniog's financial life that half of its annual traffic business is generated in the six school-holiday weeks from mid-July until the end of August. Should anything happen in those six weeks to interrupt the traffic and reduce the number of passengers, then the business is lost for good. No amount of subsequent effort or blandishments can ever bring it back, until the following year. This violently cyclical effect shows in the railway's profit and loss figures. It is fair to say that the Festiniog normally runs at a profit in July and August, breaks even in June and September, and runs at a loss for the rest of the year. The Company's bank overdraft, therefore, goes up and down, like the pumped storage scheme water at Tan-y-Grisiau – falling in summer, rising again in winter. The Festiniog's other business interests, such as catering, travel and holidays, are also seasonal (although the travel and holidays are much less seasonal than catering: the Little Wonder buffet at Harbour station is now shut in the winter, when it was found it was catering almost entirely for FR staff).

Increases in the price of petrol, redundancies in the car industry of the Midlands, where much of North Wales' holiday business originates, the day of the week, the weather – all affect the railway's daily takings. In recent years there has been a great increase in the number of self-catering holidays, so that families are no longer under the iron heels of seaside landladies over meal-times, being off the premises and so on, and can be more flexible in the times of trains they can catch. Unlike many preserved railways, the Festiniog does less business at week-ends, which are traditionally changeover days for families coming and going on holiday on the Lleyn peninsula. On a hot day, the railway cannot compete with the beaches of Black Rock. Cool windy weather, especially in the morning when families are making up their minds, is best for the Festiniog. But paradoxically, if the heatwave lasts for a few days, then the bored and/or sunburned traffic returns. But, if the hot weather persists for weeks, as in the long hot summer of 1983, then a trip on the railway seems intolerable and traffic is badly affected.

The Festiniog has its special visitors, parties, occasions or anniversaries (in fact, Festiniog cynics say 'with somebody's birth, or somebody's death, twenty-five years of this, and fifty years of that, you could have an anniversary *every* year!'). In

158

September 1965, officers and men of the Royal Corps of Transport, from 16 Railway Regiment, Longmoor, came to the Festiniog for a training exercise in various aspects of running a railway, codenamed SHISH KEBAB. They camped at Minffordd and, in spite of almost incessant rain in the wettest fortnight of a poor summer, they relaid a length of track above Tan-y-Bwlch, extended sidings in Glan-y-Mor yard and carried out mechanical work in the shops at Boston Lodge. It was the first time since 1946 that steam engines had left Boston Lodge for work as early as 6.30 a.m. Lottie's cottage had a large notice on her wall, NAFFI.

In 1968, Society officers and members met Company staff for a 'Convention', which has been held annually ever since, first at Criccieth and then at Plas Tan-y-Bwlch, to discuss work in progress, marketing and sales strategy, volunteer working, new buildings and track – railway business, in fact. In 1969, the Festiniog revived a railway letter service agreement which it had first signed with the GPO in 1891. Restarted on 28 May under the charge of one of the Company's honorary officials, Harold Creamer, erstwhile sheep-farmer and lifelong stamp collector, the service has been available every day that trains are running ever since. On high days and holidays, the Festiniog itself issues railway stamps and first-day covers. In 1972 Mrs Angela Harrington became the first woman Director of the Railway Society. In 1973, Tan-y-Bwlch celebrated its centenary as a station. In 1975, the 1,000th 'Tadpole' from Chace School, Enfield, came to work on the Festiniog.

Every year there are special trains: to celebrate the publication of the first edition of *The Little Wonder*, in May 1975; and to celebrate twenty-one years of the London Group, in the following October. In July 1976 there was a special train and a barbecue at Tunnel South to celebrate twenty-one years of the 'new' Festiniog Railway. In June 1977 there was a Very Important Train to take VIPs to open the new Moelwyn Tunnel and to inaugurate the service as far as Llyd Ystradau; a year later, almost to the day, two trains, two of the most significant 'specials' in the Festiniog's history, with distinguished guests, and Deviationists for once resting on their laurels, steamed up to Tan-y-Grisiau to mark the completion of the Deviation. Blaenau Ffestiniog was, quite literally, just around the corner. In 1979, once again in June, there were trains to celebrate the Silver Jubilee of the railway's 'rebirth'.

There were trains to mark personal occasions: in September 1977 the Jones Spooner train ran to commemorate the unveiling of a tablet at Harbour station to the late Eddie

Jones, a volunteer on the railway from the earliest days and the designer of the station building housing the new offices and the Little Wonder buffet. The same train also carried members of the Spooner family, to show them some of the railway so intimately connected with their family name.

One of the most poignant commemorative trains of modern times ran on 8 September 1973 to mark the 200th anniversary of William Alexander Madocks's birth. Miss Elisabeth Beazley, who wrote an excellent life of Madocks (*Madocks and the Wonder of Wales*) and some two hundred friends chartered a special train up to Dduallt, where they gathered round the viewpoint for an address by Sir Clough Williams-Ellis, in the midst of which a permanent way train of empty ballast wagons left by gravity for Minffordd – an unexpected but entirely appropriate image and sound from the Festiniog Railway's past.

The party then returned to Portmadoc for celebrations on the Cob. It was a perfect evening of late summer, and, as the smoke of several bonfires drifted out to sea, a cairn was built of stones brought from all parts of Great Britain. An octet from the Royal Oakeley Silver Band played. The immortal memory of William Alexander Madocks was toasted many times, whilst his spirit must surely have been hovering approvingly over the proceedings.

In July 1975, when a Royal train took HRH Princess Margaret and her children up as far as Tunnel South, with Lord Linley riding the footplate of *Blanche*, driver David Yates and fireman Philip Girdlestone appeared subsequently on TV four times inside an hour, on the Welsh and English versions of BBC Wales and ITV News. (This is believed to have been the first 'Royal Train' in the Festiniog's history.)

The Festiniog and TV have a mutual attraction. *Wales Today*, *Look North*, *Nationwide* and various holiday programmes visit the railway from time to time. The life and times of Colonel Andrew Campbell at Dduallt were given a most entertaining and informative *Look Stranger* programme. *The Singing Train* was a beautifully photographed sortie up the Festiniog, accompanied by some lusty patriotic Welsh singing; Festiniog enthusiasts inevitably complained that there was far too much singing and not nearly enough train.

For the final episode of a long-awaited BBC TV film *Go With Noakes*, a special train took John Noakes, camera crews, 240 children and a brass band up through the newly-opened tunnel, due to return to Porthmadog at seven that evening. But the BBC camera crews required so many runs through the tunnel that the light began to fade and huge spotlights were brought into play. Meanwhile, a throng of increasingly anxious parents gathered at Harbour station and had to be placated with large amounts of alcohol until their offspring finally returned at about eleven p.m. (Happily, the BBC stood the cost of entertainment.)

The membership of the Festiniog Railway Company's Board has changed little over the years. John Routly took Alan Pegler's place as Chairman in 1972 and has continued to contribute his skills as debater and negotiator, lubricator of wheels and smoother of rough places, dealing with local and county councils, electricity boards, the Atomic Energy Authority, the Welsh Office, the Welsh Development Agency, the Council for the Development of Rural Wales, the Wales Tourist Board, the EEC, and industrial companies and consultancies for the gift or loan of otherwise expensive plant, equipment, designs and advice, all in accordance with his own definition of the railway's way of doing things – 'How can it be done without spending our money?'. He has also demonstrated a sure touch for other people's money, constantly tapping hitherto un-suspected (and frequently unsuspecting) sources of grants.

Another long-serving Director is Les Smith, whose speciality is 'buildings and works'. He was the railway's chief protagonist in the negotiations over the drafting of the various Light Railway Orders relating to the Festiniog's new extension. It is a rarefied legal world, in which participants have first to learn a new language: for example, the Festiniog Railway itself, as authorised by the original 1832 Act, is baldly expressed as 'Railway No.1'; the connection with the Welsh Highland Railway, authorised by the Light Railway Order of 1923, is 'Railway No.2'; thus 'Railway No.3' is the Deviation route from Dduallt to Brooke's Quarry, authorised by the 1968 Light Railway Order; and the later Light Railway Order of 1975 authorised the remainder of the Deviation as built, known as 'Railway No.4'.

It has been a hard struggle over the years and has taken its toll. Les Smith once wrote, with feeling, that just as Mary Queen of Scots forecast that when she died 'Calais' would be found inscribed upon her heart, 'I have no doubt that so far as I am concerned there will be two names on mine, one a Welsh farmer, and the other one of our nationalised industries. I first met the aforementioned farmer when Alan Pegler, Trevor Bailey, and I first visited the line and at Tan-y-Grisiau, hired a

161

Festiniog Railway wagon (for 2/6d) which careered, with the three of us aboard, out of control into the inky and damp depths of the Moelwyn Tunnel. The nationalised industry came a little later, but the various skirmishes ranging from the House of Lords, Court of Appeal, Lands Tribunal, Public Enquiries etc., have left their marks.'

When in 1974 Gerard Fiennes insisted he wished to retire from the Board, he was replaced as Director with special brief for the Deviation by Air Vice Marshal Sir Ben Ball. A neighbour of John Routly's in Buckinghamshire, Ben Ball was almost totally unknown on the railway when he arrived, but everybody found him to be a most genial and energetic man, keen to learn and to contribute. He brought to the railway and to the Deviation the formidable organising talents he had once devoted to the planning of the RAF's communications for the D-Day landings in Normandy. He quickly endeared himself to the Deviationists and was just getting into his considerable stride as a Director of the Company and of the Festiniog Railway Society Limited when, on 24 January 1977, he died after a short illness resulting from a stroke. A memorial plaque in Minffordd hostel was unveiled by his widow Pam – who maintains his interest in the railway – on the Sunday of Convention weekend in October 1980. Speaking then, as ex-Deviation Project Engineer, Mike Schumann (who also spoke at the dedication of Andrew Campbell's memorial) said of Ben Ball that he 'regarded difficult and unpleasant people as being saddled with a burden which he regarded it as his duty to come and help shoulder': a memorable epitaph.

Ben Ball's place was taken in November 1977 by Dick Hardy, Executive Member of British Rail's Engineering Training Group, and a considerable figure in the world of 'large railways'. He had been a professional railwayman for 37 years, having started as an LNER apprentice at Doncaster in 1941. He had known Allan Garraway since 1947 and had once been his fireman, on *Linda*, when she was still coal-burning.

In 1985 Bill Broadbent stepped down from the Board, though remaining a Vice-President of the Society, honorary Mechanical Engineering Consultant to the Company, and a Trustee of the Trust. His place as the Director nominated by the Society was taken by Andy Savage. In the past, Festiniog eyebrows had been raised by the arrival on the Board of men such as, it must be said, Ben Ball, whose knowledge of railways had yet to be demonstrated and who were themselves almost complete strangers; as Festiniog people said, 'nobody had ever

162

heard of them until we saw their names on the Company's notepaper' (the Company's letterhead does not have Directors' names, but the point is made). Andy Savage could not have been better chosen to dispel all such criticisms. He was younger, by some twenty years, than the rest of the Company Board, having been a Festiniog volunteer since 1968, working on the permanent way, as buffet car staff, and on station buildings at Tan-y-Bwlch and Penrhyn. He was elected a Director of the Society at the AGM in April 1973, soon after his twenty-first birthday. He was a professional railwayman, in the civil engineering department of British Rail. He had concerned himself with all aspects of the Festiniog, on and off the track. He organised volunteer working parties and homework, edited news sheets and, as project leader, was mainly responsible for the redesigning and rebuilding of Barlwyd bridge, in the final push back to Blaenau. He was an ideal choice, for both Company and Society.

Much has been written, and will be written in the future, about the Festiniog volunteers and their achievement in recreating their railway from dereliction. But their efforts took place within the framework built by the permanent staff who live and work on the railway. The Festiniog Railway staff has grown over the years from the solitary figure of Allan Garraway in 1955 to more than fifty people in the 1970s; the summer of 1979, when there were fifty-eight paid staff, was possibly the peak. Staff members join and leave every year, but in 1983 there were eight redundancies, carried out with much painful heart-searching and coverage in the local media (which removed, at least for a time, the popular local belief that the 'Trên Bach' was 'coining the money and sending it down to London'). The usual staff number now is under fifty.

Much has also been written about the motivation of the Festiniog's volunteers. Of equal interest, though hardly ever considered, is the motivation of the permanent staff. Certainly, the main motive cannot possibly be the money. Nobody ever got rich working for the Festiniog. But there are other compensations. The staff, a highly articulate, argumentative and knowledgeable workforce, talk of 'dropping out of the rat-race' (or, as some of their workmates less kindly say, 'retreating from the real world'). Some talk of the lack of fulfilment in their 'other' jobs, the difficulty of measuring or even recognising individual achievements, the undemanding and unrewarding nature of the work.

A few have found the financial pressures too great. The

163

classical example was Roy Goldstraw, still remembered at Boston Lodge as the college lecturer who gave up his career to become a fitter-driver. He first came to the railway as a volunteer and found, as he used to say, 'it was like a holiday, so I decided I might as well be on holiday the whole time'. However, he also found, like many Festiniog employees, that he was, in their own ruefully bitter description, a 'paid volunteer' who was in a sense subsidising the railway by accepting low wages. Eventually, he returned to his lecturing.

But those who do stay tend to stay on. Evan Davies, the senior driver on the line, completed twenty-five years with the Company in 1984. He joined Boston Lodge at the age of fifteen and began his railway service even earlier, as a boy helping his parents, who looked after the Penrhyn crossing, with the gates. Several other railway employees have served twenty years or more.

Paul Dukes, for years Works Manager at Boston Lodge and now Mechanical Engineer, first visited the railway in 1954, when he got off a train at Boston Lodge to have a look round. 'I remember going through the door,' he said, in a memorable account of the day. 'There was *Merddin Emrys*, all forlorn. There was plaster down, and dust everywhere. Headlamps all askew. It had a certain enchantment though. The sun was streaming through holes in the roof. There were clouds of dust in the sunbeams. You could imagine what it had been. You could visualise it. You could see the potential of it.'

Making it clear he was not a railway enthusiast but an *engineering* enthusiast, Paul Dukes began work as a volunteer in 1957, coming down once a month from his job with International Harvesters to work on *Prince*. He actually joined the railway in 1959 at Barnstaple, travelling direct from London to start work on Operation Snapper. After working on the permanent way, he went to Boston Lodge in 1961 and became foreman in 1963.

As foreman and later as Works Manager, Paul Dukes had his own original filing system – a series of cigarette packets covered in hieroglyphics, which he would consult from time to time. This system, though still in existence, now has a powerful back-up in a computer for planning machinery maintenance and replacements.

The progression from fag-packets to computers is symbolic of the whole evolution of Boston Lodge itself. In the very early days, volunteers often used to work all night, preparing rolling stock for the next day; it is a common factor of anecdotes

164

of the era that no matter what the hour of day or night, somebody was always up and about, working at Boston Lodge. In those days, almost all the effort was expended in 'fire-fighting', running from problem to problem, from breakdown to breakdown, patching up and making do for the morrow. But Boston Lodge has suffered a transformation greater, perhaps, than anywhere else on the line. Large new extensions to the workshops and an entirely new carriage-building shop have been erected. Boston Lodge now builds its own carriages and, in 1979, rolled out a new double Fairlie locomotive, the first to be built there for exactly a hundred years. There are, of course, still breakdowns and sudden emergencies and mishaps on the line, and at the peak of the season the staff still work round the clock if need be, but Boston Lodge now has a degree of forward planning which would have been inconceivable in the early days of the restoration.

Ironically, Paul Dukes now looks upon these results of twenty-five years with mixed feelings. It seems that the bigger and more successful the Festiniog has become, the more closely it begins to resemble that 'rat-race existence' which he came to Boston Lodge to escape. Paradoxically, the harder and longer he works, the more he achieves results he does not instinctively welcome. But he still keeps his lines of communication open, still goes on his famous hunting trips, up, down and across the country, looking for bargains and doing deals – in tools and equipment and raw materials. He keeps a close eye on every visitor to Boston Lodge – closer than those visitors ever realise. 'You never know,' he says. 'If they're interested enough to come to Boston Lodge at all, they might be interested enough to have something or give something the Festiniog needs.'

The framework of the organisation of the Festiniog's heads of departments dates basically from 1969, but there was a major 'Cabinet reshuffle' in the autumn of 1983. Paul Dukes became Mechanical Engineer, responsible for design, development, procurement of materials, safety, legal requirements, off-site facilities, buildings and structures, and fuel supplies. Phil Girdlestone became Works Superintendent and when he left in October 1985, his place was taken by Steve McCallum, who first came to the railway as a schoolboy volunteer in 1970, and came to work full-time in 1974, as an electrician trainee in the winter and loco-driver in the summer. In 1980–84 the Company sponsored him to take a degree in Mechanical and Production Engineering at Sheffield Polytechnic. As Superintendent he is responsible for Boston Lodge workshops and site, locomotive, carriage and wagon repairs and maintenance, workshop plant, machinery and services, stores, materials and general administration. He is also responsible for his previous department of production control. Fred Boughey was appointed a volunteer Foreman of Works by Allan Garraway as long ago as 1955, and joined the permanent staff in 1975; he remained as Technical Officer, with a special brief for carriage building and repairs. Three supervisors were also appointed, to take charge of the three main areas of Boston Lodge's work-load: Clive Gibbard for Locomotive and Mechanical Trades, Arthur Brooks for Carriage and Wagon, and Dave Yates for Plant and Services.

All Festiniog heads of departments are expert scroungers. Ralph Taylor, once a volunteer, now Electrical Engineer, keeps tabs on all manner of unlikely sources: batteries for providing carriage lights, for example, come from ex-City of Glasgow buses, removed from a 'bus graveyard in Sheffield'. Bob MacGregor, Signal and Telecommunications Engineer, once a signals and telegraph department apprentice in British Rail, and still today, with his dramatic ginger Dundreary side-whiskers and pork-pie hat, one of the line's more notable sights, assiduously cultivates pen-friends in British Rail, British Telecom and other major concerns for equipment which may be tersely described as 'having fallen off the back of Battersea Power Station'.

Railways tend to have a powerful grip on schoolboys' imaginations, but none has ever had more effect than the Festiniog has had on Alan Heywood, the Traffic and Commercial Manager. He once won his school's senior geography prize with an essay on 'The Festiniog Railway and its relations with geography 1800–1957'. He got a BA degree in history, political theory and government at the University College of Swansea and spent six years as a teacher of history and geography to 'O' level before joining the Festiniog permanently in 1969.

Traffic and Commercial, with its timetables and tickets, books and buns, mail order and marketing, is the department with the closest interface with the travelling public: one surly, clumsy or downright bolshie buffet car attendant can in one journey undo the effect of months of careful and expensive PR effort. Alan Heywood's is also possibly the most complicated department: he is, in effect, running a travel and holiday agency, a catering business, book- and gift-shops, and a mail-order catalogue, while upstairs in 'Control' at Harbour station, Terry Turner grapples daily with timetables, telephones, graphs and diagrams, his every conversation punctuated by urgent ringing of bells.

While Traffic and Commercial is largely responsible for the face the Festiniog shows to the public, Civil Engineering deals in the bed-rock (literally) which nobody, unless they are expert, ever notices. The Manager is Fred Howes, who is the almost archetypal example of the man who grew more and more dissatisfied with his 'day job' (working in a factory at Redhill, Surrey, assembling control panels for computers) until he eventually threw it over and went to work on the Festiniog. He first visited the railway as a schoolboy in 1962 and came to work as a volunteer with the London Area Group. After one three-week visit in 1964, he joined the staff and fired *Prince* to Bill Hoole, for a time, before joining the permanent way as a novice ganger.

While the Deviation was being built, Fred Howes' responsibility ended twenty yards beyond the top points at Dduallt. Now he is responsible for the whole formation – the bridges, the embankments, walls, culverts, drains and the track. After more than twenty years of walking the line, he can rightly say he knows every single sleeper. To the uninitiated, a track is a track is a track, and a rail is a rail is a long length of metal. But in Fred Howes' company, an apparently stationary piece of line has an astounding number of moving parts. There are subtleties of curve, and cant, and camber. The Festiniog is a very old formation and has flaws and potential slips and slides every few hundred yards. Fred Howes knows them all, and still has time for public relations – making himself known to house-holders along the line at Tan-y-Grisiau and Blaenau Ffestiniog, announcing himself as 'your neighbour', forestalling possible trouble with smooth talk. Most of the line has very narrow clearances and it is vital, for the sake of life and limb, not to be caught with no escape route. Wherever he is, Fred Howes can tell, by the 'tingling' and clicking of the rails, by the pricking of his thumbs, when a train is coming.

From time to time, Fred Howes takes his department on trips, part instructional, part jollies; they went to Crewe to see how 'big brother' does it, during the massive track-works for the updating of the station in the summer of 1985. There are three supervisors, Bob Dillon for the permanent way, Howard Bowcott (part-time) for civil engineering, and Andy Putnam for plant, and normally some half a dozen full-time gangers and trackmen. Thus the department depends heavily upon skilled volunteers, especially those who can come in working parties

167

for periods of a week or more, when materials and a working plan can be prepared beforehand. For example, in one ten-day visit by experienced volunteers from the Lancashire and Cheshire Group in January 1974, a quarter of a mile of old track was taken up between Bryn Mawr and Sheepfold Curve and relaid with new rails, bolted together as they came off the wagon.

The Festiniog is also indebted to its 'honorary officials', who are strictly neither volunteers nor permanent staff, but offer advice and expertise on a great range of railway techniques. Jack Owen was an honorary official for the whole of his twenty years' service as Electrical Engineer for the line. Norman Pearce was honorary Signals and Telegraphs Engineer for twenty-six years, and is still Telecoms Engineer and deputy to Bob MacGregor: he was responsible for providing the railway with its working automatic telephone system and is still its virtuoso, the Heifetz of the high line, able to dial a number so cunningly that it bounces electronically through several exchanges, and possibly off some unwary satellite, before ringing another receiver at his elbow, so that he can literally ring himself up.

The Company's honorary Archivist is Michael Seymour, who has spent most of his holidays for the last thirty years producing order out of chaos in the railway's archives. The Festiniog must be one of the most fully recorded private transport concerns in the world, with one of the best collections of archives – documents, letters, minute-books, diaries, work and pay sheets, posters, timetables, tickets, legal leases and contracts, photographs and plans – all, at the time of the restoration, in a state of utter confusion. He has made the results of his researches available to others, and from time to time contributes learned nuggets of past railway history to the Society's magazine. He has also found time to design pottery transfers, railway letter stamps, tea towels, commemorative tickets for special trains, the orientation look-out table at Dduallt, and the memorial plaque to Ben Ball at Minffordd hostel – as well as supervising the design, layout and contents of the new Festiniog Railway Museum at Harbour station, (which, unlike the railway's lavatories, received commendations in the specialist railway press).

The Festiniog has always needed, and still does need, permanent staff with the right qualifications, but 'taking on a new chum' is a cautious process, as though both sides have first to sniff the other over. Although many of the staff will already be well-known on the line from their volunteering days, the railway have to try and decide whether the new man will fit in. He for his part will be warned about the low pay, and he will have to make up his mind whether to move his wife and family over the mountains to Porthmadog and take up a new life, in more ways than one.

Some of the younger permanent staff simply stay on after their volunteering stint is over. Terry Turner, the Controller in the Traffic Department, describes the process very well. 'They get the Festiniog bug. As the summer ends, they start getting sad. They don't want to go home. The railway is home. This is the real world for them.'

In the early 1970s, the annual number of passenger journeys on the Festiniog increased every year until it reached over 400,000 in 1974. There seemed no reason why traffic figures for the Festiniog should not go on mounting, as if by some inexorable natural law. But in 1974 the Festiniog discovered, as did local government bureaucrats and the builders of super-tankers, that the world had suddenly changed. The effects of the Yom Kippur war in 1973, the quadrupling of oil prices, and the onset of a long world-wide recession stopped the increase in traffic, and after 1974 some years actually showed a decrease.

Nobody was more quickly aware of the changed days than the Festiniog permanent staff. They are, of course, a closed society, difficult for an outsider to penetrate (almost impossible for a layman in railway affairs). But it does seem probable that their remarks about 'job-enthusiasm', the 'intangible rewards' of the railway, and so on, though sincere enough, are in a sense a 'ritual' way of speaking. Certainly, the chat at tea-breaks in the 'Den' at Boston Lodge is as much concerned with pay and conditions as in any other works canteen in the country.

For its part, the Company has long realised that the view across the Traeth Mawr, though magnificent, pays no butcher's bills. A pension scheme was introduced for all permanent staff, with benefits backdated to the early days of 1955. This was received with muted satisfaction even in the 'Den' at Boston Lodge. Further, the Company was more than once prevented from raising wages by various government pay policies, pay pauses and pay freezes.

The drop in traffic, and the sudden fear that the railway might be facing very hard times, served to concentrate minds wonderfully, especially among the permanent staff. They were not 'militant' in any 'Scargill' sense. The bolder and more intelligent spirits amongst them realised that if the railway failed, and there seemed to them at least a chance it might, then their own jobs failed with it. They needed more 'clout', as the saying went, and to 'get their act together'. The solution, as they perceived it, was union power. 'We were concerned to stop the railway failing,' they say, 'and that was the reason for the union.'

There had been members of the National Union of Railwaymen on the Festiniog for years. But they were not noted for their organisation or their solidarity. Those who were not actually involved were hardly aware that the NUR had a presence on the Festiniog. Thus, the first suggestion was to form a new staff association, which was legally feasible under current industrial relations legislation, and which might well have achieved independent status as a union eventually. But when no general agreement could be reached, it was decided to strengthen the existing NUR membership and representation.

There was much to be done. The knowledge that the Company intended to press on to Blaenau, financing the extension out of revenue, by bank borrowing (and, as it transpired, by lavish grants from various authorities) brought to a head the old argument of 'wage increases versus extending the line' which had rumbled on for many years. There were anomalies in pay and conditions. Nobody was quite sure what the one next to him was earning. Some employees were provided by the Company with accommodation, as part of their remuneration; others were not. Very few had a formal job description or contract, which had become a legal requirement. There was very little formal grading of jobs, no 'career structure'. In short, the old romantic notion of 'good companions', with an *esprit de corps* like Nelson's band of brothers, all working on their railway for the common good, was obsolete.

The final fillip to this change of mood amongst the work force was provided, unwittingly, by the Board, at a meeting in 1977 when Chairman Routly addressed the staff. This was, as those who were present recall today, 'a real eye-opener. We had always thought we were working for ourselves. We thought it was *our* railway. Now we realised that we were working for *them*.' This crystallisation of a 'them and us' situation convinced many members of the staff that a strong union was now an urgent necessity.

The union has come to the Festiniog, although the railway is by no means a closed shop. The Employment Act of 1975 required a special response from both sides. An agreement was reached whereby the National Union of Railwaymen recognised that the Festiniog was a special case; that there were great differences between the Festiniog Railway and British Rail; that the Festiniog Railway had no access to revenue subsidies and had to make profits to exist. The union agreed that it would not seek to establish demarcation of work, and would keep the Festiniog's traditional flexibility; that it would not seek to change the role of the Society or to try and restrict voluntary work; that it would consult with management before it sought to enlarge its membership amongst Festiniog Railway employees; and that negotiating procedures between non-union members and the railway would remain as before. It was altogether a most gentlemanly agreement.

The coming of the union, 'unionisation' as it is called, meant some considerable mental adjustment for some of the railway's middle management. Alan Heywood, the Traffic and Commercial Manager, says that the union has improved consultation and communication upwards and downwards 'out of all recognition. But I wouldn't be human if I didn't feel a bit nostalgic towards the old days, when everything was much more informal.' In fact, with nearly fifty permanent employees, a hard core of some twenty or thirty experienced volunteers at the height of the season, a much larger floating population of volunteers who come and go during the year, and extra manpower at the Blaenau Ffestiniog end, the railway is one of the largest employers of labour in the area. Even so, its formalised and quite complicated industrial relations structure, with its departmental committees, consultations and minutes, seems more appropriate to a much larger organisation. But this may well be the first swing of the pendulum away from the old freer and easier days.

Unionisation was only one of the aspects of the Festiniog which was getting more complicated. The traffic figures no longer showed the same startling annual increases after the mid-1970s, but in almost every other way, from the mail-order business to the extensive new works required for the return to Blaenau, the railway was growing bigger and more difficult to manage. As an even greater strain fell upon the General Manager, so the Board found themselves more and more involved in the running of affairs. The fact was that the railway had outgrown the form and structure which had served so well for so many years.

In what was intended (and proved to be) an interim step,

171

the Company appointed Bill Broadbent as Chief Executive in May 1977, the appointment to run for no longer than six months. This made many in the Society uneasy (apart from any other considerations, Bill Broadbent was not only now serving the Company as an employee, he was still Chairman of the Society). Also, there were growing rumours that the General Manager was to be dismissed.

The matter came to a head at the Society's Annual General Meeting in April 1978. John Routly made a speech attempting to clarify the position, explaining that the General Manager was not about to be dismissed but, in fact, still had more than one option open to him. This did not satisfy the Lancashire and Cheshire Group, whose spokesman got up and read a prepared statement viewing 'with grave concern the deterioration in morale among the permanent staff following the Company's declared intention of dispensing with the services of the General Manager, Mr Allan Garraway'.

John Routly said that he did not consider that this needed a reply. A 'perfectly good statement' had been made about it. There had been no attempt to get rid of Mr Garraway. 'It was a Board matter and they had to look to the future.'

There were 273 Society members present, which meant that many thousands more had to read about these proceedings with fascinated amazement in the Magazine (one suggested headline was 'Uproar in Small North Wales Town: Not Many Dead'). These 'juicy bits' as the editorial described them ('Not so much juicy as *slimy*,' retorted a member) naturally provoked some reaction. One permanent staff member, Norman Gurley, wrote to say that there had certainly not been any deterioration in *his* morale nor of anybody he knew. The editor probably summed up the feelings of many when he asked: 'What on earth was going on?'

The upshot was that the General Manager stayed, but there arrived at Portmadoc in April 1979 one of the most unexpected personalities ever to serve the railway. He was to be Chief Executive, which meant, as his 'portrait' in the Magazine described it, 'not so much a Super General Manager as portable Sessions Court and Make-It-Happener'. But, the portraitist said, 'a more completely unknown figure to our readers is unlikely to have been portraited'.

This was no understatement. His name was Dick Wollan, he came from ICI, from 'big business'. He was accustomed to running a group of a company with over 6,000 employees and an annual turnover of some £300 million. He knew very little about railways. As he said himself, 'I'm the original little boy who *didn't* want to be an engine-driver when he grew up.' But, he said, 'I'm a professional manager. I regard management as a profession. Management consists of applying the proper systems of management relationships. I am conceited enough to think that I could go and run a Chinese chocolate factory tomorrow, even though I don't speak Chinese and know nothing about chocolate.'

He was actually a research chemist by profession, but became an engineer 'by contamination, so to speak'. He served with the Royal Engineers in India during the war and joined ICI on the research side after demob. He had been in general management since 1965 but, by 1976, already had thoughts of retiring early. 'The next step was a deputy chairmanship. I was next in line for promotion, but I decided that wasn't for me. I've always thought that if you're not prepared to get on you should be prepared to get out.'

Meanwhile, the Festiniog Railway Company was employing 'headhunters' to find a chief executive with marketing expertise. The jungle drums of big business had already reached the personnel director of ICI, who suddenly said to Dick Wollan, 'How would you like to go and run a Welsh railway?' He had been on the railway once before, in 1968, and had returned to the district for walking and fishing trips. He agreed to spend three days of his week at Porthmadog.

As the man who was to take the Festiniog into the 1980s, Dick Wollan cast a bleak eye on what he found at Porthmadog. 'I had a look at the systems here. There was a tremendous inconsistency of standards. Anything to do with operating trains was first class. The other part of the business, such as training for marketing and administration, people were left to fend for themselves. Safety on the railway – first class. Safety in the works and offices – not so good. It was only through a lot of good fortune that accidents didn't happen. The philosophy here was that, if it hadn't to do with railways, then you spent as little time on it as possible.

'I concern myself chiefly with relationships between the Company and the Society. One target, straight away, was to improve wages and salaries, which were a major cause of concern and unrest. I believe that at Portmadoc now we've got more of a corporate body and much less a collection of personalities.'

Fortunately for the railway, Allan Garraway and Dick Wollan took to each other at once. They became, and remain,

173

firm friends. Dick Wollan had a natural charm of manner, coupled with an experienced executive's knack of urging matters onwards: his requests that something be done, with the postscript 'LIKE NOW', became famous on the railway. His approach to the future would certainly have found a responsive echo in Spooner. 'You may believe you're here to run a railway. You're not. You're here to run a tourist attraction. If this is going to be viable, it will not be just as a railway. Railway enthusiasts alone are not going to keep you in business. You must ask, who wants a day out? WIs, schools, Rotary clubs, over–60s clubs, local convention centres, special club outings, the holiday camps. The Vale of Ffestiniog is almost unknown in England. So you sell a package – a thumping good day out – with the railway, with Portmeirion, the potteries, the Maritime Museum, the slate caverns, the woollen mills – the whole package. When we get there,' Dick Wollan used to say, 'we stand a good chance of doing for Blaenau Ffestiniog what the railway did for Porthmadog, which they always used to say was "a graveyard with lights".'

For Allan Garraway there was a very happy surprise. For some time, Festiniog Railway 'stalwarts' had been working to obtain some form of official recognition for his efforts on the railway. When Garraway himself heard about it, he was sceptical, feeling 'it was not the sort of thing for which awards were given'. But a letter arrived from the Prime Minister's office. Moyra was 'agog for me to come home and open it'. To Allan Garraway's intense surprise, 'they wanted to know whether I would accept an award if it was agreed'. The upshot was that Allan Garraway received an MBE in the Queen's Birthday Honours List in 1979 – the first such award to anyone in the preserved railway movement.

Allan and Moyra, with Miss Ruth Garraway, went to Buckingham Palace in October – actually on their wedding anniversary. 'It was a beautiful day, and as we came out of the Palace, waiting at the gates was Alan Pegler himself, who walked with us across Green Park. On the day the awards were published he had been up early scanning the newspapers and telling everyone. In the evening, the Board had arranged a party at the Banqueting Room of the Beefeater by the Tower, where at that time Alan Pegler was Master of Ceremonies. He told the whole banquet not only where we had been that morning but that it was our wedding anniversary. He had had a special *gâteau* made for us and our party. All very typical of AFP, who had a marvellously gentlemanly way of enhancing great occasions.'

Chapter 17

'If we'd had all this planning in the early days,' said Chairman Routly, at the Society's Convention at Plas Tan-y-Bwlch in October 1980, 'we'd never have started!' That was true enough, but as everybody present knew and as the Magazine later put it, those were 'happy days when you could unload the turf over the wall and ask afterwards, do your thing and go home without telling anyone – it got us a railway . . . But too many of us remembered how temporary a railway it got and what a dramatic difference advance planning and full-time site organisers made to progress and volunteer enjoyment on the Deviation.'

By October 1980, the prospect of a return to Blaenau bulked so large in everybody's imaginations that, hard as Dick Wollan tried to preach the gospel of marketing, nobody could think of anything except Blaenau. Expectations were running even higher than usual because an earlier return to Blaenau, which had been hoped for in 1978, had been frustrated by a number of factors, not least the delays over the completion of the new tunnel. Now that the Deviation was complete and the railway was running to only just over a mile from its proper destination, Blaenau seemed almost at hand – although nobody was in any doubt that it would require more advance planning, full-time site organising and volunteer effort than ever before.

As early as June 1973, in yet another of those famous Festiniog meetings, Arthur Lambert and Norman Pearce for the Society met Les Smith at the Comet Hotel, Hatfield, Herts, to tell him that the Society wished for greater involvement in the works above Tan-y-Grisiau, assuming that extra volunteer labour could be managed. After this meeting, Arthur Lambert became (for the first time) Project Co-Ordinator for the return to Blaenau. At a Company Board meeting in November 1973,

175

when the budget for 1974 was approved, money was officially allocated for work at the top end of the line for the first time. This was the go-ahead for a programme of work to be followed, and for permanent staff labour to be provided, as available or as needed.

In the winter of 1973/4 and during the following year, there was a new air of expectancy and signs of fresh activity at the top end of the line. Volunteers from the London Area and the East Midlands began work at Glan-y-Pwll engine shed, and lifted track from Stesion Fain (Exchange) which at that time was intended to be the new terminus for the Festiniog in Blaenau. A new Light Railway Order was prepared and sent to the Railway Inspectorate of the Department of the Environment. Discussions began with the River Board over a new design for the Barlwyd Bridge; a temporary repair was made and a tramway ran from Glan-y-Pwll, over the bridge and some way down the line. At Glan-y-Pwll, the roof of the house was repaired, the top three inches of turf and topsoil removed by contractors to prepare for the new yard, and a protective stockade and temporary Terrapin buildings erected. Ron Lester, who was the foreman in charge of permanent way, was appointed supervisor for the Blaenau Project (together with permanent way and fencing work above Dduallt), while Fred Howes was placed in charge of permanent way for the rest of the railway. Contractors began work on stabilising two rock buttresses supporting an embankment above Tan-y-Grisiau. Another Simplex, to work mainly dumping spoil at Dinas, was purchased and overhauled, and arrived at Glan-y-Pwll in August 1974, to be named *Diana* in October (and later to be renamed *The Lady Diana*). The Secretary of State for Wales announced a three-year, £8–million programme to reclaim some 1,400 acres of industrially derelict land in the Principality; included in the current financial year was the intention to remove Glan-y-Don slate tip and spread the spoil on low-lying land (including the future site of Stesion Fain) in the vicinity. There were plans for a road scheme to improve access to Blaenau from the north, for providing land for industry and housing, and in particular for car parking and public open spaces near the future extension of the Festiniog Railway. Clearly, at last, things were moving in Blaenau Ffestiniog, and the railway was going to be fully involved.

Local opinion about all this activity, and the Festiniog's part in it, was as always difficult for an outsider to assess. It would not be impossible to rebuild the railway in the face of local hostility, but it would obviously be very much more

176

difficult. There was, and remains today, a small minority, implacably xenophobic in general and anglophobic in particular, who were quick to take offence, to see slights where none was intended, and who were keen to cast the Festiniog Railway in the role of agent of an alien occupying power. Conversations with railway employees, or with volunteers, would be taken as official Company policy. Casual remarks in Blaenau Ffestiniog public houses led to 'scenes'. The basic stock of much Welsh humour is lavatorial, and exhortatory graffiti such as '*Twll Din Bob Sais*' (though an anatomical impossibility) were no doubt sincerely meant.

Just how sensitive certain local opinion could be, and how quickly a *cause célèbre* could be created, was vividly shown in March 1979 when seven members of the Blaenau Ffestiniog branch of the Welsh Language Society appeared in court, charged with travelling on the Festiniog without paying their fares. For the completion of the Deviation to Tan-y-Grisiau in June 1978, the railway had erected bilingual signs, of which the Welsh version read 'Rheilffordd Festiniog'. When it was pointed out that 'Festiniog' was incorrect the Company replied that 'Festiniog was part of the legal name of the Company. Answering complaints by correspondence, the Company had stressed that its name had been laid down by Act of Parliament and could not be changed without a great deal of trouble and expense. The Society were not impressed by this 'poor excuse' as they called it. Spurred on by the usual green paint daubed over its signs, and by the knowledge that 'Rheilffordd' was not part of the Company's Parliamentary title either, the Company gave way and changed the signs to 'Rheilffordd Ffestiniog'. But some damage to the railway's standing had been done. (The Festiniog Railway Society's Magazine reported the whole incident under the headline: 'Even Writing F*******g Doesn't Look Polite'.)

There is also, to be fair, another small minority which is genuinely in favour of the railway and wholeheartedly on its side, who looked forward to its return and helped in every way they could. But the majority remained neutral, although friendly in principle. They rarely helped the railway actively, but they were most unlikely to hinder it. They would wait and see what happened. It might be good. They hoped it would.

It was at this passive majority that the railway directed its main PR effort. In March 1974, for example, bilingual leaflets were distributed to houses in Tan-y-Grisiau and Glan-y-Pwll, inviting everybody to a meeting in the Library Room in

Blaenau Ffestiniog, where representatives of Company and Society explained what the railway was proposing to do, asking for co-operation, and giving a chance to ask questions. At the end of the meeting, a local Plaid Cymru stalwart got up quite unexpectedly and thanked the platform sincerely for what they had already done and what they were going to do for the people of Blaenau. After which some seventy-eight passengers, including some children along for the ride, were taken by bus down to Porthmadog, for a trip up the line to Dduallt and back to Tan-y-Bwlch, where buses were waiting to take them home again. Everybody seemed to have a good time and wished the railway well.

It was widely believed that the Company intended the railway to return to Blaenau in 1978. This plan was first put forward in a memo, containing a forecast for figures and works necessary, by Robin Scott, then Secretary to the Company, in May 1972 and promulgated at the Society's AGM in April 1973 by Gerry Fiennes, who was then the Company's nominee Director on the Society's Board, and with special responsibility for the Deviation. But this forecast did not last much beyond 1975, the year of the Dduallt Shuttle, which was perhaps the Festiniog's last fling of the pre-recession era.

The 1969 Development of Tourism Act had empowered the Wales Tourist Board to give grants to assist selected projects. The Company were quick to apply for assistance. The Board gave grants for the new crossing loop at Rhiw Goch, for new carriages, extensions to Boston Lodge, for a link building at Harbour station, and a contribution towards the construction of the Deviation above Dduallt, as far as and including the new tunnel.

Having given their grants, the Board obviously wanted to see some results for tourists. A diesel push-pull shuttle from Dduallt up to Gelliwiog began in May 1975. But only some 1,400 passengers could be persuaded to use it. People were reluctant to change trains just for an extra mile. In any case, trains were crowded and many passengers were worried that, having once left their train, they might not be able to get a seat on another. However, the railway had at least done its best to keep faith with the spirit in which the Wales Tourist Board's grants were given.

'Blaenau '78' was still the Company's slogan and battle-cry as late as the autumn of 1976, but by then the outlook both on and for the railway had changed very much for the worse, and not all the problems were within the railway's own hands to solve. The recession was properly under way. That year expenditure for the top end of the line was severely pruned. An order for 100 tonnes of rail (a quarter of the total order) was cancelled.

Problems multiplied on every side. The rock-fall at Pen Craig in November 1975 would clearly require major repair works and a realignment of the track. The matter of Dolrhedyn bridge – who should restore it and for what size of vehicle – was still unresolved. There was a massive earth-fall after very heavy rain at Tunnel South, which blocked access to the tunnel; tunnel spoil could not be removed until the clay and boulders from the slippage had been cleared. Inside the tunnel, the rock was not as stable or as solid as had been thought. The roof of the tunnel was only a few feet below the surface of the hillside (indeed, there had been a strong debate as to whether the tunnel should not be a cutting, and Allan Garraway was not alone in favouring a cutting). Parts of the tunnel had to be lined with concrete using the shot-creting process. At Glan-y-Pwll, the slate tip was at last being cleared, after some hesitation; the owners of Glan-y-Don had insisted they wanted to keep it as a tip and Merioneth Council had actually recommended the clearance be abandoned. When the clearance finally got under way, the route of the contractors' heavy earth-moving machinery passed so close to Glan-y-Pwll depot as virtually to cut it off from the outside world. And, of course, there still remained the vast programme of work necessary, the civil engineering, walling, fencing, bridge-building and track-laying, between Tan-y-Grisiau and Blaenau. Unsurprisingly, 'Blaenau '78' was quietly dropped, while work on the Deviation, and particularly the tunnel, absorbed more and more of the railway's full-time and volunteer labour and resources.

But while the Festiniog Railway grappled with its problems and, temporarily, put Blaenau from the forefront of its thoughts, others were coming to realise, just as the Central Electricity Generating Board had done during the latter stages of the Great Law Case, that the railway was quite serious in its intentions and a return to Blaenau was inevitable, if not sooner, then later. The railway, whose PR was generally excellent, had made a point of running special trains so that people who might be able to help the railway could see what was happening. In July 1973 a train took a large number of guests, including elected representatives of various councils, large and small, up on to the Deviation as far as Barn Cutting. In September 1974 another train took permanent staff members of newly reorganised local government bodies, the Wales Tourist Board, the CEGB and the two tourist quarries, the Llechwedd and the Oakeley, up to Gwelliog. The special trains to launch 'The Little Wonder' in May 1975, and for Princess Margaret in July, both carried local VIPs and dignitaries and, of course, the media.

These and other promotional efforts, and constant lobbying, finally had its effect upon British Rail, for whom the siting of the Festiniog's new terminus in Blaenau was clearly of importance, although British Rail themselves took some time to appreciate it. As late as the spring of 1980 the Society's Magazine editorial said that BR 'have only just woken up to the fact that these nutters in the hills are not only serious about sticking a mini New York Grand Central on the end of a branch that should have been laid to a decent rest years ago, they've been and gone and got a big pile of Government money to prove it. Vague layout agreements with the FR conducted in a spirit of yes-maybe-one-day have been snatched back and are being gone over with a different eye.'

Of the Festiniog's three original stations in Blaenau Ffestiniog, Duffws was in the centre of the town but it was no longer feasible as a terminus: the sidings were car parks, the station building was (and still is) public toilets, and the short access tunnel under High Street, though still there well into the 1970s, was to vanish in road-works. The site of the central station, the old exchange between the Festiniog and the Great Western Railway, seemed too restricted. By far the best site, it seemed to the railway, was Stesion Fain, on the opposite side of the track from the old FR/LNWR Exchange station. The seven-acre site was big enough, and if necessary the station complex could extend around the corner and face the A496. The railway had first refusal to purchase the land from the Council, including the part compulsorily purchased for road building by the CEGB in 1956, which the Board was now prepared to sell to the railway (not directly, but through the Council as intermediaries). Glan-y-Don spoil had been spread on the site and levelled, and the railway had even had some say in the way the work was done, so that the contours of the slate waste safeguarded the formation of what would be the bottom of a Dinas branch, if it were ever to be reactivated. It was a prominent site, highly visible from the main road and from the main BR line. There would be the usual hurdles – committee meetings, planning permissions, Light Railway Orders – but these could be surmounted. On every count, therefore, Stesion

Fain was the obvious solution, and in 1975 *Princess* was placed on a plinth there, as a sign of things to come.

But, as some of the more perceptive citizens of Blaenau realised, Stesion Fain was on the outskirts of the town. It would be of commercial advantage to Blaenau if the Tren Bach could run into its centre. Thus, ironically, townspeople who had once regarded the railway and its new owners with suspicion and hostility were now anxious to welcome them back into the town. Prodded by local traders, Merioneth District Council asked if the Festiniog Railway could run through to the old Central FR/GWR exchange area.

On the face of it, this meant that the Festiniog would then have *two* stations, Central (FR/GWR) and Exchange (FR/LNWR), within half a mile of each other, which would increase operating difficulties without increasing traffic revenue. The suggestion was then made that BR also move their station to a joint site (BR/FR) in the area of the old Central station. This idea had much local support. Merioneth District Council began a survey and feasibility study towards the end of 1976. The Welsh Development Agency indicated they would make a one hundred per cent grant for land clearance. Gwynedd County Council undertook to carry out main road diversion schemes.

In October 1977, the grandly named Planning, Highways and Transportation Committee of Gwynedd County Council approved a scheme (to cost £340,000) to provide a new terminus in Blaenau Ffestiniog for British Rail and for the Festiniog Railway. Using (unacknowledged) plans and ground work prepared by his brother bureaucrats on Merioneth District Council (whereat there was great indignation in Cyngor Dosbarth Meirionnydd) the County Planning Officer described the scheme to realign North Western Road; build a new bridge across both railways; realign British Rail track and lay a new Festiniog track; build a new Central station and a footbridge across to Isallt where the booking and information offices would be; develop what remained of the old GWR station site for a hundred parking spaces; reclaim land above Diffwys yard for more car parks; and landscape the area between the new Central station and the new primary school. There was also an option, if funds were available (they were) to remove the old High Street bridge over the railway.

This was, in effect, the scheme as it was eventually carried out, although the cost was nearer £1 million than £340,000. One councillor spoke of 'our dream for a long time to see something like this happening to Blaenau Ffestiniog'. The county council

181

said they were selecting 'one town for special treatment'. As for the cost, the Welsh Development Agency would pay for land reclamation, and additional funds would be sought from the EEC Regional Development Fund, the Development Board for Rural Wales, the Welsh Development Agency (again), the Welsh Office, and the Wales Tourist Board. A target date for opening was set: Easter 1980, which, in local government terms, was breakneck speed and in fact proved to be wildly optimistic.

Needless to say, the new station was not ready by Easter 1980, but the contractors, Lilley Constructions Ltd, were on the site in March of that year, to find a prevailing atmosphere of haste unusual in public works. Many details had not been settled because of financial pressures to get the project started, but the contractors were able at least to start clearance and excavation.

The feeling that the whole project was being hurried along unduly quickly surfaced at the Society's AGM in April 1980. Mr Ifor Richards, the senior consultant for Robinson, Jones Partnership, the consultant engineers engaged by Gwynedd County Council, gave Society members a presentation of the plans for Central station. It had started, he said, as a 'pipe dream' but 'it was a viable scheme and not a waste of public money'. The money involved for civil engineering work was around £700,000 divided between the North Western Road end and the old Great Western site. With other plans for the area, in all some £1.3 million would be spent by April 1981. The 'financing was complicated', with contributions from many sources and, hopefully, from EEC funds.

For the Society members, this was all heady talk – of money in 'telephone numbers' for a railway which had once been bought, lock, stock and barrel and with difficulty and much argument for some £3,000. Dr Peter Jarvis, a persistent questioner at AGMs, said he had the impression that the Company and the Society were being hurried. The last extension was not finished yet, and there was a great deal of tidying up work to be done on the Deviation. He said the whole scheme ought to be looked at carefully before it was started (the scheme had actually started at that time).

Chairman Routly replied that there was no commitment to time. It had been agreed that the Festiniog could be in Blaenau by May 1981, but the aim was really to be there as soon as possible. Later, Chairman Routly was pressed more closely by Mr Evans, who reminded Routly that at the AGM three years before he, Routly, had said that when the railway reached Tan-y-Grisiau there would be a period of consolidation, as there had been at Dduallt. The railway had been at Dduallt for ten years: why then was the railway already pushing ahead? Mr Evans asked how much the scheme was costing the railway and how much of the bank loan taken to get to Tan-y-Grisiau was still outstanding?

Chairman Routly did not answer the first question, as to cost, directly, but said that the timing was not of the Festiniog's making and was in other hands. The bank overdraft varied seasonably between £100,000 and £300,000, with an average of £160,000. The Company was being operated to take the maximum advantage of tax allowances and no tax would be payable on profits for some years ahead.

The timing was certainly not in the railway's hands any longer. Large sums of public money and, much more important, the reputations of politicians and bureaucrats, both local and national, were now at stake. There was a favourable tide running and Chairman Routly was quite right to point out to the AGM that if the railway appeared at all reluctant, if it indicated it was not in any position to go ahead, then the whole scheme might be lost. The scheme would put some strain on resources, he said, but he was sure it was everybody's wish to go ahead.

It certainly was not *everybody*'s wish to go ahead. There were not a few who thought that there should now be a period of digestion and consolidation. The railway was also under pressure from the CEGB to 'clean up' the line, especially in landscaping, between the top end of the tunnel and Tan-y-Grisiau. But the railway was under even greater pressure from local councils to complete the final stretch into Blaenau and start running trains on it as soon as possible, and therefore Chairman Routly's point, that the railway should press on, was well taken, especially as the CEGB took a more lenient view over the 'cleaning up'.

As Chief Executive, Dick Wollan began to prepare an appreciation of the task ahead, taking past information from earlier reports, calling for fresh information from heads of departments, and costing out the work which would be required to restore the existing track-bed between Tan-y-Grisiau and Stesion Fain for traffic. After paying for the tunnel, and the power station end of the Deviation, labour costs would have to be kept to a minimum. Clearly, much depended upon the volunteers, who would be called upon for one more supreme effort, perhaps the greatest since 1954. In one sense, it would be a return to the early days: volunteers had shown that they much preferred the challenge of pioneering. It was always more fun to build a new line, or to restore a derelict one, than merely to go on maintaining an existing line which was already in good working order. Blaenau would be the last great challenge.

As the final act of the planning stage, a 'task force' of permanent staff and volunteers walked the length of the last mile to see for themselves exactly what work need or need not be done to accomplish a return to Blaenau. A programme was prepared for a resumption of services to the centre of Blaenau Ffestiniog at Easter 1982, to coincide with the 150th anniversary of the original Act of Parliament of May 1832.

Easter 1982 was less than two years ahead, so 'Project Blaenau' as the Company designated it, would have to be closely and skilfully organised. As a first move, Adrian Shooter, a professional railwayman with BR and then Managing Director of the Festiniog Railway Society, Colin James, a professional surveyor who was to be Project Engineer, and Dick Wollan, forming a 'Communication and Action Panel', met at Dick's house to discuss organisation. Colin James made out an organisational chart which, after some amending by heads of departments, became the broad plan of action.

Basically, the work was to be broken down into a series of mini-projects, each to be controlled by a project leader, the projects varying greatly in size, and priority from a medium size, medium priority project like mending a section of boundary wall, to a large size, high priority like rebuilding Barlwyd bridge. (This system was really a return to the early psychology of volunteering on the railway, when tasks were deliberately kept to a size where a small group, or even an individual, could identify with them.) Adrian Shooter himself had had success with it as a founder member of the Milton Keynes Group and earlier of the North Staffs Group. 'There was a tremendous amount of wringing of hands over the awful lot of things to do and no wherewithal to do them,' he said. 'We thought if we could package up those things that wanted doing, groups or individuals could take them on.'

In June 1980 Adrian Shooter wrote to all 600 who regularly received Group Information Memoranda (GIMs: a quarterly bulletin of news and gossip from the line, edited separately from the magazine, and circulated to the 'hard core' of volunteer groups and others with a closer interest than usual in the railway) inviting them to a meeting at the Royal Hotel, Crewe,

184

on 19 July, to explain the task and to 'sell' the idea of mini-projects. Some sixty attended, a third of them 'not well-known to the railway', and another fifty wrote to excuse themselves from the meeting, but said they had 'got the message' and would visit the line more often over the next two years.

Dick Wollan addressed the meeting to explain the 'Project Approach', that it was designed to give people a greater sense of ownership and identity with their work on the railway, to link contribution and achievement more closely, and above all to make sure everybody knew '*what* had to be done, *how* and *when* it had to be done, *who* was going to do it, *what* resources were required, and *how*, *when* and by *whom* were those resources to be provided'.

The size of the task ahead was formidable enough to make the most eager volunteers pensive. Put briefly, four footbridges had to be reconstructed; Barlwyd bridge had to be reconstructed and Groby bridge laid with decking for access; two pedestrian underpasses had to be rebuilt, and one filled in and sealed off; three major culverts, of which two were known to be in poor condition, had to be rebuilt, and several other culverts had to be repaired; 760 yards of surface drains had to be laid. On the track itself, 220 yards of wall or rockface, 585 yards of retaining wall, 2,270 yards of boundary wall and fencing, and 835 yards of ballast wall had to be built or rebuilt or repaired or cemented or grouted to a greater or smaller extent. On the permanent way, two hundred yards of track-bed had to be cleaned and graded, 640 yards of single and 200 yards of double new track had to be laid, and all 1830 yards of track had to be ballasted, levelled and aligned. Also, a level crossing had to be constructed at Glan-y-Pwll. For all this it was estimated that, in the twenty-two months remaining, 6,570 volunteer working days would be needed, an average of 70 per week, every week; this meant 25 people every weekend, with a weekday party of at least four. Further, at Blaenau Central itself, the formation would be provided, and the extra track paid for, but the track had still to be laid, with points and a run-round loop, a water-tank erected, and the platform finished. At Glan-y-Pwll, a great deal of work remained to be done on the depot, and the security stockade needed replacing (where it had been removed for the Glan-y-Don earth moving machinery access).

As Dick Wollan explained, there were some 'political' changes. He himself would be in charge of all works as far up as Stesion Fain; Allan Garraway, the General Manager, would look after the railway's involvement in the Blaenau Central scheme.

185

Colin James, Project Engineer, would be aided by Brian Hollingsworth, the Company's Civil Engineering Consultant, by Andy Savage, who was a civil engineer with British Rail, and Keith Tyler, as footbridge designer. The Civil Engineering Group was reshuffled to deal with the extra work: a new full-time Site Agent, David (Fluff) Fuller was appointed; the specialist post of Plant Engineer was created for Andy Putnam, with Howard Bowcott as sub-ganger. Arthur Lambert was given, for the second time, the job of Project Co-ordinator (although his original appointment had never really lapsed).

Amidst the welter of problems facing the railway, two at least were resolved: Dolrhedyn bridge was rebuilt, and the rock-fall at Penlan repaired. Over the years, the long-running saga of Dolrhedyn had become a journey through bureaucracy, like an anecdote by Kafka. The bridge had been taken down in 1957 by McAlpines, who undertook to replace it when the pumped storage scheme was completed. Some time later, Blaenau Ffestiniog Urban District Council asked for permission to remove one abutment. This was allowed, on condition the Council paid for any extra costs involved in replacing the bridge. In the event, the road gradient was altered and the formation widened so that it became impossible to relay the original girders.

Local government bureaucrats, who had never dreamed the bridge would ever be required again for railway purposes, attempted to repudiate their authorities' responsibilities when they were called upon to make good the bridge and the right of way. After much argument, and meetings with Merioneth County Council, Les Smith was able to produce copies of all the relevant correspondence which, fortunately, his secretary had kept. As a result, the Council eventually agreed that it was their responsibility to replace the bridge.

Les Smith had also suggested that, because there was a lack of height under the bridge, the CEGB road up to Stwlan be made a public highway, with a new bridge across the river to give access to Cwmorthin and Dolrhedyn for fire engines, refuse vehicles and ambulances. This was done although, in the event, there was enough headroom under the bridge to allow a small van to pass. In fact the new deck was well proud of the old formation and the Council had to add retaining and coping walling on both sides of the bridge to take the additional fill of ballast.

At Penlan, where ten tons of rock had fallen against the kitchen of a house below, loose rock was barred down and,

186

inevitably, the situation was found to be worse than expected from previous surveys. Although the railway's shelf was not directly affected, rock strata over the whole area had to be stabilised before trains could run. Sixty feet of scaffolding was erected, from which drilling and rock-bolting could be carried out. A concrete underpinning, placed there five years earlier, was itself rock-bolted, more concrete under-pinning was added, and gaps in the rock filled with concrete. During the reconstruction, the cottage below was demolished.

Unsurprisingly, Project Blaenau was almost the sole topic at the next Convention held at Plas Tan-y-Bwlch in October 1980. It was an excellent chance to get the Project's message over to another and wider audience. Dick Wollan defined the objects once again: to run trains to Blaenau Ffestiniog in May 1982; to operate an hourly train service, with trains crossing at Rhiw Goch and Dduallt; and to use the minimum of expenditure and resources to achieve these objects.

On the question of expenditure, it had always been Dick Wollan's intention not to use any of the Company's resources at all. With a blackboard and an air of 'My next trick is impossible', he explained to a slightly bemused Convention how local, national and international money could be conjured up. There would in the end still be a shortfall of some £200,000 but Dick Wollan's listeners were left with the feeling that the Society would somehow find this in its trouser turn-ups.

Other speakers followed. Arthur Lambert reminded the Convention how drastically times had changed since 1955. There was now a Health and Safety at Work Act. There were Company rules and regulations. Most important of all, there were *neighbours*: the Tan-y-Grisiau to Glan-y-Pwll section ran through 'a very *very* Welsh district', whose inhabitants were mostly indifferent to the railway but could easily be upset. Arthur Lambert stressed the need for a good trackside manner: do not throw rubbish over walls, or trespass on railside property, do not divert water into somebody's back yard, or start minor avalanches, or build a wall over a gap somebody was obviously using without telling that somebody first. Above all, watch what you say to the locals' . . . because you are strange and the FR is strange and you are part of it, your personal opinions will be taken to represent the Festiniog's official position'.

Bob MacGregor spoke of the signals and telegraphs position and projects, for a department which under Norman Pearce and now under him had always been unobtrusively

187

successful. The extension to Blaenau was 'planned not with a minimum of gimmicks, but no gimmicks at *all*'. This meant a 'Lottie Edwards' style gate crossing at Glan-y-Pwll, 'one engine in steam' section all the way up from Dduallt, the Tan-y-Grisiau loop being padlocked out of use, and a single telephone line to an automatic exchange already installed at Glan-y-Pwll.

Allan Garraway explained the political 'divide': Dick Wollan responsible below Glan-y-Pwll, himself above. Blaenau Central was on a fixed budget. There had already been unexpected expenses. The railway would not now get its second track to Glan-y-Pwll, and the old Duffws station building was to stay where it was, in the car park.

Paul Dukes described some of the works needed at the top end: steel roof trusses from the old Britannia Foundry at Porthmadog to cover the roofless locomotive shed at Glan-y-Pwll, an ex-Post Office 'Polecat' post-hole borer to be rail-mounted, and some small diesel locos exhausted from their exertions on the Deviation to be overhauled. What was really needed, Paul Dukes said, was somebody to find some welders who would like a holiday in North Wales and, having got them there, arrange for the holiday to be postponed!

Having discussed Project Blaenau, having planned it and organised it and costed it and got grants for it and thought it and dreamed it, it now only remained to do it. There were eventually about seventy 'mini-projects'. The first Group Project to get under way was by Dick Smith and the Sheffield and District Group, who took on the job of clearing and lining a culvert with eighteen-inch pipe. Andy Savage formed a group to redesign and rebuild Barlwyd bridge, with the help of an EEC grant. Lancashire and Cheshire Group, and the Midland Group, each took on the rebuilding of a footbridge. Leicester took on a culvert, drainage and railing jobs, Milton Keynes walling, with Dr Peter Jarvis taking on an individual length of wall himself, while Manpower Services Commission labour also did walling between Barlwyd terrace and Groby sidings, and Scouts and individual volunteers cleared up debris and rebuilt walls below Penlan.

The Midland Group went further, making efforts to recruit new pairs of hands. They spent £250 on a series of public meetings to explain and promote 'Project Blaenau'. In February and March 1981, they mounted displays with the joint themes of 'Slates to the Sea' and 'Project Blaenau' in the foyer of Aston University, Birmingham, and in the Art Gallery, Wednesbury. At the time, the group were somewhat disappointed by their efforts. But their bread returned to them after many days. A year later they realised their £250 had been repaid in kind many times over, and some of the new volunteers recruited were (and still are) regular workers on the railway. As Rod Weaver, their Vice Chairman, says 'you *can* market involvement, and to survive you must'.

The work went on in the spring of 1981 despite atrocious weather. In February the Sheffield and District's plans to concrete an underpass at Fron Wen were snowed off and the volunteers spent their working day digging drainage channels at Groby in a blizzard. In March, Lancashire and Cheshire, Dee and Mersey, London Area and White Rose Groups joined forces for a mammoth track-laying evolution, to lay seventy-five pound flat-bottomed rail on jarrah sleepers to join the existing sixty-pound rail track by the end of May. Walling went on steadily, the regular volunteers being joined by occasional visitors to the line, augmented by Manpower Services Commission employees, pupils of Evesham High School and the Army Cadet Force.

By September 1981, nearly all the under-track work above Tan-y-Grisiau had been completed. The footbridges had been partly demolished and were being rebuilt as sturdy, well-designed, and pleasing structures which blended admirably with their surroundings. Barlwyd bridge was finished. By November, apart from the rails still under Glan-y-Pwll crossing, the only remnant of the 'old' Festiniog's railway furniture was the 'down' signal post for the level crossing at Pont Bryn Twrog.

Heavy snow fell in December and four separate working weekend parties at the top end of the line were lost just before Christmas. However, track work above Dolrhedyn bridge was finished, and on 11 December *Blanche*, with Phil Girdlestone driving and fireman Barlow, took a works train up as far as Glan-y-Pwll. This was the first steam train to go beyond Cwmorthin Siding since 1946: an historic occasion.

December 1981 and January 1982 had some of the coldest and wettest weather in Blaenau Ffestiniog for many years. A weekend of constant driving rain would be followed by four days of just workable weather until the Friday, when there would be a blizzard and a biting east wind. However the Dee and Mersey Group, led by Jim Parrish, arrived for their usual January working week. They did not beat the *Guiness Book of Record*'s tally of fifty-eight lengths of rail laid in a week, which dated from 1977, but thirty-six lengths were laid in three days, an amazing achievement in the conditions. Heavy snow blocked many North Wales roads, but a Lancashire and Cheshire group working party, led by Neil Clayton, arrived safely on a Saturday morning having driven round by Bangor and Caernarvon. By the third week in January the platform road, top points and headshunt were down and the loop was nearly completed at Blaenau Central. There was now track all the way from buffer stops at Porthmadog to the (future) buffer stops at Blaenau Central – another historic landmark.

Yet another historic date in a sequence of them was 22 March 1982, when the buffer stop for the headshunt at Blaenau Ffestiniog was delivered and *Blanche*, with a short train of one wagon and one van, with John Routly, Les Smith and members of the Civil Engineering Groups and Permanent Way staff, approached the new Central station – the first steam locomotive to do so. By accident, design or coincidence, that day was also the opening of BR's new station and *Blanche* came up the gradient with the first BR train. The BR driver, though apparently not warned beforehand, took in the situation at once, slowed to match *Blanche*'s speed and both trains arrived together – as one watcher Eileen Bradbury said, 'it was one of the most moving moments of my life. None of us could speak.'

Major Peter Olver, Royal Engineers, the Railway Inspecting Officer for the Department of the Environment, made his inspection of the top end on 17 May 1982. By the following Saturday, the Permanent Way department had finished all major works to re-establish train services to Blaenau Ffestiniog, but Fred Howes still wanted to carry out a dynamic clearance test on the new extension. Clearances were very tight up there and a Welsh Highland coach, especially with its projecting footboards, would be the severest test. Thus the idea of 'Freddie's Fantastic Rail Tour' was born.

Freddie's Fantastic Rail Tour was not a passenger train, but it was the first with passenger coach stock into Blaenau Ffestiniog. It was a 'pirate' trip (indeed, Fred Howes was given and wore a pirate's cocked hat, with skull and crossed pick and shovel) which left Porthmadog for Blaenau at 8.00 a.m. on the 22nd with *Moelwyn*, an ex-Welsh Highland Railway coach, and Nos 1 and 2 vans, full of volunteers and permanent way department staff. Arrival at Blaenau was something of an anti-climax. 'We all felt we'd got to Blaenau on March 22nd, when BR got there,' said Fred. 'Everything that followed was slightly let down. But the thing uppermost in a lot of people's minds was that we'd pipped the rest of the outfit to the post. We'd built the bloody thing and it was right we should have the first go. The mucky-handed brigade very seldom get the credit they deserve.' However, Fred had an added bonus of not one but three working parties for the day – to work on odd jobs, ballasting, junk clearance and general clearing up, before going back to Minffordd in one of the longest permanent way trains ever run: *Moelwyn* and the Fantastic Rail Tour, tool wagons, junk wagons, the Baby Planet loco, the signals and telegraphs train and various odds and ends.

The first proper passenger train to Blaenau Central ran on Sunday evening, 23 May 1982, exactly one hundred and fifty years to the day after the date of the original Act of Parliament. It was officially described as a 'training run'. The locomotive was *Linda*, the driver most appropriately Allan Garraway, with Keith Catchpole and David Yates also on the footplate, and the guard was Alan Heywood. The train had six coaches and the passengers included almost the whole of the permanent staff and a large number of volunteers.

Previously the Company had sent out invitations, couched in the same form of language as Charles Spooner had used on the occasion of the 'Opening of the Line for Traffic by Steam' on 23 October 1863: 'SIR, THE FESTINIOG RAILWAY COMPANY propose restoring their Steam Train Service to BLAENAU FESTINIOG on Tuesday, the 25th May and intend starting a Train from PORTHMADOG at ten minutes after ten on the morning of that day to the New Station.'

The first guests for the VIP special arrived at Harbour station early on Tuesday morning and the air of excitement began to build up. The public address system announced a train to Blaenau Ffestiniog for the first time. Long before departure, the platform was thronged with people who had been connected with the railway in some way over the last thirty years, and almost every face was familiar, or half-familiar, for one reason or another. The traffic staff wore carnations in their button-holes. The BBC's 'Nationwide' interviewed the train crew; the driver was Evan Davies, the fireman Sean McMahone, the guards were Sean Britton and Alan Tibbett, the buffet car crew were Peter Dennis, David Embery, Mandy Evans, Laurie James and Paul Thomson. Colin James obtained the autograph of every person on the train, the autograph book to be placed in the museum. For historical record, the train was made up of car Nos 16, 15, 20, 18, 26, 104, 110, 118, 116, 103 ('Charles Spooner' Buffet Car), 120, and 101 (Observation Car). The first four cars dated from the 1870s, 104 from 1964, the next

191

three from the 1970s. 'Charles Spooner' from 1968, 120 from 1980, and the Observation Car from 1970.

The locomotive was the new *Earl of Merioneth*, with the headboard 'Blaenau Ffestiniog 1832–1982'. With the whistle wide open, the *Earl* pulled out of Porthmadog at 10.15. Photographers were waiting all across the Cob, and indeed most of the way up to Blaenau. At Minffordd, strengthening vehicles were added, and after a slightly extended delay the train was off up the hillside, with familiar landmarks on every side. It passed through Tan-y-Bwlch non-stop, halted at Dduallt to cross the 'down' service train (the last train to have Tan-y-Grisiau as its terminus), and then moved onwards, non-stop, to Blaenau.

For those at the top, waiting on the platform or on the bridges to greet the train and some to join it as VIPs for its second special trip back down the mountain again, it was typical volunteering weather: a bitterly cold day, with a fierce wind blowing up the valley. But the whooping of that whistle, echoing back off the hillside as the train approached Glan-y-Pwll, was one of the most thrilling sounds of a lifetime. The feelings of those on board are best described by Dan Wilson, an insider on that day and in more ways than one, for the Magazine:

> The train slowed at Tanygrisiau, but did not stop. As the locomotive hit the gradient of the old line and opened up, drawing us smoothly and even faster along that precipitous ledge where for so many years we have walked, day-dreamed, planned and finally worked, there were unashamed tears in many of the coaches. This was the first passenger train to Blaenau Ffestiniog since 1939 – and, by golly, didn't Blaenau do us proud! Folk who by no caprice could be described as train spotter material were lining the route, leaning from their windows, standing at their doors and giving us a warm and genuine welcome. Metcalfe's, the food machinery factory the Railway skirts just before Glanypwll yard, had apparently knocked off spontaneously to come out and say hello.
>
> And the new station! As *Earl of Merioneth* swung through the old site of 'Stesion Fain' and approached the final sharp 1 in 60 up into the terminus Evan Davies opened her out again and we burst through the Benar Road bridge to see a station entirely covered by humanity. What a noise! It was a Royal arrival minus the decorum and security . . .
>
> Everyone congratulated everyone else. Not only was there almost everyone from the early Festiniog revival days

who could still stand upright, there were a lot of people we wouldn't have minded meeting a lot earlier – many ex-quarrymen who remembered the bards and card-sharpers sitting on the 'donkey' (the vacuum brake cylinder in the quarrymen's coaches, which doubled as a central seat), a great-great-great-grandson of James Spooner, at least two guards from 'Old Company' days and the Duffws booking clerk from before 1914, if you can believe it. We had no fear of any criticism from any of these folk, for the trains looked their absolute best, the ride felt like one welded length of rail all the way from Tanygrisiau and the organisation of the whole event was pin-perfect.

The organisation needed to be pin-perfect; after drinks for VIPs in the Queens Hotel, and the reading of a telegram of good wishes and congratulations from the Prince of Wales, there were those VIPs to be taken down, and other VIPs to be brought back up; trains for medal-holders, who had paid for the right to travel on the first day to Blaenau; and a regular service, though not quite a full one, for paying passengers to Blaenau. Rain fell heavily later in the day, especially at the top end, but nobody bothered. Besides *Earl of Merioneth*, *Merddin Emrys*, *Blanche*, *Linda*, *Prince* and *Upnor Castle* all worked trains that day. *Prince* ran two trips with seven coaches in heavy rain – a sure sign of how hard and well Boston Lodge had worked; at one time, only four coaches and a slight shower of rain would have been enough to defeat *Prince*.

May 1982 was, of course, the month when services were resumed to Blaenau. The official opening of Blaenau Central was carried out by the Rt Hon. George Thomas, Speaker of the House of Commons, in a ceremony well concealed from Society members on 30 April 1983. The head-board read 'Trefn Trefn! Order Order!' and the voice which quelled the most unruly Members spoke eloquently of Wales and the railway. And that, after thirty years, was that.

It was left to Dick Wollan to compute the cost over the years:

	Expenditure in material, wages, salaries, contractors	Estimated value of volunteers contributions
1954–1965 To Dduallt	£150,000	£250,000
1965–1979 Deviation to Tan-y-Grisiau	£800,000	£925,000

	Expenditure in material, wages, salaries, contractors	Estimated value of volunteers contributions
1980–1982 Project Blaenau inc. FR part of Central Station	£550,000	£275,000
	£1,500,000	£1,450,000

1950s and 60s figures not adjusted for inflation

The £1,500,000 expenditure can be broken down into components, including grants, of which Chairman Routly wrote on 8 December 1981: 'The last and most important one to come through without which we actually could not complete the line next year was signed by Nicholas Edwards, Secretary of State, yesterday – that brings the total up to £705,000.' Wollan's figures for the grants content of the £1,500,000 spent by the Company differ, but both give some perception of the scale of grants received.

Of the £1,500,000 spent by the Company to restore the line to Blaenau Ffestiniog:

Wales Tourist Board	£217,500	(14½%)
Development Board for Rural Wales	£97,500	(6½%)
Manpower Services Commission	£127,500	(8½%)
European Regional Development Fund	£142,500	(9½%)
Festiniog Railway Co. (Inc. loans, overdraft, compensation, revenue)	£915,000	(61%)

Thus it seems reasonable to suppose that the thirty-year return to Blaenau cost £3 million, give or take the odd penny, of which nearly £2½ million, or over eighty per cent, was found by the Company and (in cash and kind) by the Society.

Chapter 18

'We've got to Blaenau,' said the Group Information Memorandum editorial in November 1982. 'Well done everybody. Self administer several pats on the back for tireless, sustained, damned hard work . . .But what next?'

That question hung, like a cloud of anti-climax, over the whole railway. The return to Blaenau had been a tremendous achievement, of which any organisation in the world could be proud. Everyone had looked forward to Blaenau for so long and had worked so hard to reach it that, when the fact was accomplished and the trains were running to and fro and the first euphoria had evaporated, there was a pause to consider the future.

There was, firstly, the fear that all the volunteers would down tools now that (as they thought) the end had been reached. In fact, there was a noticeable slackening of effort; but too many volunteers enjoyed working on the railway too much to stop, whether or not Blaenau had been reached. There was, however, a feeling amongst some of the more senior members of the Society that their generation's aim had been achieved and it was now time to hand over the torch to younger generations who would doubtless have their own dreams and objectives.

Secondly, the railway had now to grapple with the extra problems their success had brought. The line to Blaenau was safe for passenger traffic, but had no frills whatsoever and nothing to spare. It was calculated that there was at least ten more years' work, using all the volunteer effort presently available, to bring the top end of the line to an acceptable standard of appearance and amenity. Meanwhile, the railway had to be operated with the extra mileage, which meant more track to be maintained and more wear and tear, on stock and staff.

It so happened that 1983, the first year after Blaenau, was exceptionally difficult, even by the financial standards of the Festiniog Railway. Grant money had, of course, stopped when the various grant projects were finished. The railway was more or less back in its familiar stance of having to generate revenue through traffic and its other commercial undertakings to service its bank loan and to continue in operation. It was a long hot summer and traffic dwindled alarmingly. By mid-June the figures were down by some twenty per cent and emergency action was needed. It was decided to give free travel for one child travelling with a paying adult. The concession was actually put into effect on the line only a week after the decision was taken. It was, in a sense, mortgaging the future to pay for present necessity, but it worked: it generated an increase in traffic which produced some £30,000 additional income.

There were 330,000 passenger journeys in 1983, which was three per cent down on 1982, but marginally up on 1981, so the year ended better than anybody could have hoped at one time. But the railway made a trading loss for the year and there were redundancies at the end of the season. Ironically, there had been fifty-nine paid staff, the highest number ever, in October 1982 (albeit for that month only), but a year later there were eight redundancies: the entire Building Section of three men; one from the Electrical Department; one each from Catering and Administration; the Supervisor of The Little Wonder cafeteria; and the Boston Lodge Works tea boy. The chatter in Vale of Ffestiniog pubs about the money the Tren Bach was coining stopped suddenly, at least for the time being. Eight people were a large number to lose from a small business concern. A cold wind seemed to blow along the platform at Harbour station.

Dick Wollan left at the end of September 1983. He knew, indeed he suggested to the Company Board, that the railway did not need a Chief Executive *and* a General Manager. Dick Wollan left to the regret of many of the permanent staff, who admitted that they had learned a great deal from him. He had drastically overhauled the railway's administrative structure, which in some ways had survived unchanged from the 1930s (some would even say the 1830s) and his good manners and business acumen had helped the railway through a tricky period. Dick Wollan's place in Festiniog lore was secure.

At the beginning of August 1983 Allan Garraway was replaced as General Manager. His departure from day-to-day involvement with the running of the railway, to become a part-time consultant to the Company, was carried out with little fuss or fanfair, considering the pivotal part he had played in the Festiniog's progress over the years. The fact was that the railway had changed from the one he had loved. Some vital ingredient of enjoyment had been lost and he had recently tended to become, as Bertrand Russell said of himself in his own obituary, as isolated as John Milton after the Restoration.

Allan and Moyra had spent holidays at Boat of Garten, in Inverness-shire, and had fallen under the spell of its scenery. They had plans to build a retirement bungalow there and Allan had become closely involved with the Strathspey, a standard-gauge section of the old Highland Railway running for five miles from Aviemore down the whisky-distilling Spey Valley. Allan is still chairman of the Association of Minor Railways, an organisation dating from before the war, which he helped to revive to provide a forum for managers of operating railways. As he says: 'For about twenty-five years the Festiniog was my whole life. Bit by bit its attractions slowly diminished, and with it many dreams and aspirations. Another railway has now won its way into my heart for my time and effort. The wheel has turned full circle, and I am back with standard-gauge steam in conditions reminiscent of the early days of Boston Lodge, in scenery even more beautiful.'

But the Festiniog is an ungrateful mistress. The December 1984 'Directory of Company and Society Officials', both paid and honorary, runs to twenty-one pages and lists more than 250 names – of chairmen, and trustees, and secretaries, and treasurers, and auditors, managers of several kinds, consultants and advisers, lecturers, waste oil co-ordinators, presidents and vice-presidents, hostel wardens, liaisons officers, archivists, lecturers, sales retailers, group travel refund representatives, newsletter editors, publicity officers and working party organ-isers, with committees of all shapes and sizes all over the United Kingdom, but not, not even on the bottom line of the back page, not even as the latest afterthought of a footnote, the name of Allan Garraway as part-time consultant to the Com-pany. A year after he was replaced, and thirty years after he first came to the Festiniog, it is, so far as the railway's official directory is concerned, just as though Allan Garraway never existed.

Allan Garraway's replacement was virtually unknown on the railway. His appointment represented a change of style of management. His name was David Pollock, and he had just resigned as managing director of Westinghouse Brake and Signal Company, a £195–million business employing 3,500 people. In fact, there were ninety applicants for the post of General Manager and Pollock, known on the line as 'Papa Doc', had to beat off considerable competition. He had visited the railway as a child, but not as an enthusiast – he was not, in fact, a railway enthusiast by any definition, although his work with Westinghouse had brought him into contact with railways and railwaymen all over the world.

David Pollock's brief, according to Chairman Routly, was 'to improve marketing and correct the overswing of the pendulum which has gone a bit too far in bureaucratising a small business'. David Pollock had overhauled Westinghouse so that within seven years sales and profits had trebled to the point where, ironically, his success prompted a successful takeover bid by Hawker Siddeley in 1981. Unhappy with the new structure of his firm, bored by the prospect of retirement, and feeling vulnerable at a time when there was a glut of out-of-work executives on the market, David Pollock welcomed what he saw as the challenge of the Festiniog. One main theme of his management policy was 'to make the complementary businesses, the shop, the travel agency, all pay, although traffic overshadows everything'. He discovered that 'Boston Lodge had grown around personalities, and had no supervisory control. There was no clear policy for signalling. The museum was doing practically nothing. In the winter months the Little Wonder was serving only the staff'.

As a man with a nautical background, whose great-grandfather owned and skippered a tea-clipper and who is himself owner of a sixteen-ton ketch, David Pollock talks of 'running a tight ship', of 'eking the last ounce of efficiency out of everything'. 'It may not be quite as exciting, now that the railway has reached Blaenau, but it can be more efficient.' He delegates to his departmental heads, and has a brisk way: meetings that sometimes used to last all day once a week now, under Papa Doc, are one morning, once a month, with the time the meeting will finish firmly fixed in everybody's minds before they begin. 'The FR is going to be more professionally run. Those who want to fiddle with bits of equipment can go to the Welsh Highland.'

Papa Doc cast a bleak eye over the Society and its prospects. 'The Society is not improving. Its support for the railway is getting less and less. Membership is not increasing.' Of volunteers, he says: 'We are going to have to have a different type. When we were building the railway it didn't matter whether they were interested in railways or not. Now we want volunteers who actually like running railways. They have to be carefully trained. Now they are working on lines where there are trains running. It takes the same amount of training to work for the one day as for a hundred days.'

Broadly, the Society concedes most of Papa Doc's points. Membership has been stationary for some years, at about 6,000. A scheme for 'instant membership', where people could join at Harbour station and at once make use of their members' free travel concessions, has been modified, amid some controversy. The Society provides, generally speaking, an ageing work-force. The sons and daughters, nephews and nieces, of the generation who joined with such fiery enthusiasm in the 1950s and 1960s have not shown quite the same dedication, or have found other outlets for their surplus energies nearer home.

The number of volunteer working days per year by Society members was 2753 in 1980, rising (as Blaenau approached) to 3346 in 1981 and to 3514 in 1982, but slipping (once Blaenau had been reached) to 2640 in 1983. But by far the majority of volunteer days are worked, not by Society members, but by others – groups, schools, clubs, cadet corps, and individuals – who make their own arrangements and their own approaches to heads of departments. The *total* volunteer days worked in 1983, for example, was 8,035 – thus providing for the Society the sobering statistic that its members only worked one in three of the volunteer days.

In October 1983 the Company appointed a Volunteer Resource Manager – a post which some thought might have been made some twenty years earlier. He was David Green, who had worked on the railway as volunteer with the East Anglian Group and had been a professional railwayman, as an apprentice with Southern Region of British Rail, before going to do his National Service in the RAF. On his return, he found that BR was abandoning steam, 'so I abandoned them', and he went back to the RAF, serving until 1976, before joining the British Aircraft Corporation (later British Aerospace). At a time of declining volunteer effort, David Green's brief was to 'coordinate the volunteer workforce on the railway', with the aim of boosting the annual volunteer days to the required 10,000.

The organisation of the Festiniog Railway Society has always been that of a central Society with a board of directors, and a number of autonomous groups, nearly always geographically based, which have a great deal of individual freedom, with their own committees and volunteer working party arrangements. This system, though it has its critics, who argue that the Society should have a corporate national identity, has stood the test of time and the groups have survived many changes in personnel, disagreements, 'splinter groups', and in some cases financial difficulties.

There are eighteen geographically based groups, covering almost every area of England and Wales (except, oddly, until as late as 1985, North Wales), from Northumbria to Bristol and the West of England, from Dee and Mersey to Hants and Sussex, from East Anglia to Lancashire and Cheshire, from Upper Thames to Sheffield and District, from South East Wales to White Rose, from London in a band up through the Midlands, Milton Keynes, East Midlands, North Staffs and Leicester. Besides sending regular working parties to the line, the groups carry out 'homework' – repairing and refitting rolling stock and equipment; collecting and transporting thousands of gallons of waste oil from all parts of the country to Boston Lodge, there to be burned in the locomotives; selling Festiniog Railway promotional material at fairs, shows and rallies; attending lectures and film-shows on the Festiniog and other railways.

In recent years, Dee and Mersey, London, Lancashire and Cheshire, East Midlands and Northumbria have tended to head the top places in the 'league table' of working days. But groups come and go, depending upon personalities. In 1976 the East Anglia Group spent much of a very hot and dry summer in the dusty Chesterton Yard, near Cambridge, cutting up a mile of British Rail jarrah wood sleepers which had been accidentally damaged. Carefully sawn, they produced a mile of two-foot gauge sleepers, half a mile of fifteen-inch gauge sleepers, and a large quantity of wooden packing for Boston Lodge. In so doing, the group saved the railway some £6,000. But in the 'league tables' of successive years in the early 1980s, East Anglia reported no working days at all. Their Summer Group Newsletter of 1984 referred to '. . . the unofficial but spoken policy of the Railway and Society in Port is that only regular volunteers (once a month or so) will get the prime jobs and those that can turn up only occasionally (because of distance or whatever) will get the messy jobs – clearing up other people's rubbish. Well, the non-FR volunteers have got fed up with clearing up the FR's messes and have called a halt, The "regular" volunteers are going to have to clear up their own mess in future.'

With so many different people with different interests and temperaments and living at different distances from Porthmadog, all involved in the railway, such tensions are inevitable. One of the Festiniog's permanent tensions, which can often be creative but is sometimes destructive, is the relationship between volunteers and the permanent staff. All the staff have their own 'volunteer stories', of people who turned up late, or in the wrong place, or not at all, who lost or damaged tools, kept breaking off in the middle of work to photograph passing trains, or who spent hours energetically and disastrously doing the wrong thing.

Some of the staff, especially at Boston Lodge, envisage a railway without volunteers and argue that it would be economically feasible. But this is to mistake appearances for reality, to suppose that because the railway has employees, with a hierarchical structure, job definitions, unions, meetings, pension schemes and all the visible trappings of a normal commercial business, that it *is* a normal business. The Festiniog Railway enterprise started because of the volunteers – they were there before the permanent staff – and they are still vital. Without them, the whole fabric would dissolve, like Prospero's cloud-capped towers and gorgeous palaces.

Understandably, the staff prefer skilled and experienced volunteers who attend regularly, give notice in advance, and turn up on time. There are stories, too many to be discounted as malicious rumour, of 'raw' volunteers who 'have come in off the street', presented themselves at Harbour station, only to be sent (and not always too politely) away, because the person who should have taken charge of them was not there, or was too busy. The volunteer is expensive, costing a lot of time and tact and tools. The less experienced he is, the less use he is, but the more instruction and humouring he needs. Contrarily, the more experienced and more valuable a volunteer is, the more he tends to be taken for granted. Yet, paradoxically, some of the very best volunteers find their deepest satisfaction in precisely this awareness of being accepted; they are proud that nobody feels it necessary to comment upon their expertise. For their part, some of the more perceptive permanent staff do recognise that the more the attractive and skilful railway jobs are done by the staff, so the scope and the appeal of what jobs remain are reduced for the volunteers.

Only one group is functionally rather than geographically based: the Heritage Group, which was launched at the Society's AGM in April 1984 and had its inaugural meeting at the Convention in October that year, and now has some 130 members. The group was the outcome of discussions over a number of years and arose out of Michael Seymour's (now Chairman) work as archivist and Lieutenant Colonel David Ronald (a volunteer from the early days and in Seymour's words 'an important catalyst in promoting ideas') and his Festiniog Railway Museum Modelling Group. The group's aim as Seymour says, is 'to cherish the past, interpret it to the present, and safeguard it for the future'. The group was largely responsible for the designs, fitting out and displays in the new, larger Museum at Harbour station; has taken over the stocks of the Society (Sales) Ltd; and has undertaken the restoration, to museum display condition, of the double Fairlie engine *Taliesin* (once *Livingston Thompson*) which is now lying, in 'hulk' condition, at Glan-y-Pwll.

Some volunteers say, rather cruelly, that they only stay members of the Society for the sake of their copy of the Society's magazine, one of the most remarkable private-circulation journals in the world. Most closed society publications, such as club and school magazines, are deadly dull for all but insiders. The Festiniog Railway Magazine is a constant source of entertainment. It began in October 1954 as a simple typed and cyclostyled news-sheet, of 500 copies, produced by Allan Garraway. Originals are now rare; even the British Museum only has a Xerox copy. The front page of the first issue had a photograph of the Simplex and two coaches leaving Boston Lodge for Portmadoc on the first passenger trip of 23 September 1954. The news-sheet ran to twelve issues before the Society out grew it, and the first issue of the Magazine proper, a printed magazine on glossy paper, appeared in the summer of 1958, and quarterly ever since. Its first editors were jointly Trevor Bailey, Mr F. Gilbert and J.B. White. Its distribution manager was Norman Gurley. That first issue carried a 'Message from the Chairman', Bill Broadbent, and a biography of him, a piece from Allan Garraway called '*Prince*'s Peculiar Motion', 'Platform Gossip' and various items of Society news.

The Society Magazine has become over the years the authentic voice of the whole railway. It carries scraps of information, non-committal biographies of Society and Company personalities, news from individual groups of volunteers, reports of Annual General Meetings, regular contributions telling members what was going on on the permanent way, in the traffic department, at Boston Lodge, and in the signals and telegraphs world. New faces were bid welcome, departing ones wished farewell. Minutiae were recorded, such as the two platform seats obtained from Pwllheli promenade, and the theft of a special A4 New Zealand whistle from *Linda*. There were obituaries, marriages and engagements. The letters to the editor have provided a safety-valve through which mysterious correspondents calling themselves '34526' or 'Hot Axle of Potters Bar' can let off steam. Back numbers have become collectors' items, and complete sets change hands at high prices.

The Magazine, as a chronicle of a railway growing and changing year by year, has itself had several editorial reshuffles. Norman Gurley became editor in charge of production in 1962 and remained part of the editorial team until 1981. Peter Johnson, one of the most indefatigable of Festiniog volunteers over the years, became one of the joint editors in 1974. For nearly twenty years, the editorials have been written by Dan Wilson, a telecommunications engineer from Kent. His pieces, always informative, sometimes hilarious, a fortunate combination of needle and slapstick, occasionally required expert interpretation. From time to time an irate reader would complain that he could understand only every other word, or even every other paragraph. But in general the editorials succeeded in explaining the railway's doings, politics, rows and personalities to Society members, many of whom never set foot on the railway from one year's end to another, in an unsolemn way which even railway laymen could grasp.

Here he is, describing the open weekend held at Boston Lodge on 15 and 16 September 1979 to celebrate the Silver Jubilee of the Festiniog Railway Society and the takeover of the Festiniog Railway Company by the present regime:

> It started modestly enough. Diffidently requesting a small area of the works for a celebratory display, by design or accident the Society succeeded in convincing Boston Lodge that where Open Days were concerned the Society could not be trusted, in the rather fetching American phrase, to float an ice-cream onto a root beer. Large signs appeared overlooking the main road, handbills were printed for local distribution and on the day, virtually the whole working area had been ruthlessly cleared. With the other departments not wishing to be upstaged either, it rapidly became not a Society affair but an all-Festiniog one, a memorable gala of engines shunting vans of food, huge photo displays, the 40-seater push-pull shuttle from Harbour carrying 70, a reception coach with visitor interviewers smoothly fitted out with coffee service and telephone, diagrams, films, videotapes and slide shows. You could see how to cast a firebox arch, make a bogie, cut a rail and bore railway-shaped holes in hills; or buy bits of

obscure bent pipe labelled breathlessly NWNGR – VERY
RARE – £5. If you shut your eyes, imagined how a Boston
Lodge Open Weekend ought to be, and opened them again,
that was how it was: a triumph of teamwork that surprised
even its own creators.

Maybe a few of the advertised ideas got lost and there
were other hiccups (one working party had its lunch *sold*,
Earl of Merioneth decided the occasion called for a single
Fairlie) but then there is always another time. Oh yes, you
can be sure there will be another time!

The official visitor tally was 1,768.

One veteran supporter of the magazine, whether contributing a
learned dissertation on the biological origins of Welsh dragons,
or a neo-Georgian sonnet in praise of a double Fairlie engine, is
Dr Peter Jarvis, one of three honorary medical advisers to the
Company and Chairman of the Milton Keynes Group. He might
well be called the romantic conscience of the railway – for years
he has enlivened proceedings at Annual General Meetings.
Half-Welsh, calling himself a 'half-breed', his anecdotes of the
railway merge, at some indeterminable point, into Welsh
legend. The Moelwyn tunnel was not built by anyone as prosaic
as John Smith of Caernarvon, but by Dillus the Bearded, who
was four-foot seven-inches high, threw no shadow, and struck
gold half-way through; he stayed there to mine it until 1941,
when the lease expired and he was thrown out after a furious
argument with the Company. 'In Wales,' he says, 'the boundary
between the truth and fiction is lost in Celtic twilight of varied
opinion, and our railway, our valley, and ourselves are all
perhaps become part of it. It was from *here* that Madog ab
Owain Gwynedd went to America, it was *there* that the English
built a castell at the conquest, and here that Dafydd Nanmor
sang, it was here that William Alexander Madocks came, it was
here Lord Palmerston had the matter of the horse-whips; and
did you see Shelley plain?'

Any group calling themselves 'Heritage' are bound to
revive and polarise the old argument, which always smoulders
beneath the surface, between the 'Modernists' (for want of a
better term) and the 'Traditionalists' – between those who insist
that the railway must progress at whatever cost in appearance
or tradition, and those who still hanker after a Victorian past,
who would like the Festiniog to be a 'time-machine' back into
nostalgia, who resisted the change from coal- to oil-firing, who
believe diesels are instruments of the anti-Christ, and who
would, for instance, much prefer a vintage, pre-printed

204

Edmondson card ticket, no matter how much it cost, to a limp, printed paper slip ('like a supermarket checkout').

The limits of this debate are very well set out by Rod Weaver, an aero-engineer by profession and Vice-Chairman of the Midlands Group, who regularly bombards the Magazine with what the editorial staff themselves call 'an asteroid belt' of informative articles, thought-provoking letters and challenging footnotes. His other great railway love is the London and North Western ('characterised by total professionalism in everything it did – did you know that Spooner modelled the FR on the LNWR?'). But he sums up the Festiniog Railway very well: 'There is a school of thought that history is only for the enthusiast and the only good history is that which pays for itself. This I find quite unsupportable. Without the unique history and development of the FR, nobody would have been in the least bit interested in saving it, so there wouldn't be a railway any more . . . I do sometimes disagree with some people over the role of "heritage" on a working railway. I do not advocate the creation of a static, mock-Victorian "steam railway". That is an insult to the men who created the FR, for it was by looking forward that they made their mark, not by looking backwards. But neither do I believe that one should sweep away all of the past and create a thoroughly modern railway, even though that is exactly what Charles Spooner would have done. One must steer a middle course . . . '

In fact, the whole argument is largely rhetorical. Where a volunteer or sponsor was willing to offer his own time, money and labour, the railway was happy to accept the gift. But when spending its own money, the railway has always taken a severely practical view. Coal was dropped in favour of oil because the economics of fuel prices made that necessary. But now that the balance of price between coal and oil has changed again, *Linda* has recently been re-converted to burn low grade coal, using a 'Gas Producer Combustion System' in which (to cut a highly technical description short) coal is first 'gasified' instead of being burned on the grate, and the gas is burned in secondary air admitted over the firebed; there is no clinker in the firebed, and sparks are virtually eliminated by a spark arrestor.

Similarly, despite protests and misgivings, the Festiniog now runs a selective daily diesel-hauled service, with an average of about one train in four, off-peak and with cheaper fares. The economics are overwhelmingly simple: a steam engine burns four gallons of oil to the mile, while a diesel engine does four miles to the gallon. In David Pollock's opinion, 'People don't mind diesels, provided they can *see* steam engines.'

In May 1985, the Festiniog became the first railway in Britain to have a fully computerised ticketing system. Largely due to the efforts and expertise of Brian Bushell, a volunteer guard who is also a computer programmer and who used to work for British Rail, three Apricot micro-computers were installed, one providing financial services for management, a second for maintenance records and planning at Boston Lodge and the third at Harbour station ticket-office.

The Festiniog has literally thousands of varieties of tickets, but Bushell's machine can handle some 10,000 different fares, issuing even the most complicated ticket with a discreet *'peep peep'* in six seconds. In high season the booking clerk is often a volunteer, doing his yearly few days' stint on the line, and is expected to know the price differences for first and third class fares to any one of ten destinations, single or return, ordinary, economy, period and other special tickets, rates for high season and low, off-peak, children, pensioners, group rates, pets and livestock. Now the computer 'takes the strain of the train'.

The railway expects to recover the £2,000 cost in under two years, by cutting out mistakes and saving time. David Pollock said: 'Steam purists might frown on us for going electronic.' The best summing up is, once again, by Rod Weaver: 'If Spooner had had computers available to him, he would have used them! And just as a Spooner booking office would have issued a distinctive ticket, so too does our modern one. The tradition has been maintained.'

Questions of tradition, 'heritage' and the future policy of the railway and its Society, were thrown into even sharper focus in the summer of 1983, when the Magazine carried one of its most surprising items, under the heading 'Amazing challenge offer could put *Livingston Thompson* in steam by 1986'. It was, said the Magazine, 'the most exciting sponsorship offer in the history of the Festiniog Railway'.

The full details were published two issues later. The sponsor was described as a 'long-standing active Life Member of the FR Society, who has been very active in the restoration of the Railway but who wishes to keep his name out of print'. The offer, which certainly was as improbable as any event on the Festiniog Railway, was to the Trust and was 50,000 shares in a successful and expanding public company. Shares, which the sponsor would underwrite to a minimum value of £100,000, were offered rather than cash because the donor would be exempt from Capital Transfer Tax on a gift to a registered charity and the Festiniog Railway Trust, unlike the donor, can sell the shares free of Capital Gains Tax.

Briefly, the scheme was for the shares to be held by the Trust in one fund (Fund A) and shares or money released from that fund at the rate of £12 for every Society volunteer working day above a starting threshold of 1,500 days in any one year; £1 for every £1 generated by the Society, or directly by the Trust, above a threshold of £10,000; and 50p for every £1 of cash raised from corporate bodies (with an upper limit of £5,000 for any donation from any one source in one year). The maximum sponsorship from volunteer working days and cash generated by the Society, the Trust or coporate bodies was limited to £60,000 a year. The scheme was backdated to 1 January 1983.

As sponsorship funds were earned by any of the methods described, so transfers would be made from Fund A to another fund (X) and passed to the Company specifically for such purposes as, in order of priority: restoring *Livingston Thompson* to museum standard, with its outward appearance as it was in the first half of this century, in time for the exhibition in 1985 at York; restoring *Livingston Thompson* to full working condition by 1986, its centenary year; restoring other historical working stock; rebuilding of stone walls, tunnel portals etc in stone, and other building works, including stone- or slate-clad buildings at Blaenau Ffestiniog, and signal boxes, and other projects that could be done largely by volunteer labour. The scheme was to run until 31 December 1986.

There was, at the same time, a *Livingston Thompson* Restoration Fund, to which Society members were invited to contribute. For a short period members looked forward to the heady prospect of three large double Fairlie engines – the 1879 *Merddin Emrys*, the 1979 *Earl of Merioneth*, and the 1886 *Livingston Thompson*, (under the name of *Taliesin*) – being restored, as the sponsor wished, to their 'original and aesthetically pleasing' appearances, using sponsorship funds and the Restoration Fund.

The sponsor's anonymity did not last long. He was soon revealed as Mike Schumann, who had been Site Engineer on the Deviation for some years. His original scheme, as revealed to the Society Board in January 1983 when it (unsurprisingly) caused some flutterings in the dovecots, did not last long either. As Schumann himself explained to Society members in November 1984, 'it did not take long to discover that the hulk of

207

Livingston Thompson could not be effectively rebuilt without compromising the desire [of the sponsor] to provide the railway also with a sound and efficient engine'. An alternative, to build a brand new double Fairlie of traditional (pre-1940) appearance also had to be abandoned when the estimated bill had risen to some £300,000, and Schumann himself, as he admitted, 'was getting rather nervous of the rising cost'.

When David Pollock had been General Manager long enough to assess the situation, he approached Mike Schumann with a 'reasoned argument as to why the railway did not want a third Fairlie and how he proposed that the need for larger locomotives in the future should be met'. As a result, in November 1984 Mike Schumann was writing that he 'was pleased to accept his proposal partially to fund instead the reconstruction and overhaul of *Merddin Emrys* to a traditional outline'. By 1985, as Schumann said, his 'original scheme had been effectively abandoned'. It 'became necessary to disentangle fund-raising for a locomotive from fund-raising for other activities'.

But in its final form the sponsorship scheme was still of enormous value to the railway and its value was not merely in cash. By putting his money where his criticisms were, Mike Schumann was entitled to express his views publicly and he was only saying out loud what many people knew in their hearts to be true: in general, the railway had no policy except to make ends meet. The Society needed radical change and a new infusion of life. The volunteers needed a fresh spur and another challenge. The line up to Blaenau satisfied the legal minimum requirements to carry passengers, but no more. The pressures of expediency over many years had reduced it to a 'tatty state', with what Schumann calls 'temporary and inadequate structures pushed up through the years'. Sponsorship will provide funds for solid, good quality buildings which, from a strictly accountancy viewpoint might not be justified, but which will enormously improve the railway's appearance, and might well prove cheaper in the end. 'There used to be a uniformity about the railway,' says Schumann. 'All that has been bulldozed aside. There was a house style for buildings along the railway. We've succeeded in desecrating almost every station.' Schumann regularly photographs what he calls 'Festiniog Tat'. 'There are five different types of fencing at Tan-y-Grisiau – all of them needing repair!'

According to Schumann, at the time his sponsorship scheme was launched, the railway 'had no evident locomotive policy. I myself have always felt somewhat dismayed seeing the smaller engines trying to cope with what seemed like oversized loads and every year being modified away from their traditional appearance, not only in the quest for greater efficiency but also greater haulage capacity under all weather conditions.' In Schumann's opinion, David Pollock's arrival and 'the threat of a third double Fairlie to maintain caused the development of the Railway's locomotive policy'.

Whether or not Schumann's sponsorship was quite the catalyst he claims, there certainly has been a recent policy explosion on the railway. From seemingly having no policies on anything, except to go on surviving, the Festiniog now has published policies on finance, building and works, training, locomotives, archives, museum, civil engineering, signalling and telecommunications, volunteering and marketing.

Marketing is the new 'buzz' word on the railway, although it does seem that to many people marketing is synonymous with selling, whereas selling is only part of marketing (and many of the important marketing decisions on the Festiniog were taken 150 years ago). However, there are now constant references to marketing in the Magazine, and marketing panels, marketing courses, marketing conventions, and general hints and exhortations to marketers are regular occurrences.

There are even marketing volunteers. Once again, and inescapably, the volunteers are crucial to every aspect of the railway's prosperity. The Festiniog volunteers continue to defy analysis. Their motivation remains mysterious. Some undoubtedly find on the railway a respect, a recognisable personality, which they do not have in their 'real life' job. Some, not normally Society members, came because their friends, already volunteers, knew of their special skills – in carpentry, or panel-beating, or welding – and asked them to give the railway a try. Conversely some volunteers come to the railway to submerge their workaday personalities in a group. Managers with great responsibilities on weekdays say on weekends: 'I don't want to organise anything or anybody. Just tell me where and when to shovel and I'll shovel.'

Those first volunteers of the 1950s knew of the Festiniog because they had ridden on it as children before the war, or because somebody gave them a cigarette-card, or sent them a postcard, or they saw a highly-coloured picture of a double Fairlie in a book, or simply they heard through a friend. When the news spread that a Society was being formed to revive the railway, they joined it. They were in the great majority middle-class, middle-brow, middle-income, with a high proportion of professionally qualified men – although these predominate much less now than they did at first. They were barristers, solicitors, clergymen, civil servants, doctors, army officers, architects, engineers of all specialities, schoolmasters, university lecturers and a large category of professional railwaymen from all the regions of British Rail. Managing directors of engineering firms worked as fitters and boiler-makers at Boston Lodge. Schoolmasters and civil servants acted as guards. Surgeons, it was said, could be seen manhandling sleepers, wearing gloves to protect their scalpel hands. Bishops stood on *Prince*'s footplate, as assistant firemen; one of them brought his bulldog and had to work twice as hard because the episcopal bulldog sat on the coal and bit the pukka fireman whenever he tried to shovel any coal.

The Festiniog's appeal has always been difficult to define. In the somewhat baroque prose of John Snell, well-known railway author, early volunteer on the Talyllyn, who now runs the Romney, Hythe and Dymchurch Railway in Kent, 'the thing [i.e. the Festiniog] was mathematically satisfying, aurally satisfying, visually logical, it had history and drama, it was useful to many, but it could not exist without this constructive human co-operation'.

However they describe it, there is no doubt that the Festiniog Railway has drawn a great many different people together. It appeals to the lonely and to the shy, who can merge their own personalities in a common enterprise; work on the railway made all men equal, and they could take a fresh lease of identity. Paradoxically, the railway appeals as strongly to the sociable extrovert, stimulating his need to share, to undergo common experience; shared hardships make shared reminiscences and, eventually, a shared mythology. Thus, for example, a man painting the railings at Penrhyn station, all by himself, could get as much pleasure from his efforts and feel as necessary to the railway as any one of a gang working in a team, with all the gear prepared and the moves rehearsed, to lay a set of points for the new loop at Rhiw Goch.

The railway appealed to those with a pioneering spirit, especially in those rougher, earlier days. Large parts of the line had been allowed to go back to a state of nature. So the volunteers could imagine they were setting foot where no white man had trod before, imposing order and discipline upon disorder and wilderness. They enjoyed the sensation of violent physical exertion in the open air, the wild country, and the spartan working and living conditions. Many of the best-known early Festiniog anecdotes have titles which reflect either rigorous cold or wet ('Garraway's Bath' – an expedition to recover old Welsh Highland flat-bottom rails from Pitts Head), or struggle ('The Battle of Buarth Melyn' – a famous altercation with a farmer across whose land the railway was going to run).

Yet, paradoxically again, the railway also appeals to those of a neat and tidy, finicky frame of mind. Such people make natural train guards. To dress up in a uniform with a peaked cap and give the 'Right away' to a compliant engine-driver of a little train which goes puff-puff-puff is the very stuff of nursery dreams. Nothing pleases them more than to have to make sure that all the doors are shut, everybody has a ticket, and everything is just so. They love to have to work out how much excess fare to charge a man in a wheelchair travelling off-peak with a dog. Their happiest hours are spent poring over timetables to settle on which is the best connection for the Istanbul Blue Train, via Blaenau Ffestiniog. (Nor is this an idle joke: a loudspeaker at Harbour station once announced, for the benefit of some American tourists just embarking, 'the train now standing at this platform is the train for Tan-y-Bwlch and Dduallt, with connections to Blaenau Ffestiniog, Euston, Dover, Calais and Paris'.)

There was, too – there still is – a strong sexual element. Colonel Campbell of Dduallt was convinced of it. 'You could see it plainly in the mixed working parties. The boys like to show off their strength, to show off their muscles, to work hard in front of the girls. The girls know they are supposed to be impressed. Often they are, even though just as often they are as good shovellers, excavator drivers and truck-pushers as the boys.'

The railway has also been a great debunker of the pretentious. Many a young woman, coming to work on the Deviation, has found her young man, the charmer of her home-town, shrunk to a much more humble size when viewed against the Welsh mountains.

Occasionally, sex has militated against the interests of the railway. Bob MacGregor tells the cautionary tale of a valuable volunteer, a skilled electrician called Ron, who once came, with his girlfriend, to work for a week on some highly intricate signals and telegraph gear at Tan-y-Bwlch. While Ron buckled down to it, the girlfriend was left to her own devices. 'The first day she walked by herself down to the lake and across to Maentwrog and back. The second day she walked all by herself up to Creuau and then across to Rhyd and back across the hills.

211

I could see what was happening, so on the Wednesday I said to Ron, "How about, you know, taking a little time off, you know, take the girlfriend out a bit?" No, no, says Ron, quite happy, quite happy, and on he went with his work. I was delighted of course that he was doing the job, but when they went away at the end of that week there was a look in that girl's eye. I haven't seen Ron since!' (Nevertheless, they did get married.)

For some the Festiniog is simply a part of lost youth. John Snell again remembers with nostalgia

> . . . the lunatic rides down hill with the Simplex
> in 1955. I suppose we were all younger and gayer then. The
> train usually consisted of the Simplex and one or two small
> bogie coaches, with perhaps twelve or twenty people on board.
> Athough the armour-clad Simplex got through well enough, the
> trees and bushes were well foul of the line and branches used to
> bang on the carriages as they went past fiercely enough to break
> the windows. There was hardly a whole pane of glass intact
> anywhere in the train. Coming down hill again, often in the
> dark, when Allan Garraway used to take the brake off and let
> rip, it was certainly very exciting, and I would have said we
> touched speeds between thirty and forty miles an hour,
> although it was difficult to judge speeds in the dark. As I said,
> we were younger then.

Volunteers come at all ages. About eighty per cent of the volunteer-days worked at the souvenir shop (the 'Bunny Hutch') at Blaenau in the 1984 season was contributed by children of fourteen years and under, and most of it was by five local boys from Blaenau itself. Many of the early volunteers now have families of their own – the next generation.

Another, more senior volunteer, Ron Jarvis, will for ever be associated with the renovation of the '1863 Stock', or the 'Bug Boxes' as they are better known: six little four-wheeled coaches, of which four still survive, built by Brown Marshall & Co. in or around 1864. Ron Jarvis began work on the first of them when they were required for traffic to meet peak-hour demand in 1958. When he retired from British Rail in 1971, he moved to Llanbedr, Conwy, and now has a workshop in which he rebuilt the complete bodies of these historic coaches, which were the first passenger carrying vehicles on a British narrow-gauge railway, and very possibly the first in the world.

For some, volunteering seems almost predestined, an inevitable part of life. Eileen Bradbury, as a child, lived at Hellifield in Yorkshire, an important rail junction in its day on the route across the Pennines, where she used to 'lie in bed every night and listen to the trains'. She joined the Society in the 1960s, came to the Snowdonia National Park Centre at Plas Tan-y-Bwlch as a lecturer in 1977 and at once took to volunteering; she now divides her time between firing, permanent way work, 'parks and gardens', and the Heritage Group (which she named). She has a reporter's knack of being present at the right time. She was there for *Blanche*'s historic trip above Tan-y-Grisiau in December 1981, worked on the line at Blaenau in the terrible weather of January 1982, was there again at Blaenau when British Rail opened their station in March and, of course, was there for Freddie's Fantastic Rail Tour (wearing a badge saying 'Tour Groupie').

But just as Norman Pearce is famous for his telephones, Brian Bushell for his computers, Ron Jarvis for his 'Bug Boxes', Rod Weaver for his letters to the editor, Keith Catchpole for his Tadpoles, and Steve Coulson for his Stefcomatic Matisa ballast tamping machine (which he re-gauged from standard to two-inch), so Eileen Bradbury is famous for her course, or rather several courses, on the Festiniog Railway.

The first, 'The line that refused to die', was held on Friday through to Monday at Plas Tan-y-Bwlch in February 1981, and there have been six more – all over-subscribed, with people fighting for places. The idea was to show, as Eileen says, 'how the Festiniog is so many different things to so many different people'. There were trips up and down the line, visits to the new tunnel with Mike Schumann and Andy Putnam, to Boston Lodge with Paul Dukes and Fred Boughey, to Minffordd yard with Paul Dukes and Geoff Hall, to the museum with Mike Seymour and to Dduallt signal box with Terry Turner. There were talks – on the early days, by Alan Pegler, on progress on the line by Geoff Hall, on the railway's commercial life by Alan Heywood, on the role of the regional groups by Adrian Shooter, on working parties by Jim Parrish, on permanent way work by Fred Howes, on the 'Great Legal Case' by Arthur Lambert, on 'Where are we going?' by Dick Wollan, films by Allan Garraway, and 'Go with Noakes'. The course was a stupendous success and more than one of the permanent staff who were there said they had learned more about their railway in those three days than in the previous ten years.

The flavour of working as a volunteer is best expressed by the volunteers themselves. For three days in July 1984 *Mountaineer* had Paul Ingham as driver and Dick Hardy as fireman. Paul Ingham, of Loughborough College, had 650 turns as a fireman before becoming a driver and is one of only about a dozen volunteers qualified as drivers. Dick Hardy, a Director of the Company, had forty-two years with LNER and BR, but considered himself 'only a young hand' at firing. Some of his phrases are hardly intelligible to a layman in railway affairs, but the enthusiasm is unmistakable:

> Now the *Mountaineer* makes a fireman think and scheme, and to be a step ahead of that little machine makes the job. On Monday, we were learning; on Tuesday we sought sound advice and applied the remedy but I stole an inch of water at Tan-y-Bwlch to keep up my sleeve against the last half mile of the climb. The *Mountaineer* would not permit such LNER liberties and had a little prime, which upset the boiler for quite a time and made me scheme even more. But on the third day, Paul and I put it all together and we did a good job. The little engine laid on 180 psi from start to finish; the injector did likewise, cut fine and as Paul and I passed the summit with our nine cars, we shook hands with genuine pleasure born of teamwork on such a super little machine.

At the summer peak, about sixty-five volunteers will be working on the railway on any one day, most of them in Traffic and Commercial, but over the years there have been thousands of them, all with their individual stories. John Saville heard of the Festiniog in 1953 (when it was in the past tense) and he was at school. On first visiting Porthmadog and actually seeing the railway: 'I was immediately fascinated, joined the Society, and then did nothing – not even a return visit – for several years . . . Then, in 1976, they sold off the left-over Festiniog Railway Centenary of Steam medallions at £31 each, with the inducement of a guaranteed seat on Day One of services to Blaenau.' So he bought one, but 'the next winter the appeal for volunteers was even more impassioned than usual, and I realised that I had no moral right to that seat if I had contributed nothing to the cause.'

So he wrote in, 'carefully pointing out that I was approaching middle age, wilted after half an hour's gardening, and that my job gave me too much to do with the Great British Public without being a buffet car steward as well.' He offered to do a week of anything at Boston Lodge, 'even if only sweeping the floor'. He kitted himself out with a brand new pair of boots, 'which were agonising', and brand new overalls, two pairs of 'the naviest blue'.

John Saville had been told to report as a trainee cleaner/ fireman at 8.30 a.m. on the first day of the low season service.

214

He expected on his first morning to be given a broom and shown where to start sweeping. Instead, someone looked on the roster and said, 'You're on *Mountaineer* – out there.'

'Some ninety minutes later *Mountaineer*, not in the best of health at the time, chuffled asthmatically past the Lodge under a plume of oily smoke with me already learning the rudiments of firing. One day later I was rostered for two trips on *Blanche*. The first was under the strict but friendly guidance of Joe Clulow, the ideal mentor for any novice fireman (or guard, or signalman). For the round trip I was on my own, with Warren Shepherd calling oil and atomiser settings to me across the cab. And it was still only Tuesday!

'By the time I went home I had done nine solo trips and been involved in a forest fire and a train crash (well, sort of – already looking forward to next year's visit, I had a farewell trip on the Sunday evening beer train. In the gathering dusk on the way down, half a mile from anywhere, near Crossing Bothy, *Blanche*'s tender took a sharp turn to the right, and we were stuck. Eventually the entire population of the train was herded into the two rear coaches, which were painfully dragged back to Tan-y-Bwlch by the Simplex, which happened to have been stabled there for the weekend. For me the trip ended in a terrifying drive down to Port on one of the rescue vans driven by a very irate Bunny Lewis.)

'I have been back every year since. I don't improve much as a fireman, but the boots no longer hurt and the overalls are a much lighter blue. I have my reservation at the Hilton for June and am looking forward to it as much as ever.

'One final thing: I am now a regular on the Brecon Mountain Railway, which is close to where I live. When I started there, I found that Festiniog Railway training was just assumed to be a certificate of competence. Not everyone likes or approves of the Festiniog Railway, but they don't half respect it.'

Inevitably there has been a wastage of volunteers through the years. Some early stalwarts have died, some have gone back to the Talyllyn (at one time a fate worse than death in Festiniog eyes – although they are all the best of friends now). Some, like John Snell, are now running other railways. Pat Whitehouse, still a Patron of the Festiniog, is concerned with the successful Dart Valley Railway. Alan Pratt, for years Secretary of the Midland Group, founded the Conway Valley Railway Museum at Bettws-y-Coed. Others simply dropped out as they grew older, when the demands of family or business became more pressing. Others emigrated, or stopped because they found it less fun than in the old days. They enjoyed that sense of pioneering, when you cleared a patch of brambles and never quite knew what you might discover underneath it. Now, they say, the Festiniog is too well organised, too successful, too predictable – too professional, I suspect they mean. There were very few railway restoration and preservation schemes in the early 1950s. Now a young man does not need to go as far as Portmadoc to find an old railway to work on. Some returned to the Festiniog after an absence of several years and found to their chagrin that they had only a qualified welcome. The railway is a jealous jade and is not interested in hearing of the rival claims of other women. But, like those nineteenth-century names scratched on the cutting below Tan-y-Bwlch, none of them are forgotten. Their names survive in anecdote and legend, in articles in the magazine, in faces in the old photographs; and in the evening beer trains after the Annual General Meeting or coming down the mountain on a Sunday night, their names are in all their flowing cups freshly remembered.

Appendices

Ffestiniog Railway stock list
Section 1
steam locomotives

Pre-1946 No.	Name	Wheel Arrangement	Builder	Works No.	Date of Completion	Cylinders (No.) dia. x str.
a)	**BUILT NEW FOR THE F.R. Co.**					
2	Prince	0–4–0STT	G. England & Co., New Cross, London	?	1863/4	(2) 8⅛" x 12"
10	Merddin Emrys	0–4–4–0T	Festiniog Rly. Co., Boston Lodge Works	(1)	1879	(4) 9" x 14"
–	Earl of Merioneth/ Iarll Meirionnydd	0–4–4–0T	Festiniog Rly. Co., Boston Lodge Works	3	1979	(4) 9" x 14"
5	Welsh Pony	0–4–0STT	G. England & Co., New Cross, London	234	1867	(2) 8¼" x 12"
b)	**ACQUIRED FROM OTHER SOURCES**					
	Linda	2–4–0STT	Hunslet Engine Co., Leeds	590	1893	(2) 10½" x 12"
	Blanche	2–4–0STT	Hunslet Engine Co., Leeds	589	1893	(2) 10½" x 12"
	Mountaineer	2–6–2T	American Loco. Co., (Cooke Works) Paterson, New Jersey, U.S.A.	57156	1917	(2) 9" x 14"
	(Volunteer)	0–6–0ST	Peckett & Sons, Bristol	2050	1944	(2) 9½" x 14"
c)	**PRIVATELY OWNED**					
	Britomart	0–4–0ST	Hunslet Engine Co., Leeds	707	1899	(2) 7" x 10"

Driving Wheel dia. (nominal)	Boiler Pressure (lb/sq.in.)	Notes	Major overhauls/rebuildings
2' 3"	160	One of the first four locomotives built in 1863/4; delivered in 1864. The first locomotive in steam 1955.	1892 1921 1955 1980 rebuilt boiler 1980; oil burning and superheating 1980.
2' 9¼"	160	Fairlie's Patent double-bogie locomotive, designed by G. P. Spooner.	1896 1921 1934 1961 1970 1979 new superheated boiler 1970; oil burning 1972.
2' 9¼"	160	Fairlie's Patent double-bogie locomotive; designed and built at Boston Lodge, the first Fairlie built since 1911.	bogies from 'Livingston Thompson'; superheated boiler from Hunslet Engine Co., Leeds.
2' 3"	150	The fifth locomotive built for the F.R. Boiler condemned in 1938; stored out of service awaiting renovation.	1891 1915
2' 2"	160	ex Penrhyn Quarry Railway, Main Line class; on loan 1962, and bought in 1963. Built as 0–4–0ST.	new boiler 1936, superheated by Hunslet 1969 rebuilt to 2–4–0STT 1970; oil burning 1971.
2' 2"	160	ex Penrhyn Quarry Railway, Main Line class; bought 1963. Built as 0–4–0ST.	new boiler 1955: half cab and new tender 1965: new p.v.cyls 1971; rebuilt as 2–4–0STT 1972: oil burning 1971; superheating 1972.
2' 3"	180	Built for W.D. Light Rlys. France, No. 1265; after WW1 used in France, from 1935 on Tramway de Pithiviera à Toury, no. 3–23; TPT closed 31.12.1964; 3–23 bought and brought to G.B.; donated to F.R. 1967.	modified to F.R. loading gauge 1967; oil burning 1971; new superheated SB3 boiler and piston valves 1982; new cab etc., 1983.
2' 3½"	200	ex Harrogate Gas Works (closed 1956); bought 1957.	stripped for evaluation.
1' 8"	160	ex Pen-yr-Orsedd Quarry; first steamed on F.R. July 1966.	1966 1982 coal fired.

219

Ffestiniog Railway stock list
Section 1
steam locomotives

Pre-1946 No.	Name	Wheel Arrange-ment	Builder	Works No.	Date of Completion	Cylinders (No.) dia. x str.
d) HISTORIC LOCOMOTIVES NOT IN RUNNING STOCK						
1	Princess	0–4–0STT	G. England & Co., New Cross, London	199/200?	1863	(2) 8″ x 12″
3	Livingston Thompson	0–4–4–0T	Festiniog Rly. Co., Boston Lodge Works	(2)	1886	(4) 9″ x 14″
(K1)		0–4–0–0–4–0	Beyer Peacock & Co., Manchester	5792	1909	(2) 11″ x 16″ h.p. (2) 17″ x 16″ l.p. compound

Driving Wheel dia. (nominal)	Boiler Pressure (lb/sq.in.)	Notes	Major overhauls/rebuildings
2' 3"	140/160	The first steam locomotive in the world for a public narrow-gauge railway. The first locomotive in steam on the F.R., August 1863; worked the last goods train 1st August 1946. Exhibited at Blaenau Ffestiniog 1969–1980; on show at Stockton & Darlington 150 celebrations, Shildon August 1975. Partial restoration 1981; entered F.R. Museum 22nd April 1981.	1895 1923 1937
2' 9"	160	Fairlie's Patent double-bogie locomotive, design improved by W. Williams; the last to carry the special taper boiler. Last train worked 31.10.1971, then withdrawn; fund raised to preserve boiler unit, tanks, cab and frames. In store pending restoration for museum display.	1905 1932 1956 bore name 'Taliesin' 1932–1961 and name 'Earl of Merioneth' 1961–1971.
2' 7"	195	The first Beyer-Garratt patent articulated locomotive (H.W. Garratt's Paten 13079/1907), built for N.E. Dundas Tramway. Tasmania; line closed 1929. K1 returned to Beyer-Peacock in 1947 and preserved in works until 1966. Fund raised to purchase K1; arrived Porthmadog 23.2.1966. Stored pending modification for F.R. service. To National Railway Museum, York, for long-term loan on display 2.7.1976; formal handling over ceremony 9.4.1979. Displayed in grey.	

Section 2
Internal combustion locomotives

Name	Wheel Arrangement	Builder	Works No.	Date of Completion/ Delivery	Original Power Unit
Mary Ann	4wDM	Motor Rail Ltd., Bedford	(596?)	1917	40 h.p. Dorman 4JO
Moelwyn	2–4–0DM	Baldwin Loco. Works, Philadelphia U.S.A. (possibly sub-contracted)	49604	1918	45 h.p. Pittsburgh
Ashover	4wDM	F.C. Hibberd, Park Royal	3307	1948	48 h.p. Perkins P6
Upnor Castle	4wDM	F.C. Hibberd	3687	1954	Foden FD6 2–stroke 126 b.h.p. de-rated to 105 b.h.p.
	4wDM	F.C. Hibberd	3831	1958	Dorman 4DL
Model Hebog	0–4–0DM	Hunslet Engine Co., Leeds	4113	1955	Meadows 70 h.p.
(Jane)	4wDM	Motor Rail Ltd.	8565	1940	Dorman 20 h.p.
The Colonel	4wDM	Motor Rail Ltd.	8788	1943	Dorman 20 h.p.
Diana	4wDM	Motor Rail Ltd.	21579	1957	Dorman 20 h.p.
(Sandra)	4wDM	Motor Rail Ltd.	22119	1961	Dorman 20 h.p.
Andrew	4wDM	Ruston & Hornsby, Lincoln	193984	1939	13 h.p. Ruston 2VTO
Alistair	4wDM	Ruston & Hornsby, Lincoln	201970	1940	13 h.p. Ruston 2VTO
Stefcomatic	2–2–0DH	Matisa	48589	1956	Leyland 125 h.p.

Latest Power Unit	Notes	Major Overhauls/Rebuildings
Gardner 4LK	Built for W.D. Light Rlys., France, Indent No. 10350; bought 1923 from Kent Construction & Engineering Co., Ashford, Kent. First locomotive restored to working order 1954; worked first passenger train 23.7.1955.	1954; 1973 (cab added). Nameplated added 1971. Vacuum brake fitted. Original Dorman engine retained for display in Museum.
Gardner 4LK	Built for French Govt. Artillery Rlys. No. 1491. Bought Feb. 1925 from E.W. Farrow & Sons, Spalding, Lincs. Returned to service Aug. 1956, still as 0–4–0DM.	1956; 1957 rebuilt to 2–4–0DM; 1966. Vacuum brake fitted.
	Originally Ashover Light Rly.: to George Cohen 1951; to R.G. Odell Ltd. Canvey Island 23.6.1953; to E. Anglian Transport Museum Oct. 1972; to F.R. late 1981.	
Gardner 6LXB 180 h.p.	Built for R.N. Chattenden & Upnor Rly, Chatham, Kent. Yard No. 44. Line closed 1960. 13.2.1962 to Welshpool & Llanfair Lt. Rly.: No. 4 'Upnor Castle'. 13.2.1968 to F.R. Co.; in service mid August 1968.	1968 cut down and re-gauged from 2' 6" to 2'; vacuum brake fitted. 1971 re-engined.
	ex. R.N.A.D. Ernesettle, Plymouth. To F.R. 23.5.1981.	to be re-gauged from 2' 6" to 2' gauge.
	Mines loco; ex works 28.2.1955 to N.C.B. New Stubbin Colliery, Dewsbury. Yorks.; altered to 2' gauge on transfer to Shaw Cross Colliery, Rawmarsh, Yorks. To F.R. on purchase 1969.	1975; cab and name added; first service Dduallt-Gelliwiog shuttle. Vacuum brake fitted.
	Model 12428/36; ex St. Albans Sand & Gravel Co. 1966 via Col. Campbell. Early 1971 F.R. property; name carried 1972–6.	
Dorman 20 h.p. ex 'Sandra'	ex St. Albans Sand & Gravel Co. 1966, property of Col. Campbell. To F.R. stock 1982.	
	ex Minworth Sewage Works. Birmingham. Arrived Glan-y-Pwll 25.8.1974; named 7.10.1974.	
	ex. Gt. Ouse River Division of Anglian Water Authority. May 1977. Delivered to F.R. 24.6.1977.	power unit transferred to 'The Colonel'.
	ex Smith & Sons, Raunds, Northants. 1974.	dismantled 1979 for repair.
	to Bierrum & Partners 1949; donated by Mr. H. A. Bierrum 1968.	
	to B.R. (Southern Region) Oct 1956. To F.R. autumn 1968 Standard-guage ballast tamping machine.	Rebuilt 1977 and re-gauged to 2' at Boston Lodge; in service 1978.

SOURCES

I have found the following sources useful, and I acknowledge with thanks where I have quoted from them:

BADDELEY, M.J.B., and C.S. WARD, *North Wales* (Thorough Guide Series), Dulau & Co., London, 1892

BARRADELL, MARTIN, F.R., 'Volunteering Reminiscences', in MS, November 1973

BARRETT, R.J., 'The Festiniog Railway Today', *Railway World*, Vol. 17, 1956

BEAZLEY, ELISABETH, *Madocks and the Wonder of Wales*, Faber & Faber, London, 1967

BISHOP, WILLIAM H., 'Over the Narrowest Narrow Gauge', *Scribner's Monthly*, Vol. XVIII, August 1879

BOUGHEY, FRED, 'Thoughts on Driving a Double Engine', in MS, May 1974

BOYD, J.I.C., *Narrow Gauge Rails to Portmadoc*, Oakwood Press, Godstone, 1949

  Narrow Gauge Railways in South Caernarvonshire, Oakwood Press, Godstone, 1972

  The Festiniog Railway, Vol. I 1800–1889 (third revised ed.), Oakwood Press, Lingfield, Surrey, 1965, Vol. II 1890–1962 (2nd revised ed.), 1962

  The Festiniog Railway, Vol. I, 'History and Route, 1800–1953', Vol. 2, 'Locomotive Rolling Stock and Quarry Feeders', Oakwood Press, Blandford, 1975

BROADBENT, BILL, 'The Broadbent Papers', Festiniog Railway Magazine, No. 90, Autumn 1980

BROOKS, J.R., 'Cautionary Tales for Preservationists', in MS, March 1974

BURN, MICHAEL, *The Age of Slate* (abridged), Quarry Tours Ltd, Blaenau Ffestiniog

CARR, H.A.C., and G.A. LISTER, *The Mountains of Snowdonia*, Crosby Lockwood, London, (2nd ed.), 1948

DAVIES, A.M., 'Some Reminiscences of the FR Revival', Festiniog Railway Magazine, No. 85, Summer 1979

DODD, A.H., *The Industrial Revolution in North Wales*, University of Wales Press, Cardiff, (3rd ed.), 1971

DRAGE, DOROTHY, *Pennies for Friendship*, Gwenlyn Evans Ltd, Caernarvon, 1961

EDWARDS, WILLIAM THOMAS (Gwilym Deudraeth), *Chydig Ar Gofa Chadw* ('A Little Something to Keep and Remember'), Brython Press, Liverpool, 1926
   Yr Awen Barod ('The Ready Muse'), Gwasg Gomer, Llandysul, 1943

Engineering: 4 October 1867; 24 September 1869; 29 December 1871; 26 September 1884; 7 June 1957

FAIRLIE, ROBERT F., *Locomotive Engines, What they are and What they ought to be*, London 1864, reprinted for Festiniog Railway Co., 1969

FESTINIOG RAILWAY COMPANY, *A Traveller's Guide to the FR, FR Companion, FR Guide Book, FR in Pictures, Festiniog Pictorial*, various editions and dates, 1956–1985

FESTINIOG RAILWAY SOCIETY, Newsletters No. 1 (October 1954) to No. 13 (February 1958)
   Festiniog Railway Magazine, No. 1 (Summer 1959) to No. 111 (Winter 1985–86)
   The Volunteer's Manual, ed. Roy Cunningham, (rev. ed.) 1965
   Group Information Memoranda, Nos. 1 to 97

FIENNES, G.F., *I Tried to Run a Railway*, Ian Allan, London, (rev. ed.) 1973

GARRAWAY, A.G.W., 'The Festiniog Railway', Transactions of Caernarvonshire Historical Society, vol. 16, 1955
   'Restoring the Festiniog Railway', MS
   'The Story of the Revival of the Festiniog Railway: A Personal Chronicle', MS
   Garraway Father And Son, Middleton Press, Midhurst, 1985

GREAVES, J.W., & SON LTD, *Slate and Slating*, Portmadoc (2nd ed.), 1950

GREAVES, T.A., 'The Festiniog Under Military Occupation' (Operation SHISH KEBAB), *Railway World*, Vol. 30, 1969

GURLEY, NORMAN, *Narrow Gauge Steam out of Portmadoc: 25 Years of the Festiniog Railway*, Bradford Barton, Truro, 1980

HARRIS, MICHAEL, 'Little Wonder or Much Enterprise', *Railway World*, August 1978

HEMINGWAY, J., *Panorama of the Beauties, Curiosities, and Antiquities of North Wales*, London, 1848

HOLLAND, SAMUEL, 'The Memoirs of Samuel Holland One of the Pioneers of the North Wales Slate Industry', Merioneth Historical and Record Society, Extra Publications, Series 1, No. 1, Evans & Son, Bala, 1952

HOLLINGSWORTH, BRIAN, *Ffestiniog Adventure: The Festiniog Railway's Deviation Project*, David & Charles, Newton Abbot, 1981

HUGHES, EMRYS, and ALED HUGHES, *Porthmadog Ships*, Gwynedd Archives Service, Caernarfon, 1975

HUGHES, HENRY, *Immortal Sails*, T. Stephenson & Sons Ltd., Prescot, Lancs. (2nd ed.), 1969

HEATH HUMPHRYS, LEONARD A., 'The Festiniog Railway Preservation Scheme, 1950/51: How It All Started', Parts I and II, Festiniog Railway Magazine Nos 11 (Winter 1960–61) and 12 (Spring 1961)

ISHERWOOD, J.G., *Candles to Caplamps*, Gloddfa Canol, Blaenau Ffestiniog, 1980

JACKSON, DOUG, *Ffestiniog 150*, Festiniog Railway Company, City Press Services, Manchester, 1982

JARVIS, PETER, 'Twenty-Five years of restoring the FR', *Railway World*, September 1979
'Takeway Restorations', The Railway Magazine, September 1979

JOHNSON, PETER, 'Little Giant in Snowdonia: With the FR in the 1980s', *Railway World*, October 1983
The Welsh Narrow-Gauge Railways, Railway World Special, Ian Allan, Weybridge, 1985

LAMBERT, ARTHUR Ll., 'The Story of the Festiniog Railway Society', MS, 1969
'The Festiniog Railway versus the Central Electricity Generating Board', in MS, January 1974
'The Blaenau Project', Progress Reports, 1973–1982

LEE, CHARLES E., *Narrow Gauge Railways in North Wales*, Railway Publishing Co. Ltd, London, 1945
The Welsh Highland Railway, 1962; *More About the Welsh Highland Railway*, 1965, Welsh Highland Light Railway (1964) Ltd and David & Charles, Newton Abbot.

LEWIS, M.J.T., *How Ffestiniog Got Its Railway*, Railway and Canal Historical Society, Caterham, Surrey, 1968

LINK No. 100, 'LAG Newsletter Special Edition', June 1980, ed.
 Peter Wood
MASSAU, TONY, 'When Coal Was King', *Steam World*, June,
 July, August 1983
MITCHELL, VIC, 'The Rebirth of the Festiniog Railway',
 Festiniog Railway Magazine, No. 85 (Summer 1979)
MORGAN, D.W., *Brief Glory*, Brython Press, Liverpool, 1948
NORTH, F.J., *The Slates of Wales*, National Museum of Wales,
 Cardiff, 1946
PARRY, JAMES, 'Fun and Romance with the "Tren Bach" ',
 Caban, December 1960
PEACOCK, THOMAS LOVE, *Headlong Hall*, 1816
PEGLER, ALAN, 'Looking Back', Festiniog Railway Magazine,
 No. 85, Summer 1979
PENNANT, THOMAS, *Tours in Wales*, ed. John Rhys,
 H. Humphreys, Caernarvon, 1883
PHILLIPS, Rev. TIMOTHY, 'Paving the Way for the Festiniog
 Railway', *South Caernarvonshire Leader*, 4,11,18,25
 April, 2,9,16 May 1946
REID, CHARLES, 'Branch-Line Fever', *Punch*, 15 May 1957
RICHARDS, MORGAN, (Morgrugyn Machno), *Slate Quarrying
 and How to Make it Profitable*, Watts & Co, London;
 Evan Williams, Bangor, 1876
ROLT, L.T.C., *Railway Adventure*, Pan Books, London, 1971
 Talyllyn Century (ed.), David & Charles, Dawlish, Mac-
 Donald, London, 1965
SEMMENS, P.W.B., *Bill Hoole: Engineman Extraordinary*, Ian
 Allan, London, 1966
SEYMOUR, MICHAEL, 'Volunteering in 1955', MS, March 1974
SNELL, JOHN, 'The Festiniog Railway Derelict', MS, February
 1974
TALYLLYN RAILWAY, 'Photo Precision', St Ives, Huntingdon
VICKERS, H.E., 'A Moelwyn Memory', MS, March 1974
WAYNE, FRANCIS, 'The Festiniog Case', *Freedom First*, Society
 for Individual Freedom, February/March 1972
WEAVER, RODNEY, 'Double Fairlie Celebration', *Railway
 World*, January 1980
 'Prince 117', MS, July 1981
WHITEHOUSE, P.B., *Festiniog Railway Revival*, Ian Allan,
 London, 1963
 On the Narrow Gauge, Nelson, London, 1964
WILLIAMS, G.J., *Hanes Plwyf Ffestiniog* ('History of Ffestiniog
 Parish'), Hughes and Son, Wrexham, 1883

WYNNE JONES, IVOR, *Llechwedd: Its Slate and its People*, Quarry Tours Ltd, Blaenau Ffestiniog

Memoirs, reminiscences, diaries, correspondence, contributions to the Festiniog Railway Magazine, tape recordings, photographs, miscellaneous information, conversation and advice from John Alexander; Ben Ball; Martin Barradell; Fred Boughey; J.I.C. Boyd; Eileen Bradbury; Bill Broadbent; J.R. Brooks; Brian Bushell; Andrew Campbell; Keith Catchpole; Chris Chitty; Harold Creamer; Geoff Crine; Roy Cunningham; A.M. Davies; Paul Dukes; Lottie Edwards; John Williams Ellis; David Fuller; Allan Garraway; Philip Girdlestone, Roy Goldstraw; David Green; Norman Gurley; Geoff Hall; John Halsall; Angela Harrington; Bob Harris; John Harrison; Alan Heywood; Brian Hollingsworth; Leonard Heath Humphrys; Fred Howes; Doug Jackson; Peter Jarvis; Ron Jarvis; Peter Johnson; E.N. Kneale; Arthur Lloyd Lambert; Brian Leech; Ron Lester; Bunny Lewis; Sandy Livingstone Learmonth; Vic Mitchell; Bob MacGregor; Jack Owen; Norman Pearce; Alan Pegler; David Pollock; Alan Pratt; Andy Putnam; John Reynolds; Brian Rogers; E.J. Routly; John Saville; Mike Schumann; Michael Seymour; Warren Shephard; Adrian Shooter; Les Smith; John Snell; Ralph Taylor; Herbert Thomas; Paul Thomson; Terry Turner; Harold Vickers; Francis Wayne; Rodney Weaver; Richard Weir; Pat Whitehouse; Eddie Wilkinson; Gwen Williams; Charles Wilson; Dan Wilson; Dick Wollan; John M. Worley.

Index

Aberglaslyn Pass, 84, 85
accidents, 42, 65, 71, 72, 75, 82, 86
accounting system, 141
Afon Cwmorthin bridge, 156
Alexander, John, 125
Allott, Paul, xiii
Aluminium Company of
  Dolgarrog, 100
Archer, George, 17, 19
Archer, Henry, 17–19, 31, 32, 33,
  34–6, 38, 49
Archer Dam, 26
Arup, Ove, 23
Association of Minor Railways,
  197
Atomic Energy Authority, 28
Ayres, Jane, 150

Bailey, Trevor, 99, 101–4, 109, 161,
  202
Bailey's Gap, 109
Baker, Sir William, 59
Bala and Festiniog Railway, 64
Ball, Lady Pamela, 162
Ball, Sir Ben, 162, 168
Bantock, Sir Granville, 27
Barlow, 189
Barlwyd, 22
Barlwyd Bridge, 163, 176, 184, 185,
  188, 189
Bate, J. L. H., 98
Bate, John, 137
Bath Committee, 98

BBC, 88, 110–11, 154, 160–1,
  191
Beazley, Elizabeth, 160
Beddgelert, 84, 85
Bellamy, Bill, 103, 117, 141
Bethesda, 10
Beud-y-Gwyn, 50
Billington, H. W., 4
Bingley, Reverend, 11
Bishop, William B., 61–4
Blaenau Central, 21–2, 180–2,
  190–3
Blaenau Ffestiniog
  and the electricity storage
    scheme, 135
  local support for the
    restoration, 128–9, 135, 176–8
  origins, 43
  quarries, 12
  restoration of line to, 21–2, 128,
    175–94
  stations, 64, 66, 77, 118, 180–2,
    190
Blanche, 155, 156, 160, 189, 190,
  193, 215
Blanche's Bump, 29
Bleasdale, R. H., 123
Bobrinskoy, Count Alexei, 59
Boocock, Sabrina, 71
Borrow, George, 3, 11
Boston Lodge Works, 5, 28, 30, 40,
  41, 54, 68–9, 73, 75, 77, 84, 91,
  109, 113, 118, 164–6
Boston Lodge Halt, 113, 116

Boughey, Fred, 113, 118, 125, 129–31, 166, 213
Bowcott, Howard, 24, 167, 186
Boyd, J. I. C., 51–2, 95, 123
Bradbury, Eileen, 190, 212–13
Bradshaw, Paul, 147
brakesmen, 39, 41–2, 69–70
Brex, Twells, 30
Bristol Meeting, 97
Bristol Railway Circle, 97
Britannia Foundry, 188
British Electric Authority, 111
British Rail, 118, 180–1, 190
Britton, Sean, 191
Broadbent, Bill, 94–5, 103, 104, 162, 172
Brooks, Arthur, 166
Brown Marshall & Co., 212
Bushell, Brian, 206, 213
Busta, 111

Cabanau, 45
Caednyfydd, 40
Caldecot, William Lloyd, 16
Cambrian Railway, 61, 87
Campbell, Col. Andrew, 27, 146, 151, 160, 162, 211
Campbell, Douglas, 150
Campbell, Mary, 146
Carreg, Edward, 35
carriages, 68
    early, 54
    restoration, 113, 119, 126
    workmen's, 67
Casson brothers, 11, 19, 39
Catchpole, Keith, 112, 121, 125, 191, 213
Cei Mawr, 29
Centenaries Express, 101
Central Electricity Generating Board (CEGB), 24–5, 133–44, 180, 183
Chace School, 121, 159
chairs, 34
Chitty, Chris, 150, 156
Chwarel Lord, 12
Cilgwyn, 9

Citrine, Lord, 134
City of Truro, 123, 125
Clayton, Neil, 190
Cliffe, Charles Frederick, 43
Clulow, Joe, 215
Cob, 30
    breaches, 7
    construction, 4–7
    horse drawn trains over, 39
    low walls built, 57
    restoration work, 113
    road over, 34, 36
Coed Dduallt, 26
Coed-y-Bleddiau, 27
Cogl-Wal, 12
Cohens, 118
Conventions, 159, 187
Cooper, Alison, 154
Coulson, Steve, 213
Craig-Ddu, 41
Creamer, Harold, 159
Creuau, 16, 32
Crick, A. G., 71–2
Crick, F. G., 71
Croesor Junction, 85
Croesor Tramway, 85, 86
Crosville Bus Company, 81
Cunningham, Roy, 121, 122
Currant, David, 148
cuttings, 28
Cwmorthin, 41, 69
Cwmorthin Bridge, 24
Cwmorthin Falls, 24
Cwmorthin Incline, 53

Daniels, Robin, 153
Davies, David, 45
Davies, Dick, 156
Davies, Evan, 45, 78, 87–8, 94, 95, 100, 164
Davies, Tom, 45, 88, 91
Davies, W. Cradoc, 94
Davies, Will, 45, 91
Dduallt, 24, 26–7, 55
    restoration to, 127–8, 143, 157
'Dduallt Diddy', 128
Dduallt Manor, 146

Dee and Merseyside Group, 189
Dennis, Peter, 191
Development Board for Rural
    Wales, 24, 194
Deviation, 24, 71, 145–56, 179
Deviation Mess, 27
Deviationists, 145–56, 162
Dewdrop, 75
Diana, 176
Dillon, Bob, 167
Dinas, 41, 55, 85, 86
Dinas Junction, 41, 84
Dinorwic, 10, 12
Diphwys, 10–11, 16
Diphwys Casson Company, 11, 64
dividends, 1
Dol-y-Moch, 16
Dolmelynllyn, 3
Dolrhedyn bridge, 23, 179, 186
double engines, 58, 59–60, 119,
    131
Doyle, George, 42
Drage, Dorothy, 39
Duffws, 39, 41, 70, 77, 180
Duffys, 55, 88, 112
Dukes, Paul, 164–5, 188, 213
Duncan, Martin, 154
Dwyryd, river, 13, 28

Earl of Merioneth, 60, 119, 131,
    192–3, 207
East Anglia Group, 120, 200
Easton, James, 18
Economic Forestry Group, 146
Edwards, Lottie, 29–30
Elizabeth Anne, 72
Elvey, Mike, 143
Embery, David, 191
employers, 45
England, George, 50, 52, 56, 57–8
enthusiasts, 115, 147
European Regional Development
    Fund, 194
Evans, Mandy, 191
Evans, Mr, 182–3
Evans, Robert, 82, 91, 93–4, 101,
    108, 109–10

Evershed, Mr, 146
Evesham High School, 189
expenditure, 193–4
Experiment, 14

Fairlie, Robert Francis, 57–8, 59,
    60
Fame, 72
Farthing, A. F., 143
Fenton, Richard, 4, 11
Festiniog and Blaenau Railway, 64
Festiniog and Port Madoc
    Railway, 16–17
Festiniog Railway
    Abandonment Order sought,
        95–6
    building of, 31–7
    closure, 2, 92
    description of route, 20–31
    early business on, 38–9
    early employees, 45
    early passengers, 53–5
    first run after restoration, 108
    freed from speed restrictions,
        61
    introduction of steam, 48–53
    origins, 14–19
    revival attempts, 93–6
    revived, 96–106
    run down, 1–2
    slate business, 38–43, 47, 56, 76,
        88, 91–2, 95
    unreliability, 81
Festiniog Railway Company
    apply for Abandonment Order,
        95–6
    and the beginning of the
        Society, 99–100
    Board Members, 103, 161, 162
    builds the railway, 31–7
    closure, 92
    and the Electricity Authority,
        133–44
    expenditure, 193–4
    goes public, 74
    opens the railway, 36–7
    Pegler buys, 102–4

relationship to the Society,
103–6, 117–18, 126–7
and revival attempts, 95–6
run down of the railway, 88–92
stocks and shares, 103, 118
and the West Highland
Railway, 87, 100
Festiniog Railway Magazine,
202–3
Festiniog Railway Society
foundation, 98
membership, 104, 198–9
organisation, 199–200
relationship with the
Company, 103–5, 117–18,
126–7
Festiniog Railway (Sales)
Limited, 94
Festiniog Railway Society Ltd., 94
Festiniog Railway Trust, 94, 104,
117–18, 126–7
Festiniog Railway Works, 5
Festiniog v. Electricity Authority,
133–44
Fiennes, Gerry, 45–6, 148, 162,
178
fines, 42, 69
fish-plates, 61
Fitzgerald, Sir William, 139
Five Valleys Tour, 87
Flying Flea, 125
footplate work, 129–31
Fox, Gerald, 142–3, 145, 146–7, 153
'Freddie's Fantastic Rail Tour',
190–1
Fron Wen, 189
Fuller, David 'Fluff', 186

Galn-y-Don, 176
Gandon, James, 35
Garnedd, 42
Garnedd Tunnel, 27
Garraway, Allan, 20, 98, 99, 107–9,
111–15, 119, 134, 147–8, 162, 163,
172–4, 179, 185, 188, 191, 196–7
Garraway, Moyra, 114–15, 174,
197

Garraway, Ron, 99, 104
Garraway, Ruth, 174
gauge, 33, 49
Gestiana, 43
Gibbard, Clive, 166
gifts, 125–6
Gilbert, F., 98, 99, 101–2, 103, 104,
202
Girdlestone, Philip, 160, 165, 189
Glan-y-Don, 22, 179
Glan-y-Mor, 123
Glan-y-Pwll, 41, 69, 70, 176, 179,
188
Glan-y-Pwll level crossing, 22,
112, 185
Glaslyn, River, 5, 7
Glaslyn Foundry, 34
Glynceiriog, 9
Glynrhomwy, 12
Goldstraw, Bob, 164
Goode, 137
gradients, 39
Grand, K. W. C., 119
gravity trains, 39–41
Great Western Railway, 64
Greaves, John Whitehead, 11–12,
46
Greaves, Marianne, 46
Greaves family, 3
Green, David, 199
Gregory, Ross, 125
Grimshaw, John, 150, 151
Groby, 189
Groby bridge, 185
Groby Granite Quarry, 69, 88
Groesffordd, 23
Groeslon, 126
groups, 120–1, 126–7, 184–5, 200–2
Guard-Day, Derek, 121
Gurley, Norman, 99, 121, 154, 172,
202–3
Gweunydd Band, 46
Gwynne, Eliza Anne, 15

Hafod-y-Llyn, 29, 40, 55
Hafoty Cwmbowydd, 12
Hall, Geoff, 213

Hall, R. A. B., 143
Halsall, John, 125
Harbour station, 30, 77, 158, 178
Hardy, Dick, 162, 213–14
Harlech Castle, 28
Harman, Lord Justice, 140
Harrington, Angela, 159
Harris, L. Taylor, 99, 104
Harrison, John, 27–8, 150
Harvey, Bill, 20, 108
Hatcham Ironworks, 50
Hay Railway, 15
Heath Humphreys, Leonard A.,
    96–8, 104
Hemingway, J., 42–3
Heritage Group, 201–2
Heywood, Alan, 166, 171, 191, 213
Holcroft, H., 98
Holland, Charles Menzies, 49
Holland, Samuel Jr, 11, 17–19, 31,
    36, 38, 46, 47, 48–51, 58, 64, 72
Holland, Samuel Sr, 14, 16, 31, 38
Holland, William, 11
Hollingsworth, Brian, 22, 24, 134,
    147–8, 156, 186
Homfray, George, 16, 17
Homfray, William, 46
Hoole, Bill, 111, 131, 167
Hoole, Dolly, 131
horse power, 39–41, 48
hostility, local, 135
Hovenden, 27
Howes, Fred, 121, 167, 176, 190–1
Huddart, George Augustus, 61
Hughes, Hugh, 84
Hughes, J. S., 65
Hughes, Peter, 153
Hunter, Bob, 99

Ingham, Paul, 213
inspection cars, 65
Iorwerth, Ffilys, 13–14
ITV, 160

Jack, H. J., 78, 80, 86
James, Colin, 184, 186, 191
James, Laurie, 191

James Spooner, 61
Jamieson, Peter, 143, 147
Jarvis, Peter, 182, 188, 204
Jarvis, Ron, 212
Jevons Sons, 34
Johnson, Geoffrey, 120
Johnson, Peter, 203
Jones, Bessie, 88, 113, 120
Jones, David, 72
Jones, Eddie, 159–60
Jones, Griffith, 70
Jones, Janet, 116
Jones, John, 34
Jones, Methusalem, 10, 14
Jones, Morgan, 40
Jones, Morris, 84, 91, 94, 108, 110,
    115
Jones, Thomas, 34
Jones, W., 14
Jones, Will, 79, 113
Junta, 147–8

Keleher, G. J., 143
King, Tom, 98, 99, 101, 103, 104
Krena, Norman, 88

The Lady Diana, 176
Lady Vaughan, 43
Lambert, Arthur, 121, 140–1, 175,
    186, 187, 213
Lancashire and Cheshire Group,
    120, 168, 172, 188, 190
Lands Tribunal, 138–40, 143
Lascelles, Thomas Spooner, 123
Le Marchant, Bob, 153
Lester, Ron, 176
Lewis, Bunny, 150, 151, 154, 215
Lewis, Michael, 34, 62
Lilley Constructions Ltd, 182
Linda, 114, 162, 191, 193
Linda's Leap, 29
Lindsay, Earl of (formerly Lord
    Garnock), 105
Linley, Lord, 160
Little Giant, 56, 57
Little Wonder, 58, 59–60, 62

Little Wonder Buffet, 158, 160
Livesey & Henderson, 137
Livingston Thompson, 61, 68, 119, 206–8
Llan Ffestiniog, 28
Llandudno and Colwyn Bay Tramway, 119
Llansannan, 9
Llechwedd, 12, 41, 66, 88, 91
Llechwedd-Coed, 54
Lloyd, Richard, 36
Llyn Mair, 27
Llyn Ystradau Halt, 26, 157
local authorities
  and closure, 91
  and reopening of the railway, 95, 183
local support, 128–9, 135, 176–8
locomotives, 61
  at the time of closure, 106
  double engines, 58, 59–60, 119, 131
  early, 49–53, 56, 57–8
  maintenance, 68–9, 77
  restoration, 119, 123
London and North-Western Railway (LNWR), 64, 91, 92
London Group, 121, 159
Londonderry and Coleraine Railway, 57
Long Tunnel, 26, 36, 53, 111
Lord Palmerston, 51, 52, 71, 86, 106
Low, R. C. S. (Michael), 94–5
Lucas, Margaret Bright, 71
Lyn Ystradau Deviation, 145–56

McAlpines, 23, 155, 186
McCallum, Steve, 165
MacGregor, Bob, 166, 168, 187, 211
McMahone, Sean, 191
McMullen, Colonel, 107–8, 115
Madocks, Eliza Anne, 15, 19, 32, 35
Madocks, John, 19
Madocks, William Alexander, 3–8, 14–17, 19, 160
Maenofferen, 41, 91, 92

Maentwrog, 7, 65
Maenyferram, 16
Manod, 89
Manpower Services Commission, 24, 155–6, 188–9, 194
Margaret, Princess, 155, 160
marketing, 209
May, John, 83
Merddin Emrys, 61, 68, 72, 90, 106, 123, 152, 154, 156, 193, 207, 208
Midland Group, 120, 188
Milton Keynes Group, 188
Minffordd, 16, 24, 29–30, 41, 50, 55, 61, 69, 113, 118–19, 157
Ministry of Transport, 92, 95–6, 107
Mitchell, J. C. V., 98, 99
Moel Tryfan, 86, 106, 109
Moelwyn, 16, 34, 35–6
Moelwyn, 79, 190
Moelwyn Mawr, 17
Moelwyn and Portmadoc Railway, 16–17
Moelwyn Railway Company, 17
Moelwyn Tunnel, 69, 86, 101, 107, 112, 145, 153–5
Morgan, Arwyn, 110, 115
Morgan, D. W., 75
Morgan, T., 78–9, 82, 83
Morris, William, 10
Mountaineer, 51, 52, 215
Mulvany, Herr, 59
Museum, 123, 202

Nantlle, 10, 17
Nantmor, 85
National Provincial Bank, 100, 102
National Shell Factory, 75
National Union of Railwaymen (NUR), 170–1
Nazareth, Bryn, 70
Nelson, W. K., 99, 104
Nevitt, 78, 81
New Tunnel, 26
Newborough, Lord, 12, 15, 16, 39
Newburger, Rosalind, 150, 151
Nicholls, E. H. R., 84

Nicholson, E. D., 102, 103
1949 Group, 95
Noakes, John, 160–1
North Wales Hydro-Electric Act,
    136
North Wales Narrow Gauge
    Railway (NWNGR), 84–5
North Wales Power and Electric
    Traction Company, 86
North Wales Quarrymen's Union,
    44
Northesk, Lord, 101

Oakeley, W. G., 11, 16, 32, 38
Oakeley family, 28, 55, 68, 72
Oakeley Quarry, 41, 55, 70–1, 74,
    91
oil firing, 115, 128, 205
Old Vein Slate, 12
Olver, Major Peter, 154, 190
Operation Snapper, 125–6, 164
Owen, David, 6
Owen, Jack, 112, 118, 168

Palmerston, Lord, 11, 16, 19
Parrish, Jim, 189, 213
Parry, James, 66–7
passenger services, 56, 66, 76
    after complete restoration, 196
    renewal of, 109, 113, 115–16
    restoration, 123, 127, 143, 191
    season for, 157–9
    suspension, 90
    unreliability, 81
    Welsh Highland Railway, 87
    winter services suspended, 88
    workmen's carriages, 66–7
passengers, 131–2
    early, 43, 53–5
Payne, David, 154
Peacock, Thomas Love, 7
Pearce, Norman, 99, 104, 168, 175,
    187, 213
Pegler, Alan, 100–5, 110, 117–18,
    126, 134, 161, 174, 213

Pen Cob, 90, 115
Pen Craig, 23, 179
Pen-y-Groes, 17
Penlan, 186–7
Pennant, Richard, Lord Penrhyn,
    9–10
Pennant, Thomas, 10
Penrhyn, 24, 29, 55
    downgraded to halt, 77
    hostel, 121
    restoration, 123, 157
Penrhyn Cottage, 5
Penrhyn Isa, 4
Penrhyn Quarry, 114, 127
permanent staff, 163–74
    redundancies, 196
    relations with volunteers, 201
    unionisation, 170–1
Philby, Kim, 27
Philby, St John, 27
Philistines, 13, 19, 39
Phillips, Tim, 54, 67, 69, 129
Pihl, Carl, 59
Pinfold, G. A., 143
Pitts Head, 85
Plas Tan-y-Bwlch, 28, 55
Plymouth, Devonport and South-
    Western Junction Railway, 78
Pollock, David, 197–9, 206, 208
Port Penrhyn, 10
Porthdinlleyn, 35
Porthmadog, 55, 63
    creation, 43
    decline, 75–6
    harbour, 14, 72, 75
    terminus at, 30–1
Portmadoc, Beddgelert and South
    Snowdon Railway Company
    (PBSSR), 85, 86
Portmadoc Mutual Ship
    Insurance Company, 46
postal service, 159
Powick, 62
Pratt, Alan, 215
preservationists, 115, 122
Prichard, Thomas, 18, 32, 40, 49
The Prince, 52, 106, 110, 115, 116,
    119, 131, 164, 167, 193

The Princess, 51, 52, 62, 90, 106, 116, 181
Pring, Mr, 6
Project Approach, 184–5
Putnam, Andy, 155, 156, 167, 186

quarry-owners, 46
quarrymen, 44–5

rails, 34, 70, 77
railwaymen, 45
  see also permanent staff; volunteers
Rastrick, John Urpeth, 49
Rear, Mr, 98
redundancies, 196
Rees, Dewi, 156
refreshment rooms, 71
Reid, Charles, 123–4
Rhiw Goch, 29, 40, 178
Rhiwbryfdir, 11, 16
Rhoslyn bridge, 150
Rhosydd, 69
Rhyd, 16
Richards, Ifor, 182
Richards, Morgan, 44, 46
Richards, Richard, 52–3
Richmond, D. A. H., 143
Roberts, John, 54
Roberts, Robert, 40
Roberts, William, 63
Robinson, Jones Partnership, 182
Rogers, Samuel, 7
rolling-stock, 68
  see also carriages; wagons; etc.
Rolt, L. T. C., 99
Ronald, David, 202
Rother Valley Railway, 78
Rothschild, Baron Nathan Meyer, 11, 16, 17
Routly, John, 102, 103–4, 134, 137, 144, 161, 170, 172, 175, 182–3, 194
Royal Cambrian Company, 16
Royal Corps of Transport, 159

Royal Oakeley Silver Band, 46, 160
Royal Trains, 155, 160
Rudgard, R. H., 104

safety, 81, 173
St Paul's School, 108
Salmon, Mr, 111
Sandberg, C. P., 59
Savage, Andy, 162–3, 186, 188
Saville, John, 214–15
Schumann, Mike, 143, 147, 153, 154, 162, 207–9, 213
Scott, Robin, 178
Seaborne, 88
season, 157–9
Semmens, P. W. B., 131
Seymour, Michael, 116, 123, 168, 202, 213
Sheffield and District Group, 188, 189
Shelley, Percy Bysshe, 3, 7
Shelton, Edwin, 12
Shephard, Warren, xii
Shooter, Adrian, 184, 213
Short Tunnel, 27
shot-creting, 155
shunting, 69
Sidmouth, Lord, 16
Silver Jubilee, 203–4
Simons, Roger, 147
Simplex tractor, 79, 108, 111, 112, 115–16, 134, 176
slate industry
  decline, 74
  opening of quarries, 9–19
  quarry-owners, 46
  quarrymen, 44–5
  rail transport, 38–43, 47, 56, 76, 88, 91–2, 95
sleepers, 34, 77, 126
Smalley, 152–3
Smallman, Bob, 99
Smart, Ian, 99, 111, 112, 126
Smith, Assheton, 10, 12
Smith, Benjamin, 16, 18
Smith, Dick, 188

Smith, James, 19, 31, 32, 36
Smith, Jinks, 111, 116
Smith, Les, 101–2, 111, 115–16,
    134, 137, 161, 175, 186
Snapper Halt, 125–6
Snell, John, 210, 212, 215
snow, 62–3, 72
Somervell, Dave, 151
South Snowdon, 85
special excursions, 72
speed restrictions, 61
Spey Railway, 197
sponsorship, 207–9
Spooner, Charles Easton, 33, 35,
    48, 58, 59–61, 64–5, 70, 84, 123
Spooner, Charles Edwin, 64
Spooner, George Percy, 61, 64,
    72
Spooner, Henry, 40
Spooner, James, 17, 18, 31, 32, 48–
    52, 61–2
Spooner family, 72
Spring, G. C., 76–7
staff
    early railwaymen, 45
    permanent, 163–74
    see also volunteers
Stainer, A. B., 143
stations, 61
    original, 55
    see also individual stations
steam engines, introduction, 48–
    53
Stein, Dafydd, 13
Stein, Ebenezer, 13–14
Stein, Ffilys, 13–14
Stephens, F. G., 78
Stephens, Holman Frederick, 77–
    80, 81, 82–4, 86–7
Stephenson, Robert, 18, 36, 49
Stephenson Meeting, 98
Sterling Plant Hire, 153
Stesion Fain, 22, 176, 180–1
Stewart, Louise, 71
strikes, quarry, 74
Stwlan, 25
Summit Cutting, 24
Sutherland, Duke of, 59

Swinton, James, 18
Szechenyi, Count, 59

Taliesin, 61, 106, 116, 119–20, 202
Talyllyn Railway, 20, 98–9, 101,
    103, 113, 118
Tan-y-Bwlch, 24, 27–8, 55
    centenary, 159
    restoration, 125, 157
Tan-y-Grisiau, 23, 24, 42, 55, 77,
    79
    restoration, 157
Tan-y-Grisiau reservoir, 25,
    133–4
Tan-yr-Allt, 3, 7, 12
Taylor, Ralph, 166
Taylor Woodrow, 146
Thomas, George, 193
Thomas, Herbert, 109, 129
Thomas, Mrs, 109
Thompson, Livingston, 35, 59
Thomson, Paul, 191
Tibbett, Alan, 191
ticket system, 206
timetables, 157
Tonbridge, 78
Topsy, 59
tourist trade, 88
Towyn machine, 5
Trawsfynydd, 25, 28
Tregunter, 15
Tremadoc, 4
Trematon Castle, xii
Tro Peudy, 27
Trwyn-y-Garnedd, 14
Tunnel Fach, 27
Tunnel Mess, 148, 156
Tunnel South, 26, 179
Turner, Terry, 166, 169, 213
Turner, William, 10–11, 19, 39, 46
Tyler, H. W., 53, 55–6, 59, 61
Tyler, Keith, 186
Tyler's Cutting, 71
Tyrwhitt, S. E., 78, 80, 83

unions, 170–1
Upnor Castle, 193

vans, 68
Vaughan, A. B., 27
Vaughan, Frederick, 73
volunteers, 108, 111, 120–2, 126,
  145, 163, 183–4, 198–202, 209–16
Votty, 91, 92
Votty and Bowydd, 41
Vulcan Foundry, 119

wagons, 68
Wales Tourist Board, 178, 194
Warburton, Anne Susannah, 9
Watkins, Hugh, 151
Wayne, Francis, 136, 139–42
Weaver, Rod, 189, 205, 206
Welsh Development Agency, 181,
  182
Welsh Highland Railway, 2, 80,
  81, 84–8, 90, 102, 128
Welsh Language Society, 177
Welsh Pony, 56, 106
Welsh Slate Company, 11, 16, 39,
  41
Welshpool and Llanfair Railway,
  120
Westinghouse Brake and Signal
  Company, 198
White, J. B., 202
White, John, 99

Whithead, Peter, 11
Whitehouse, Pat, 78, 86–7
Wilks, John, 16
Williams, Harry, 50
Williams, Job, 50
Williams, John, 14
Williams, Johnny, 72
Williams, Lady, 110
Williams, Robert, 75, 79, 82, 84
Williams, Sir Osmond, 110
Williams, William, 72–3
Williams-Ellis, Clough, 160
Wilson, Charles, 151–2
Wilson, Dan, 121, 192–3, 203
Winter, 98, 104
Wollan, Dick, 172–4, 175, 183, 184–
  5, 187–8, 193, 196, 213
Woodhouse, E., 98
The Woods, 28
World War I, 1, 74–5
World War II, 2, 89–91
Wrexham, 5
Wrysgan, 41, 69, 91

Yates, David, 160, 166, 191
Ynys Cyngar, 14
Ynys Towyn, 4, 43
Ynyscynhaiarn, 43
Youell, Mr, 153